Evelyn Turn
9-17-2002

W9-BXZ-475

A Handbook *for* Christian Maturity

Bill Bright

NewLife
PUBLICATIONS
A MINISTRY OF CAMPUS CRUSADE FOR CHRIST

A Handbook for Christian Maturity

Published by
New*Life* Publications
100 Lake Hart Drive
Orlando, FL 32832 -0100

Printed in the United States of America.

ISBN: 1–56399–040–7

Thomas Nelson Inc., Nashville, Tennessee, is the exclusive distributor of this book to the trade markets in the United States and the District of Columbia.

Distributed in Canada by Campus Crusade for Christ of Canada, Surrey, B.C.

Unless otherwise indicated, all Scripture references are from the *New International Version,* © 1973, 1978, 1984 by the International Bible Society. Published by Zondervan Bible Publishers, Grand Rapids, Michigan.

Scripture quotations designated TLB are from *The Living Bible,* © 1971 by Tyndale House Publishers, Wheaton, Illinois.

Scripture quotations designated NKJ are from the *New King James* version, © 1979, 1980, 1982 by Thomas Nelson Inc., Publishers, Nashville, Tennessee.

Scripture quotations designated NASB are from the *New American Standard Bible,* © 1960, 1962, 1963, 1968, 1971, 1972, 1975, 1977 by the Lockman Foundation, La Habra, California.

Scripture quotations designated Phillips are from the *Letters to Young Churches, A Translation of the New Testament Epistles,* by J. B. Phillips, © 1947, 1957 by the MacMillan Company, New York, New York.

Any royalties from this book or the many other books by Bill Bright are dedicated to the glory of God and designated to the various ministries of Campus Crusade for Christ/*NewLife2000.*

For more information, write:

Life Ministries—P. O. Box 40, Flemington Markets, N5W 2129, Australia
Campus Crusade for Christ of Canada—Box 300, Vancouver, B.C., V6C 2X3, Canada
Campus Crusade for Christ—Fairgate House, King's Road, Tyseley, Birmingham, B11 2AA, England
Campus Crusade for Christ—P. O. Box 8786, Auckland, New Zealand
Campus Crusade for Christ—Alexandra, P. O. Box 0205, Singapore 9115, Singapore
Great Commission Movement of Nigeria—P. O. Box 500, Jos, Plateau State Nigeria, West Africa
Campus Crusade for Christ International—100 Sunport Lane, Orlando, FL 32809, USA

Contents

❖   ❖   ❖

Acknowledgments

The *Ten Basic Steps Toward Christian Maturity* series was a product of necessity. As the ministry of Campus Crusade for Christ expanded rapidly to scores of campuses across America, thousands of students committed their lives to Christ—several hundred on a single campus. Individual follow-up of all new converts soon became impossible. Who was to help them grow in their new-found faith?

A Bible study series designed for new Christians was desperately needed—a study that would stimulate individuals and groups to explore the depths and the riches of God's Word. Although several excellent studies were available, we felt the particular need of new material for these college students.

In 1955, I asked several of my fellow staff associates to assist me in the preparation of Bible studies that would stimulate both evangelism and Christian growth in a new believer. The contribution by campus staff members was especially significant because of their constant contact with students in introducing them to Christ and meeting regularly with them to disciple them. Thus, the *Ten Basic Steps Toward Christian Maturity* was the fruit of our combined labor.

Since that modest beginning, many other members of the staff have contributed generously. On occasion, for example, I found myself involved in research and writing sessions with several of our staff, all seminary graduates, some with advanced degrees and one with his doctorate in theology. More important, all were actively engaged in "winning, building, and sending men" for Christ.

A Handbook for Christian Maturity combines the eleven-booklet series into one practical, easy-to-follow volume. For this latest edition, I want to thank Don Tanner for his professional assistance in revising, expanding, and editing the contents. I also want to thank Joette Whims and Jean Bryant for their extensive help and for joining Don and me in the editorial process.

A Personal Word

As reporter Clarence W. Hall followed American troops through Okinawa in 1945, he and his Jeep driver came upon a small town that stood out as a beautiful example of a Christian community.

"We had seen other Okinawan villages down at the heels and despairing," he reported. "By contrast, this one shone like a diamond. Everywhere, we were greeted by smiles and dignified bows. Proudly," he continued, "the old men showed us their spotless homes, their terraced fields, and their prized sugar mills."

The newsman saw no jails and no drunkenness, and divorce was unknown in the town.

Why was this village so unusual? An American missionary had come there thirty years earlier and had led two elderly townspeople to Christ and left them with a Japanese Bible. These new believers studied the Scriptures and started leading their fellow villagers to the Lord Jesus.

The reporter's Jeep driver was equally amazed at the difference and exclaimed, "So this is what comes out of only a Bible and a couple of old guys who wanted to live like Jesus!"

The faithfulness of one missionary changed an entire village. You, too, can make a difference in your home and your community for the Lord Jesus Christ. Since I received Christ as my Savior and Lord in 1944, I have had the exciting privilege of sharing the Lord Jesus Christ with many millions of students and lay people around the world. On the basis of their remarkable response, I am deeply convinced that the world is more ready for the gospel of Christ today that ever before.

With a world so ready, we cannot afford to sit back and hope they will be reached. Our relatively few full-time ministers of the gospel, no matter how gifted and dedicated they may be, will not be able to accomplish the task alone. We, too, as lay men and women, have the privilege—and responsibility—of participating with our living Lord in the fulfillment of His Great Commission in our generation.

Jesus promised, "Follow me and I will make you fishers of men." It is our responsibility to follow Him and obey Him. He, then, will make us fishers of men.

My prayer is that the studies in this *Handbook* will bless and enrich your life and increase your effectiveness as a personal witness for our Lord and that this Bible study series will encourage your growth toward full maturity in Jesus Christ. I assure you that there is no experience in life more exciting and spiritually rewarding than helping to introduce men and women to Christ—and seeing the change He brings to their lives and your life as well.

Bill Bright

What This Study Will Do for You

Years ago as a new Christian, I felt frustrated about the way my ministry was going. Along with others, I had been sharing my faith on the UCLA and USC campuses for some time as a representative of our church. But we had little success. It seemed as if our efforts were fruitless. I wasn't sure what God wanted me to do.

Then one day, Dr. Henrietta Mears, the Christian education director at Hollywood Presbyterian Church, presented a challenge that caught my attention. She had just returned from a world tour and had seen the devastation left by World War II in Europe.

"The world's on fire!" she exclaimed. "Evil is rampant and people are hurting. Jesus Christ is what the world needs. I'm convinced that we need to make an impact on the whole world, not just here..."

As she shared her vision for the world, I began to catch her enthusiasm. Later, as I again thought of her words, it was as if a huge canvas of the world were spread before me. Like an artist's hand sketching a sky, mountains, streams and brooks, the painting only showed the high points, not the details. I sensed that the Lord was showing me a broad plan for taking the gospel to the whole world. I was to invest my life in helping to

❖
You are about to begin one of the most life-changing Bible studies ever developed.

fulfill Christ's Great Commission in this generation—to win and disciple people for Christ.

Today in my travels all over the world, I see hundreds of thousands of people from every walk of life getting excited about Jesus Christ as their lives are transformed by the power of the Holy Spirit and God's holy Word.

This edition of *A Handbook for Christian Maturity* has been prepared to help you catch a vision for introducing men and women to Jesus Christ and to help you experience a deeper, more intimate fellowship with our Lord.

The study is divided into eleven parts—called Steps—each designed to build on the previous one to give you a well-balanced, in-depth study of the Christian faith. When used during your personal quiet times or in a group setting, the *Handbook* can give you an efficient way to study the Bible and understand the Christian faith.

The lesson material in these Steps have been revised, expanded and updated. The Leader's Guide for the *Ten Basic Steps Toward Christian Maturity* can be used with the *Handbook* for group study.

You will benefit from this study series in several ways. You will discover:

◆ Why Jesus is truly a "man without equal"

◆ How God's power can change your life

◆ Who the Holy Spirit is and why He came

◆ How to get answers to your prayers

◆ How to witness more effectively

◆ How to trust God for your finances

◆ How to study the Bible more effectively

When you complete the introductory Step, I encourage you to go on to Step 1 and continue through the series until you have completed Step 10. Study the lessons diligently and review each Step periodically to make the principles you learn your own.

If you are a new Christian, the study will acquaint you with the major doctrines of the Christian faith. By applying the principles you learn, you will grow spiritually and find solutions to the problems you are likely to face as a new believer.

If you are a mature Christian, you will discover tools to help others find Christ and grow in their faith. Your own commitment to our Lord will be affirmed, and you will discover how to develop an effective devotional and study plan.

A faithful study of the material will also show you how to walk daily in the power of the Holy Spirit, enabling you to live a more joyous and triumphant Christian life.

You are about to begin one of the most life-changing Bible studies ever developed. Millions of people throughout the world today are following Jesus Christ and experiencing the power of His resurrection because this study helped them build a strong foundation for their faith.

I encourage you to pursue each study with an open, eager mind. As you work through the lessons, continually pray that God will show you how to relate the principles you learn to your situation. Begin to apply them on a daily basis and you will experience the joy, victory and power that a study of the Bible will bring to your life.

How to Use This Study

On page 17 of this *Handbook,* you will find the preparatory article, "Take the Challenge; Change Your World." The article will give you a clear perspective on how you can influence your world for Christ. Read it carefully before you begin this series of studies. Review it periodically as you go through the lessons in the *Handbook.*

This book contains eleven Bible studies called Steps. Each Step contains several lessons plus a "Recap" or review. Each lesson is divided into two sections: the Bible Study and the Life Application. Whether you are studying on your own or with a group, I encourage you to buy a notebook to carry with your Bible and *Handbook.* Be sure the notebook has ample space for recording your answers and thoughts for each lesson.

Casual Bible reading uncovers valuable spiritual facts that lie near the surface. But understanding the deeper truths requires study. Often the difference between reading and studying is a pen and your notebook. By using this notebook to record answers for all the studies in the series, you will have on hand the answers and application points for the series of study. You may want to add other scriptural topics you are interested in to make a great resource for future reference. Also, you will be able to use your

❖

Your most important objective is not to acquire knowledge but to meet with God in a loving, personal way.

13

notebook and your recorded answers to begin your own Bible study group.

How to Study the Lessons

Every lesson in this *Handbook* covers an important topic. Plan to spend a minimum of thirty minutes each day—preferably in the morning—in Bible study, meditation, and prayer.

Remember, the most important objective and benefit of a quiet time or Bible study is not to acquire knowledge or accumulate biblical information but to meet with God in a loving, personal way.

Here are some suggestions to help you in your study time:

◆ Plan a specific time and place to work on these studies. Make an appointment with God; then keep it.

◆ Use a pen or pencil, your Bible, the *Handbook* and your notebook.

◆ Begin with prayer for God's presence, blessing and wisdom.

◆ Meditate on the Objective to determine how it fits into your circumstances.

◆ Memorize the suggested verses.

◆ Proceed to the Bible study, trusting God to use it to teach you. Prayerfully anticipate His presence with you. Work carefully, reading the Scripture passages and thinking through the questions. Answer each as completely as possible, writing enough so you can understand your answers later.

◆ When you come to the Life Application, answer the questions honestly and begin to apply them to your own life.

◆ Prayerfully read through the lesson again and reevaluate your Life Application answers. Do they need changing? Or adjusting?

◆ Review the memory verses.

◆ Consider the Objective again and determine if it has been accomplished. It not, what do you need to do?

◆ Close with a prayer of thanksgiving, and ask God to help you grow spiritually in the areas He has specifically revealed to you.

- ◆ When you complete the lessons of the Step, spend extra time on the Recap to make sure you understand every lesson thoroughly.

- ◆ If you need more study of the Step, ask God for wisdom again and go through whatever lesson(s) you need to review, repeating the process until you do understand and are able to apply the truths to your own life.

Divide your notebook into eleven sections corresponding to each Step. For each section, write the title and number of the Step in your notebook.

Turn to the section for the Introductory Step and begin by writing "Lesson 1: Who Is Jesus Christ?" Underneath, put the Objective for Lesson 1. The Objective states the main goal for your study. Keep it in mind as you continue through the lesson.

Then take time to memorize the referenced Scripture verse and write it in your notebook. As you work through the lessons, review daily the verses you have memorized. Our Lord has commanded that we learn His Word. Proverbs 7:1-3 reminds us:

> My son, keep my words and store up my commands within you. Keep my commands and you will live, guard my teachings as the apple of your eye. Bind them on your fingers; write them on the tablet of your heart.

As you use the verses you have memorized and claim God's promises, you will experience the joy, victory, and power that God's Word gives to your Christian walk.

Now go on to the Bible study itself. After the Objective and verse to memorize, write "Bible Study" and the first topic to be studied under the Bible Study section of the lesson. You can either write each question and its answer or write just the number of the question and the answer. When you have finished, write the second topic in your notebook and answer those questions.

When you get to the Life Application, write it in your notebook under that lesson. Then answer the questions as completely as possible and write down the specific things you plan to do this week to apply the lesson to your life.

These studies are not intended as a complete development of Christian beliefs. However, a careful study of the material will give you, with God's help, a sufficient understanding of how you can know and apply God's plan for your life. The spiritual truths contained here will help you meet with our Lord Jesus Christ in an intimate way and discover the full and abundant life that Jesus promised (John 10:10).

Do not rush through the lessons. Take plenty of time to think through the questions. Meditate on them. Absorb the truths presented, and make the application a part of your life. Give God a chance to speak to you, and let the Holy Spirit teach you. As you spend time with our Lord in prayer and study, and as you trust and obey Him, you will experience the amazing joy of His presence (John 14:21).

Take the Challenge; Change Your World

Driving through the barren desert between Los Angeles and Las Vegas, you can see a 300-foot tower. The top of this tower holds a black receiver 45 feet high and 23 feet across which is surrounded by seventy heat-conducting tubes. During the daylight hours, a brilliant ball of fire glows from the top of the tower creating the world's largest solar-powered electrical generating station, Solar One.

How can a black receiver turn into a glowing ball with a temperature exceeding 1,175 degrees Fahrenheit? The secret is on the ground. The desert floor surrounding the tower holds 1,818 computer-controlled frames. Each frame holds twelve giant mirrors that track the sun from the time it rises until it sets.

The sunlight strikes these mirrors called heliostats. The mirrors reflect the sunlight onto the black receiver at the top of the tower. The heat generated at the receiver is transformed into electrical energy through a system of thermal storage and a turbine generator.

The power generated is really nothing new; it is from the sun. The process is possible only because a network of mirrors reflects sunlight onto a helpless receiver where the power is generated.

❖

Our challenge is to reflect God's love and power to a world that is dark with sin and despair.

We have an even greater Source of power with which to generate change in our world—the power of God's Holy Spirit. Our challenge is to reflect God's love and power to a world that is dark with sin and despair.

We live in a world of rapid and radical change. Men's hearts are filled with fear and dread, frustration and hopelessness. Mankind has proven capable of inventing tremendous technical feats but incapable of managing his own heart or of coping with the pressing problems of our time: the population explosion, pollution, crime and violence, sexual rebellion, alcoholism and other addictions, abortion, pornography, and widespread political, social and moral decay.

What an hour for Christians to reflect the love of Christ! We can become involved in the greatest spiritual harvest since New Testament times. This dark hour in the history of mankind is also an hour of destiny, a time of unprecedented opportunity for Christians to shine as lights in the darkness. This is the hour for which we were born—to set in motion a mighty, sweeping spiritual revolution that will turn the tide of sin and despair and reveal to mankind that the glorious gospel of our Lord Jesus Christ offers the power to change the way we live.

The Greatest Challenge

If I had the privilege of writing a news story about the greatest events of the centuries, one of the most important would be a meeting on a mountain near Galilee where a small group of men were commanded to carry God's love and forgiveness to a dark and dying world.

On this mountain these men received the greatest challenge ever given to mankind, by the greatest Person who ever lived, concerning the greatest power ever revealed and the greatest promise ever recorded. I refer, of course, to the Great Commission of our Lord Jesus Christ, which He gave to His disciples and through them to us. Jesus said:

> I have been given all authority in heaven and earth. Therefore go and make disciples in all the nations, baptizing them into the name of the Father and of the Son and of the Holy Spirit, and then teach these new disciples

to obey all the commands I have given you; and be sure of this—that I am with you always, even to the end of the world (Matthew 28:18-20, TLB).

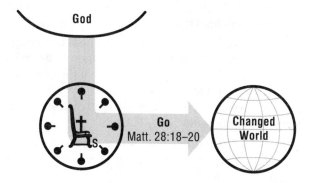

Later, on the Mount of Olives, our Lord gave His final word to His disciples and to us before He ascended to the Father. He said:

When the Holy Spirit has come upon you, you will receive power to testify about me with great effect, to the people in Jerusalem, throughout Judea, in Samaria, and to the ends of the earth, about my death and resurrection (Acts 1:8, TLB).

Like the mirrors that reflect the sun's power to generate electricity, God has given us the power of His Holy Spirit to enable us to introduce others to His Son and help them mature in their faith. Had our Lord's command and promise not been given, we could not share the love, forgiveness, joy, and purpose of God's matchless grace available to all who believe in Christ.

The Focus of Jesus' Ministry

The Great Commission was the focus of Jesus' ministry on this earth. The fifth chapter of Luke records an incident in the life of a seasoned fisherman—Simon Peter. He and his fellow workers had spent the entire night casting and gathering their nets but had not caught a single fish.

Jesus observed these men as they were washing their nets and asked Peter to push out a little into the water so He could sit in the boat and speak to the crowds that were pressing around Him.

When He had finished speaking, Jesus made a promise to this fisherman—a promise that I believe Peter, weary from his futile night of fishing, initially thought foolish. Jesus told Peter to go out a little further and let down his nets. If he did so, he would catch fish. Luke records Peter's response and what happened as a result:

> "Sir," Simon [Peter] replied, "we worked hard all night and didn't catch a thing. But if you say so, we'll try again." And this time their nets were so full that they began to tear! A shout for help brought their partners in the other boat and soon both boats were filled with fish and on the verge of sinking (Luke 5:5-7, TLB).

Jesus told the fishermen who were so awestruck with this demonstration of His power, "From now on you'll be fishing for the souls of men!"

They were so overwhelmed with the presence and power of Jesus that they left their occupation to follow Him.

How are you reflecting the power of the Holy Spirit in the lives of others? How is God's power at work in your life?

The most exiting and spiritually rewarding experience in life is the adventure of fishing for people. Through the studies in this *Handbook,* I want to help you be a successful fisherman for our Lord wherever you are and wherever you go. As you follow the principles outlined in the studies, your net too can be filled—even if you have never introduced anyone to Christ—even if you may be skeptical like Peter. If you are obedient like Peter, the Lord Jesus will honor you, and you will see miracles happen through the power of the Holy Spirit in your life!

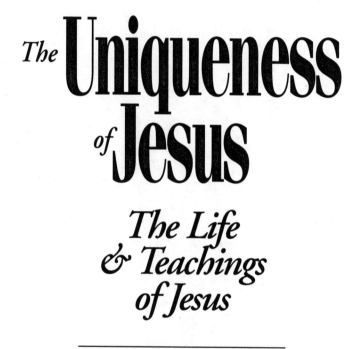

The Uniqueness of Jesus

The Life & Teachings of Jesus

INTRODUCTION

Who Is Jesus Christ?

What if you could predict that a major world event would take place five minutes from now?

What if you could accurately describe what would happen?

Would knowing the future give you unusual power?

Would anyone believe you?

Possibly some would, but how many would not?

Many people do not believe the Bible, yet it miraculously foretells hundreds of events, sometimes in minute detail, and usually hundreds—sometimes thousands—of years ahead. Some prophecies concern cities and countries, such as Tyre, Jericho, Samaria, Jerusalem, Palestine, Moab, and Babylon. Others relate to specific individuals. Many have already been fulfilled, but some are still in the future.

Jesus Christ is the subject of more than 300 Old Testament prophecies. His birth nearly 2,000 years ago, and events of His life, had been foretold by many prophets during a period of 1,500 years. History confirms that even the smallest detail happened just as predicted. It confirms beyond a doubt that

❖

Objective: To recognize Jesus Christ as the Son of God

Read: John 1:1–34

Memorize: John 14:6

Jesus is the true Messiah, the Son of God and Savior of the world.

The following chart lists some of the amazing predictions concerning Jesus Christ, together with the record of their fulfillment:

EVENT	OLD TESTAMENT PROPHECY	FULFILLMENT IN JESUS
His birth	Isaiah 7:14	Matthew 1:18,22,23
His birthplace	Micah 5:2	Luke 2:4,6,7
His childhood in Egypt	Hosea 11:1	Matthew 2:14,15
The purpose for His death	Isaiah 53:4–6	2 Corinthians 5:21 1 Peter 2:24
His betrayal	Zechariah 11:12,13; 13:6	Matthew 26:14–16; 27:3–10
His crucifixion	Psalm 22	Matthew 27
His resurrection	Psalm 16:9,10	Acts 2:31

❖

Bible Study

Jesus' Claims Concerning Who He Is

1. In your own words, write the claims Christ made concerning Himself in the following verses:

   Mark 14:61,62

   John 6:38; 8:42

   John 5:17,18

   John 10:30

   What did those who heard what Jesus said think He meant?

   John 14:7

   John 14:8,9

2. What did Jesus claim to do in the following verses?
John 5:22
Matthew 9:6
John 6:45–47

3. What did Jesus predict in the following verses?
Mark 9:31
Luke 18:31–33
John 14:1–3

4. What characteristics of Jesus are attributes of an omnipotent God?
John 2:24
Matthew 8:26,27
John 11:43–45

According to the above passages, Jesus claimed to be God. He made the kinds of claims that only a person who presumed he was God would make. Both His friends and His enemies called Him God, and He never attempted to deny it. He even commended His followers for believing He was God.

The Importance of the Truth About His Identity

1. Suppose Jesus Christ were not God. If He knew He was not God and that none of those claims were true, what could we conclude about Him?

2. Suppose Jesus were sincerely wrong. Suppose He sincerely believed all these fantastic claims, even though they were not true. What could we conclude about Him?

3. Why is it important to investigate His claims?

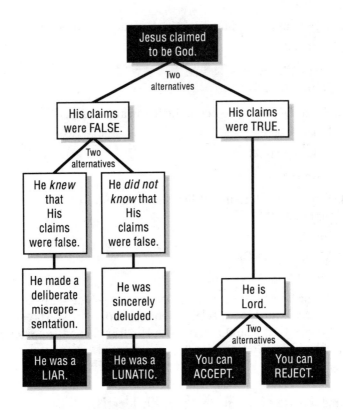

What Others Said About Who He Was

1. His followers:

John the Baptist (John 1:29)

Peter (Matthew 16:16)

Martha (John 11:27)

Thomas (John 20:28)

Paul (2 Corinthians 5:21; Titus 2:13)

How did Jesus respond to what Peter said (Matthew 16:17)?

How does Christ's response to what Thomas said
(John 20:29) apply to you?

2. His enemies:

The Jews (John 10:33)

Judas (Matthew 27:3,4)

Pilate (Matthew 27:22,23)

The Roman soldier (Matthew 27:54)

3. Who do *you* believe Jesus is and on what do you base that belief? List the facts that particularly help you know that He is God.

LIFE APPLICATION

1 Why is it important that you personally recognize who Jesus Christ really is?

2 Have you invited Jesus Christ into your life?

3 What changes do you expect to experience in your life as a result of receiving Christ as your Savior and Lord?

❖ ❖ ❖

The Earthly Life of Jesus Christ

Jesus Christ is the greatest person who ever lived. His moral character, His teachings, and His influence upon history demonstrate that He is indeed God. Through two thousand years of advancements in education, technology, philosophy, medicine, and science, mankind has never produced a person who is worthy to be compared with Jesus.

His divinity and humanity are without parallel. His life, death, and resurrection were mandatory for man's salvation. With His ascension into heaven, He completed His mission and made possible man's restoration to his original destiny.

❖

Bible Study

Objective: To recognize that Christ's earthly life confirmed His deity

Read: John 17

Memorize: John 1:12

The Entrance of Jesus Christ Into the World

1. On the basis of His statement in John 17:5, where was Jesus Christ before He came into the world?

2. Read Matthew 1:18–23. In your own words, summarize the circumstances that surrounded Jesus' birth.

The New Testament passes over the next thirty years of Jesus' life almost in silence. Apparently the gospel writers were more anxious to portray the character and ministry of Jesus than to give us a chronological biography.

The Character of Jesus

1. From these verses, describe the character of Jesus:

Mark 1:40–42

Luke 23:33,34

John 2:13–17

John 13:1–17

Romans 5:8–10

2. How does Jesus' attitude contrast with the attitude of His contemporaries toward the following?

Adults (Matthew 14:15–21)

Children (Mark 10:13–16)

Those who offend (Luke 9:51–56)

3. Why did the following people love Christ?

The widow of Nain (Luke 7:11–15)

The sinful woman (Luke 7:36–50)

Mary and Martha (John 11:30–44)

4. From the beginning of His life, Jesus demonstrated unfailing grace, amazing wisdom, and astounding understanding and knowledge. He consistently pleased God.

The crowds found His compassion constant, and He was humble and meek before His enemies. He treated the poor with respect and the children with love and tenderness. His character was pure, selfless, and sinless.

Jesus also proved His divine character through His immeasurable love, an unconditional love unique in history. He willingly offered Himself as a sacrifice for all sin and evil, and He gave the free gift of everlasting life to every person who would accept it. Only God in the flesh could have embodied all these characteristics.

Read Hebrews 4:15. How can Jesus understand our feelings so completely?

According to Luke 2:42–47, when did Jesus first demonstrate His depth of knowledge and commitment?

What was the general reaction to Jesus' remarks?

5. Read Matthew 7:28,29. What other reactions do you think the people had to His teachings besides amazement?

Imagine yourself in Jesus' day, listening to Him teach and observing His behavior. What would your reaction be?

6. How do you feel about Jesus?

Why?

Jesus Christ as a Teacher

1. What did Christ teach about the new birth (John 3:1–8)?

Why did He describe salvation in this way?

2. What did Christ teach regarding His claims about Himself?

John 10:11

John 13:13,14

John 15:1,5

Matthew 5:17

John 11:25,26

Which of these claims do you think is most important? Why?

Which has meant the most to you personally? Why?

3. What did Christ teach about His demands of His followers?

Mark 8:38

Mark 10:29,30

Matthew 9:9

Matthew 11:29

Luke 9:23

John 13:34,35

Which of these demands do you find easiest to follow?

How do you think Jesus wants you to deal with the difficult ones?

4. Many view Jesus as the greatest teacher in history. No other man has been quoted as often or has inspired as many books and articles. His teachings have given us clear, profound insights into the deepest questions of life. People flocked to hear Him speak. The disciples left everything to follow Him.

   What kind of teacher could inspire such loyalty? (See John 6:66–69 for help in formulating your answer.)

   From the following verses, list characteristics of Jesus that made Him such an excellent teacher:

   Mark 6:34

   Luke 21:29–38

   Luke 4:14–30

   John 3:1–8; 7:50,51; 19:38–42

5. Carefully read Matthew 7:7–12 from the Sermon on the Mount. How did Jesus use the following teaching methods to emphasize His lessons?

   Repetition of ideas

   Practical application

   Clear summarization

6. What was even more important than Christ's effective teaching methods (Matthew 7:29)?

   Where did He get this authority (John 12:49,50)?

   Summarize how Jesus' earthly life confirmed His deity.

LIFE APPLICATION

1 Give at least three reasons you can trust Jesus' teachings.

2 List in your notebook three ways these teachings can change your life.

3 Plan how you will implement these changes.

❖ ❖ ❖

The Death of Jesus Christ

When did you last talk about death? Did you enjoy your conversation?

People don't usually like to talk about death, do they? But the Bible has some very important things to say about it.

According to God's Word, death means "separation," not "cessation of existence." Physical death is the separation of the spirit (the immaterial part of us) from the body. As a result, the body decomposes. Spiritual death is the separation of man from God. Both physical and spiritual death are the results of sin.

The results of this separation are not only sins like murder, immorality, and stealing, but also worry, irritability, lack of purpose in life, frustration, the desire to escape reality, and fear of death. These and many other conditions are evidence that we are cut off from God, the only One who can give us the power to live an abundant life.

The most important question in life becomes, "How can I be reconciled to God?" In our own power, we can never bridge the gulf between us and God. But God has provided a way to bring us to Him.

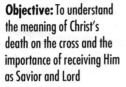

Objective: To understand the meaning of Christ's death on the cross and the importance of receiving Him as Savior and Lord

Read: Romans 3:10–28; 5:1–21

Memorize: Romans 5:8

❖

Bible Study

The Need for the Death of Jesus Christ

1. Carefully read Romans 3:10–12 and 3:23.

    How many times does the writer, Paul, use terms like *all, none,* or their equivalents?

    Why do you think he repeats these terms?

    What does this tell you about moral, respectable people?

2. What is the result of sin (Romans 6:23)?

The Result of the Death of Christ

1. Read 2 Corinthians 5:21 carefully.

    How good does it say Christ was?

    But what happened to Him when He died on the cross to pay the penalty of our sins?

    What was the result for you?

2. What did Christ teach concerning His death (Mark 8:31,32)?

3. How did Christ feel about such a death (Hebrews 12:2)?

4. Describe the effect of Christ's death with respect to God's holiness (Romans 3:25; John 4:10).

5. Why did He die for us (1 Peter 3:18)?

6. How did Christ's death affect your relationship with God (Colossians 1:21,22; Romans 5:10,11)?

Significance of the Death of Christ

1. What is the only thing we can do to make sure that the death of Christ applies to us so we can be saved (Acts 16:31)?

2. Can we work for salvation (Ephesians 2:8,9)?

    Why not?

L I F E   A P P L I C A T I O N

 Read John 3:18 carefully. What two kinds of people are described here?

What is the only reason any person will be condemned?

 According to what the Bible says here, are you condemned?

According to 1 John 5:11,12, do you have eternal life? (Do not confuse 1 John, the Epistle, near the end of the New Testament, with the Gospel of John.)

According to that same passage, how can you know?

Have you made the decision to accept Christ's death on the cross for you, and have you received Him into your life as Savior and Lord? If you would like to receive Him as your Savior right now, pray a prayer like this one from your heart:

> *Lord Jesus, I want to know you personally. Thank You for dying on the cross for my sins. I open the door of my life and receive You as my Savior and Lord. Thank You for forgiving my sins and giving me eternal life. Make me the kind of person You want me to be. Amen.*

❖ ❖ ❖

The Resurrection of Jesus Christ

Jesus' crucifixion demoralized His followers. The terror-stricken little band scattered; Jesus' enemies were celebrating their victory. But three days after the crucifixion a miracle occurred: Jesus rose from the dead.

Within a few weeks His once cowardly followers were fearlessly proclaiming His resurrection, a fact that changed the course of history. Followers of Jesus Christ were not people who promoted an ethical code of a dead founder, but rather those who had had vital contact with a living Lord. Jesus Christ still lives today, and He is anxiously waiting to work in the lives of those who will trust Him.

The new life and fresh courage demonstrated by the early Christians is vividly described by J. B. Phillips in the Preface to his *Letters to Young Churches*:

> The great difference between present-day Christianity and that of which we read in these letters is that to us it is primarily a performance; to them it was a real experience. We are apt to reduce the Christian religion to a code, or at best a rule of heart and life. To these men it is quite plainly the invasion of their lives by a new quality of life al-

❖

Objective: To recognize the importance of Christ's resurrection, and how it relates to us personally

Read: John 20

Memorize: 1 Corinthians 15:3,4

together. They do not hesitate to describe this as Christ "living in" them.

Mere moral reformation will hardly explain the transformation and the exuberant vitality of these men's lives—even if we could prove a motive for such reformation, and certainly the world around offered little encouragement to the early Christian! We are practically driven to accept their own explanation, which is that their little human lives had, through Christ, been linked up with the very life of God.

Many Christians today talk about the "difficulties of our times" as though we should have to wait for better ones before the Christian religion can take root. It is heartening to remember that this faith took root and flourished amazingly in conditions that would have killed anything less vital in a matter of weeks.

These early Christians were on fire with the conviction that they had become, through Christ, literal sons of God; they were pioneers of a new humanity, founders of a new kingdom.

They still speak to us across the centuries. Perhaps if we believed what they believed, we might achieve what they achieved.

❖

Bible Study

Five Proofs That Jesus Actually Rose From the Dead

1. *The resurrection was foretold by Jesus Christ, the Son of God.*

   What did Jesus tell His disciples in Luke 18:31–33?

   If Jesus had clearly predicted that He would rise from the dead, then failed to do so, what would this say about Him?

2. *The resurrection of Christ is the only reasonable explanation for the empty tomb.*

What did Jesus' friends do to make certain His body would not be taken (Mark 15:46)?

What did Jesus' enemies do to make sure His body would not be taken (Matthew 27:62–66)?

But on Sunday morning the tomb was *empty!*

Note: If Jesus had not been killed, but only weakened and wounded by crucifixion, the stone and the soldiers would have prevented His escape from the tomb. If Jesus' friends had tried to steal His body, the stone and the soldiers would likewise have prevented them. Jesus' enemies would never have taken the body since its absence from the tomb would only serve to encourage belief in His resurrection. *Only His resurrection can account for the empty tomb!*

3. *The resurrection is the only reasonable explanation for the appearance of Jesus Christ to His disciples.*

List all the individuals or groups who actually saw the risen Christ, according to 1 Corinthians 15:4–8:

If Christ had not risen from the dead, what could we then conclude about all these witnesses (1 Corinthians 15:15)?

What else would be true if Christ had not risen from the dead (1 Corinthians 15:17)?

When Christ appeared to His followers, what things did He do to prove He was not a hallucination (Luke 24:36-43)?

4. *The dramatic change in the lives of His followers.*

Look up these verses and describe the differences in these people:

Peter (Luke 22:54–62; Acts 4:1–22)

Thomas (John 20:24–28; Acts 1:12–14)

Paul (Acts 7:54–8:3; Acts 16:16–40)

5. *The resurrection is the only reasonable explanation for the beginning of the Christian church.*

Within a few weeks after Jesus' resurrection, Peter preached at Pentecost, and the Christian church began. What was the subject of his sermon (Acts 2:14–36)?

If Jesus' body were still in the tomb, how do you think Peter's audience would have responded to this sermon?

But how did they respond (Acts 2:37,38,41,42)?

The Results of the Resurrection

1. What does the resurrection tell us about the following:

Jesus Christ (Romans 1:4)

The power God can now exercise in our lives (Ephesians 1:19,20)

What will eventually happen to our bodies (Philippians 3:21)

2. How would your life be affected if Christ had not risen from the dead (1 Corinthians 15:12–26)?

3. If we can believe the resurrection, why is it then logical to believe all the miracles Jesus performed?

The Visible Return of Christ

1. Describe the way in which Christ will return to earth (Matthew 24:30; Acts 1:11).

2. How does this compare to the first time Christ came to earth?

3. What will happen to the Christian when Christ comes for him (1 Corinthians 15:51,52; Philippians 3:20,21)?

4. What will be the condition of the earth when Christ returns (Matthew 24:6–8)?

5. What will happen to those who are not Christians when He returns (2 Thessalonians 1:7–9)?

6. What is our present hope (1 John 2:2,3)?

LIFE APPLICATION

Hebrews 13:8 says Jesus is the same today, and He can transform your life.

 How would your life be different from what it is if Jesus had not risen from the dead?

2 How do you think His "resurrection life" can be seen in you on a daily basis?

3 How can your life be different if you allow Jesus to transform it?

❖ ❖ ❖

Jesus Christ Living in the Christian

Are you a member of a church? Are you committed and active in your church? And do you have a close relationship with Jesus Christ?

Chapters 2 and 3 of Revelation emphasize the fact that merely to be a church member offers no guarantee of a right relationship with Jesus Christ. Notice in Revelation 3:20 that the reference is to individuals, not to a group as a whole: "If anyone hears my voice and opens the door, I will go in and eat with him, and he with me."

When you invite Jesus Christ to come into your heart and life to be your Savior and Lord, confessing your sin and need of forgiveness, He answers your prayer. He enters your heart and life. Why?

One reason is so He can empower you. The Christian life is more than difficult; it is humanly impossible to live. Only Jesus Christ can live it through you as He dwells within you. He wants to think with your mind, express Himself through your emotions, and speak through your voice, though you may be unconscious of it.

❖

Objective: To realize the importance of total surrender to Christ

Read: Revelation 2 and 3

Memorize: Revelation 3:20

But as worldly Christians examine their lives, they often find themselves filled with many areas of activity—studies, finances, social life, home life, business, travel—but with no real purpose or meaning. The reason for this is that they are controlling these areas themselves instead of allowing Jesus Christ to control them.

There is a throne in each of our lives (see diagram below). Until Jesus Christ comes into our lives, our self, or ego, is on the throne. But when Jesus comes in, He wants to assume His place of authority on this throne. We must step down and relinquish the authority of our lives to Him. As you can see from the diagram, when Christ becomes the controller of our lives, He becomes Lord of every activity, and that results in purpose and harmony.

Thus the Christian life is not a person trying to imitate Christ; rather, it is Christ imparting His life to and living His life through the person. The Christian life is not what you do for Him; it is what He does for and through you. The Christ-controlled life always produces the fruit of the Spirit as listed in Galatians 5:22,23.

- Love
- Joy
- Peace
- Patience
- Kindness
- Faithfulness
- Goodness

- Life is Christ-centered
- Empowered by Holy Spirit
- Introduces others to Christ
- Has effective prayer life
- Understands God's Word
- Trusts God
- Obeys God

❖

Bible Study

The Need for Jesus Christ to Live in the Christian

1. What was Jesus unwilling to entrust to men (John 2:24,25)? Why?

2. What kinds of things are in our hearts (Mark 7:21–23)?

3. How did the apostle Paul, one of the world's greatest Christians, evaluate his human nature (Romans 7:18)?

4. What is our condition apart from Jesus Christ (John 15:4,5)?

The Fact that Jesus Christ Lives in the Christian

1. Restate Revelation 3:20 in your own words:

Note: The word *sup* that appears in some translations is Old English for "eat" or "dine," and it describes the idea of fellowship in its original meaning.

2. What guarantee does Jesus Christ give in this verse, and how can we believe Him?

3. How do you know that Jesus Christ has entered your life?

4. How do you know that Jesus will never leave you even when you sin (Hebrews 13:5)?

5. If you do sin, how can you renew your fellowship with Him (1 John 1:9)?

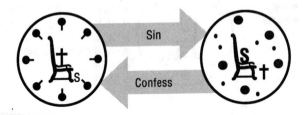

Note: *Salvation* differs from *fellowship*. Salvation is having our sins forgiven and receiving eternal life. Fellowship is our daily relationship, or communion, with Christ. Through sin we may often lose our fellowship in the same way a child loses fellowship with his father through disobedience. However, the child does not lose his relationship as a son, nor do we lose our relationship with God. He is still our heavenly Father. (See John 10:27-29.)

Jesus Christ at Home Within the Christian

When Jesus Christ lives within us, what can He do for us as we face the following problems?

1. Emptiness (John 6:35)

2. Anxiety (John 14:27)

3. Unhappiness (John 15:11)

4. Lack of power (Philippians 4:13)

LIFE APPLICATION

1 What must we do so that Jesus Christ can live His victorious life through us (Romans 6:13; 12:1,2)?

2 Read and meditate on John 3:16. On the basis of this verse, why do you think we should give control of our lives to God?

3 Right now, surrender control of your life to God. Be willing to give Him every area—your family, job, finances, even your health. Pray this simple prayer:

> *Dear Father, I need You. I acknowledge that I have been directing my own life and that, as a result, I have sinned against You. I thank You for forgiving my sins through Christ's death on the cross for me. I now invite Christ to again take His place on the throne of my life. Fill me with the Holy Spirit as You commanded me to be filled in Ephesians 5:18, and as You promised in Your Word that You would do if I ask in faith. I now thank You for directing my life and for filling me with the Holy Spirit. Amen.*

❖   ❖   ❖

The Church of Jesus Christ

What is the strongest organization on earth? It is the church. Composed of every person who has received Jesus Christ into his or her life, the church is also called the Body of Christ or the Bride of Christ. It is the one organization for which He gave His life (Ephesians 5:25).

The Bible describes the church in two senses:

1) The universal church, which refers to all true Christians

2) The local church, which is an individual group of Christians who gather for worship, instruction, and mutual encouragement

❖

Objective: To recognize the importance of the church in the Christian's life

Read: Hebrews 10:19–25; 1 Corinthians 12:12–31

Memorize: Hebrews 10:25

❖

Bible Study

The Universal Church

1. Paul frequently compares the church to a body. Who is the only head (Ephesians 5:23)?

Who are the members (1 Corinthians 12:27)?

2. How does Christ see the church (1 Corinthians 12:12,13)?

3. As members of His body, how should we feel toward each other (1 Corinthians 12:25,26)?

Name some specific ways we can express these feelings.

4. Read Acts 1:6–11 carefully.

According to verse 8, what is to be the church's great concern?

Where does the Bible say Jesus went physically (verse 9)?

Describe in your own words how Jesus will come again for His church (verse 11).

Who knows when that will be (verse 7)? (See also Mark 13:32,33.)

Although Jesus is spiritually present in our hearts, He is also with God the Father in heaven. In the future, He will return to judge the world and rule the nations (Matthew 25:31,32). In the meantime, the church is to be His witness on earth and bring as many people as possible into a personal relationship with Him.

5. In light of this, what should be one of your main purposes while here on earth?

The Local Church

1. What are Christians *not* to do (Hebrews 10:25)?

Note: The "meeting together" refers to the regular assembling of the local church.

2. We are saved by faith. But the church has two simple, yet meaningful, ordinances that we are to observe: baptism and communion.

According to Matthew 28:18,19, why should we be baptized?

What is the purpose of the communion service (1 Corinthians 11:23–26)?

3. Write your own one-sentence description of each of the following local churches:

The church in Jerusalem (Acts 4:32,33)

The church in Thessalonica (1 Thessalonians 1:6–10)

The church in Laodicea (Revelation 3:14–17)

Just as some New Testament churches are dynamic and others powerless, so it is today. Not all churches are vital, and great variety exists even within a single denomination. To stimulate your Christian growth, you should attend a church that exalts Christ, teaches the Bible, explains clearly what a Christian is and how to become one, and provides loving fellowship.

4. What could happen to your spiritual growth if you:

Do not attend church regularly?

Attend a church that is powerless?

LIFE APPLICATION

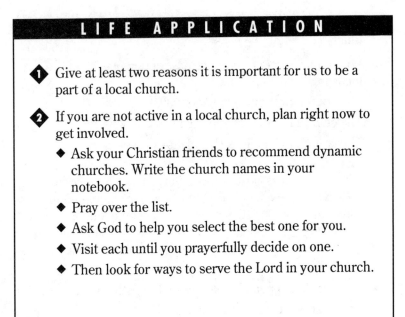

1 Give at least two reasons it is important for us to be a part of a local church.

2 If you are not active in a local church, plan right now to get involved.

- ◆ Ask your Christian friends to recommend dynamic churches. Write the church names in your notebook.
- ◆ Pray over the list.
- ◆ Ask God to help you select the best one for you.
- ◆ Visit each until you prayerfully decide on one.
- ◆ Then look for ways to serve the Lord in your church.

❖ ❖ ❖

Recap

The following questions will help you review this Step. If necessary, reread the appropriate lesson(s).

1. List ways the memory verses have helped you in your daily life during the weeks of this study.

2. What do you think is the most important way in which Jesus Christ is different from other people?

   What does that mean to you?

   How does it affect your life?

3. Who is Jesus Christ to you?

   What has He given you?

4. Why do you suppose Jesus' enemies did not want to believe His claims about who He was?

5. Why did Jesus' friends, who had watched Him die, believe in the resurrection?

❖

Reread: John 1:1–34; Romans 3:10–28; Romans 5:1–21; John 20

Review: Verses memorized

LIFE APPLICATION

1 What does it mean to you now to have Jesus living within you?

2 How does your present relationship with Christ help you develop a rich fellowship with your local church?

3 How can you improve your relationship with other Christians?

4 How does your fellowship in your church help your relationship with God?

5 Write down ways you could make the relationship more vital.

❖ ❖ ❖

The Christian Adventure

*Beginning
the Exciting
Journey
of Faith*

STEP 1

The Christian's Certainty

Believers of Old Testament times looked forward to the coming of their Messiah. New Testament believers look back to the cross and the resurrection. Both of these events culminate in the unique person of Jesus Christ.

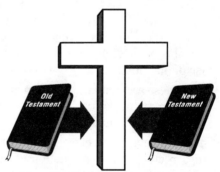

The apostle Paul says, "It was through what His Son did that God cleared a path for everything to come to Him—all things in heaven and on earth—for Christ's death on the cross has made peace with God for all by His blood...and now as a result Christ has brought you into the very presence of God, and you are standing there before Him with nothing left against you...the only condition is that you fully believe the Truth, standing in it steadfast and firm, strong in the Lord, convinced of the Good News that Jesus died

❖

Objective: To give the new Christian assurance of eternal life and of Christ's presence in his life

Read: John 3:1–20 and 1 John 5:9–15

Memorize: 1 John 5:13

for you, and never shifting from trusting Him to save you" (Colossians 1:20–23, TLB).

Hundreds of millions of people around the world have discovered this marvelous "path" because of Jesus' death on the cross and His bodily resurrection from the dead.

Jesus' death bridged the gulf between the holiness of God and the sinfulness of man. He died to pay the penalty of our sin and rescue us "out of the darkness and gloom of Satan's kingdom" and bring us "into the Kingdom of His dear Son, who bought our freedom with His blood and forgave us all our sins" (Colossians 1:13,14, TLB). But without His resurrection and ascension, His sacrifice would have been incomplete, and we would have remained under the penalty of death (1 Corinthians 15:17).

To believe in Jesus Christ as the Savior of the world is to believe in a living person. People often ask, "What is the meaning of belief?" *The Amplified New Testament* expresses the full meaning of the term *believe* as "adhere to, trust in, and rely on." The Gospel of John has been called the Gospel of Belief. The word *believe* occurs many times in the book of John. Chapter 20, verse 31, expresses the purpose of that book:

> These are written that you may believe that Jesus is
> the Christ, the Son of God, and that by believing you may
> have life in His name.

The living Savior, therefore, is the basis for Christian confidence. The resurrection is the foundation of our certainty that we have eternal life in Christ and that we experience daily the indwelling presence of our living Savior.

❖

Bible Study

Christian Certainty

1. What must one do to become a Christian (John 1:12)?

2. To be a son of God is to be born of whom (John 1:13)?

3. To believe in Jesus Christ is to possess and to be free from what (John 5:24)?

4. What did Christ do with our sins (1 Peter 2:24,25)?

How should this affect our lives?

5. What three things characterize Jesus' sheep (John 10:27)?

6. What is your relationship with Christ, as He Himself states in John 10:18–30?

7. What are the implications of failing to believe the testimony that God has given regarding His Son (1 John 5:10,11)?

8. The resurrection of Jesus is history's most revolutionary event. How does it prove Christ's claim to be God (Romans 1:4)?

Why is the resurrection so essential to our faith (1 Corinthians 15:17; Ephesians 2:4–10)?

New Life

1. In John 3:3–7 what did Jesus tell Nicodemus about seeing and entering the kingdom of God?

2. At physical birth one receives many things he is not aware of: family name, privileges, wealth, love, care, and protection. At spiritual birth one becomes a son of God and receives eternal life, a divine inheritance, and God's love, care, and protection. God has given us these because of His great love. God's gifts are never based on man's changing emotions, but on His own unchanging Word.

In your own words describe what you have, according to these verses:

Ephesians 1:7

Romans 5:1

Romans 3:22

Colossians 1:27

3. As you begin to live the Christian life, what three
   evidences in your life will assure you that you know
   Jesus Christ?

   1 John 2:3

   1 John 3:14

   Romans 8:16

LIFE APPLICATION

1 Who is Jesus Christ to you?

2 What is your relationship with God?

3 What kind of life do you now possess?

4 What about your sins?

5 Why are you sure (or doubtful) of your salvation?

6 What changes do you believe have taken place because Christ is in your life?

❖ ❖ ❖

The Christ-Controlled Life

There is a throne, a control center—the intersection of one's intellect, emotions, and will—in every life. Either self or Christ is on that throne. Let me illustrate.

I like to plan as far in advance as possible, especially for key events. But occasionally I get so busy with the many details of our worldwide ministry that an important item slips through.

With a key conference only a couple of weeks away, I had just realized the need for a set of printed materials that would be of tremendous benefit to the attendees.

As I shared the urgency with the department director responsible for this need, he responded, "Bill, we're full up already. Two weeks just isn't enough time."

I became impatient. Couldn't my associate see that we are in a war for men's souls, that we must seize opportunities when they arise and not limit our efforts to 8-to-5 workdays? I made my point clear to him.

"But if we had more notice…," he protested. "There just is no way we can squeeze

❖

Objective: To show how the indwelling Christ is the key to the Christian life

Read: 1 Corinthians 2:11; 3:5; Galatians 5:16–24

Memorize: Philippians 4:13

in such a huge job with so little time. There's the writing, then the design, typesetting, and artwork, then the printing…"

It seemed obvious that he did not share my burden for the upcoming event. I pressed my point. "Look, this is an important international conference," I said firmly, my voice rising. "And this is no time for 'business as usual.' Please find a way to finish this project in time for the conference, even if you have to work around the clock."

I could tell that my colleague was frustrated. But I reasoned, *We need those printed materials. Whatever it takes, we need them.*

Within a few moments after our conversation, I sensed the conviction of the Holy Spirit. Yes, even in our well-intended service of the Lord, we can stumble—and in the name of godliness I had offended a dear brother in Christ. I had failed to give him and his staff the benefit of the doubt—failed to take into account the tough workload they already were facing each day.

Instead of asking him to think through the possibilities with me and helping him rearrange his priorities to accommodate the new task, I had virtually ordered him to get the project done and shown little appreciation for the many late evenings his team was already devoting to their work. I had reacted impatiently rather than in a spirit of love, understanding, and teamwork.

At this point I had a choice to make.

On the one hand, I could let it go. After all, doesn't the head of a large organization have the right to ramrod projects through when necessary? Didn't the end (the strategic international conference) justify the means (get the job done no matter what it takes)? And didn't my associate's hesitant attitude warrant a stern talking-to about the urgency of the hour?

By all human standards, I probably could have justified letting the incident go. But deep inside I would have been restless and uncomfortable as the Holy Spirit continued to point out my sin to me, and God would not have blessed my efforts on His behalf as long as this sin remained unconfessed. On top of that, several of my dear co-workers would have continued to hurt as a result of my callous attitude.

On the other hand, I could deal with the problem by taking scriptural action to clear the slate. The unrest in my conscience was the Holy Spirit cross-examining me as I tried to rationalize my behavior. What I had thought was forceful leadership, He was identifying as the sins of impatience and unjustifiable anger.

I knew that taking scriptural action was the only choice I could make that would please my Lord. I confessed my sin to Him and appropriated His forgiveness.

Then came the toughest part.

I drove down to the office complex where my associate and his team were located and asked their forgiveness. We cried and laughed and prayed together, sensing a fresh outpouring of God's love in our midst. Then we talked through our mutual needs and found a way—as teammates—to rearrange priorities and accomplish the task—on time!

That is what the Christian life is all about—just keeping Christ on the throne. You do this when you understand how to walk in the control and power of the Holy Spirit, for the Holy Spirit came for the express purpose of glorifying Christ by enabling the believer to live a holy life and to be a fruitful witness for our dear Savior.

Many people have misconceptions about the Christian life. Some argue that once they have received Jesus Christ into their lives by faith, it is up to them to live a life pleasing to God in their own strength. Others believe that Christ has entered their lives to help them live and work for God's glory. These ideas of Christian living look good on the surface, but each contains a weakness that actually undermines the basis of vital Christian living.

In light of Romans 7:18, Galatians 2:20, and Romans 1:17, what do you think the basic approach should be?

Someone said, "the Christian life is not difficult—it is impossible." Only one person has ever lived the Christian life, and that was Jesus Christ. Today He desires to go on living His life through Christians whom He indwells. J. B. Phillips, in the Preface to his translation of a portion of the New Testament, *Letters to Young Churches,* said:

The great difference between present-day Christianity and that of which we read in these letters is that to us it is primarily a performance; to them it was a real experience. We are apt to reduce the Christian religion to a code, or at best a rule of heart and life. To these men it is quite plainly the invasion of their lives by a new quality of life altogether. They do not hesitate to describe this as Christ "living in" them.

Before His death, Christ told His disciples that it was best for Him to leave them so that the Spirit of God might come to dwell in each of them (John 14:16–20; 16:7). In other words, Christ was physically departing from His disciples so that He might always be present spiritually within each of them.

Today when a person places his faith in Christ, Christ comes to dwell within him by means of the Holy Spirit (Romans 8:9). His purpose for dwelling in us is that He might live His life through us. Many Christians are trying to operate on their own finite ability instead of Christ's infinite power.

Have you ever asked yourself, *How can I experience the victorious life of Christ?*[1] To find the answer, let's examine the three types of persons in the world today: the non-Christian (natural man), the spiritual Christian, and the worldly or carnal Christian.

❖

Bible Study

The Non-Christian or Natural Man

In the following diagram, this circle represents the life of the person who has never received Christ as Savior and Lord. Christ stands outside the door of the life, seeking entrance (Revelation 3:20).

Self-Directed Life
S – Self is on the throne
† – Christ is outside the life
● – Interests are directed by self, often resulting in discord and frustration

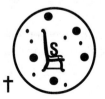

1. What adjective do you think best describes the man who does not understand the things of the Spirit of God (1 Corinthians 2:14)?

2. What terms describe self in the following verses?

   Romans 6:6

   Galatians 5:16,17

3. List at least three characteristics of the man without Christ, as described in Ephesians 2:1–3.

4. What is the condition of the heart of the natural man (Jeremiah 17:9)?

5. List the thirteen sins that Jesus said come from the heart of man (Mark 7:20–23).

6. Summarize the relationship between God and the non-Christian (John 3:36).

7. How, then, does one become a Christian (John 1:12; Revelation 3:20)?

The Spiritual or Christ-Controlled Christian

This circle represents the life of the person who has invited Jesus Christ to come into his life and who is allowing Him to control and empower his life. Christ is occupying His rightful place on the throne of the life. Self has been dethroned.

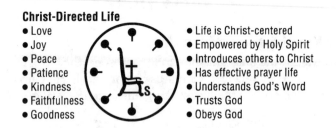

Christ-Directed Life

- Love
- Joy
- Peace
- Patience
- Kindness
- Faithfulness
- Goodness

- Life is Christ-centered
- Empowered by Holy Spirit
- Introduces others to Christ
- Has effective prayer life
- Understands God's Word
- Trusts God
- Obeys God

1. What are some other characteristics of a life controlled by God's Spirit (Galatians 5:22,23)?

2. In what sense could the Spirit-controlled life be called the exchanged life (Galatians 2:20)?

3. Where does the Christian receive the power to live this otherwise impossible life (Philippians 4:13)?

4. What does the spiritual Christian have that will enable him to understand the things of God (1 Corinthians 2:14–16)?

The Worldly Christian and the Solution

In 1 Corinthians 3:1–3, the apostle Paul addresses the Christians as "worldly" ["carnal," King James Version] (self-centered), rather than spiritual (Christ-centered). The following diagram represents a life in which the person's ego has asserted itself. Self has usurped the throne of the life, and Christ has stepped down. The result is the loss of the individual's fellowship with God though he is still a Christian.

Self-Directed Life

- Legalistic attitude
- Impure thoughts
- Jealousy
- Guilt
- Worry
- Discouragement
- Critical spirit
- Frustration
- Aimlessness
- Fear

- Ignorance of his spiritual heritage
- Unbelief
- Disobedience
- Loss of love for God and for others
- Poor prayer life
- No desire for Bible study

1. Describe the worldly Christian as presented in 1 Corinthians 3:1–3.

Name five or six practices that result from worldliness (Galatians 5:19–21).

Summarize in your own words the relationship between the worldly mind and God, as described in Romans 8:7.

2. The solution to worldliness (the self-controlled life) is threefold:

1) We must confess our sins, recognizing that we have been rulers of our own lives. When we confess them, what will God do (1 John 1:9)?

   Read Proverbs 28:13. What is the result of not admitting sin?

   What is the result of admitting sin (Proverbs 28:13; Psalm 32:1)?

2) We must *surrender,* or yield, the throne to Christ. State in your own words how Paul describes the act of presenting ourselves to God in Romans 12:1,2.

3) By *faith* we must *recognize* that Christ assumed control of our lives upon our invitation. How can you be sure that if you ask Jesus Christ to assume His rightful place on the throne of your life, He will do so (1 John 5:14,15)?

   We receive the Lord Jesus Christ by faith. How then do we allow Him to control our lives moment by moment (Colossians 2:6)?

   Give three reasons faith is so important (Hebrews 11:6; Romans 14:23; Romans 1:17).

LIFE APPLICATION

The secret of the abundant life is to allow Jesus Christ to control your life moment by moment through His Holy Spirit living within you. When you realize that you have sinned, confess your sin immediately; thank God for forgiving you and continue to walk in fellowship with God.

1 In prayer, examine your attitude. Do you honestly want Christ to control your life? If not, ask God to change your heart. Thank Him, by faith, that He has begun to do so.

2 List areas of your life that you believe should be brought under the control of Jesus Christ.

3 Ask God to show you ways to bring these areas under His control.

4 To make 1 John 1:9 meaningful in your life:
   - ◆ List your sins and failures on a separate sheet of paper.
   - ◆ Claim 1 John 1:9 for your own life by writing the words of the verse over the list.
   - ◆ Thank God for His forgiveness and cleansing.
   - ◆ Destroy the list.
   - ◆ Make restitution wherever appropriate and possible.

❖ ❖ ❖

Five Principles of Growth

Y ou made the most important decision of your life when you chose to receive Jesus Christ as your Savior and Lord. At that moment you were born into God's family, and you received everything you need to live the abundant Christian life.

But that does not mean you are as spiritually mature as someone who has walked with Christ for many years. The Christian life is a process that begins with an act of faith and is lived by faith.

What do you suppose would happen to a child who doesn't grow properly in his physical body? In his emotional life? In his spiritual maturity? Just as physical life requires air, food, rest, and exercise, so does spiritual life require certain things for growth and development.

This lesson deals with five principles of Christian growth. The first two, *We must study God's Word* and *We must pray,* help us deepen our relationship with God. This could be called our vertical relationship. Through the Bible, God communicates to us; through prayer, we communicate with Him.

The next two principles, *We must fellowship with other Christians* and *We must wit-*

❖

Objective: To understand the essentials of Christian growth and put them into practice

Read: James 1:18–27; Matthew 26:31–75; 1 Corinthians 12:12–27; Acts 26:12–29

Memorize: 2 Timothy 2:15

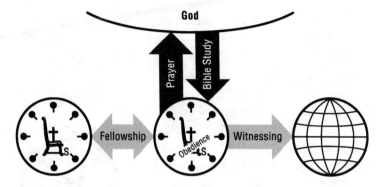

ness for Christ, help us reach out to others. This could be called our horizontal relationship. In fellowship, we communicate with other Christians about our Savior and the bond He gives us with one another. In witnessing, we communicate with non-Christians. We tell them about Jesus, what He has done for us, and what He desires to do for them.

Principle five, *We must obey God,* is the core of the growth. As we obey Him, we experience increasing joy, peace, and fellowship with the Lord Jesus Christ and fellow believers. We also become increasingly more mature in our Christian walk.

If you follow these principles, you can be sure that you will grow toward spiritual maturity in Christ.

❖

Bible Study

Principle One: We Must Study God's Word
Read James 1:18–27.

You would not think of going without physical food for a week or even a day, would you? It is necessary for physical life. Without food, we become weakened and eventually may become ill. Lack of spiritual food produces the same results in our spiritual lives.

1. What is the food of the young Christian (1 Peter 2:2)?

In what ways have you made it a consistent spiritual diet?

Read Psalm 119. Write down several ways that God's Word can help you in your daily life.

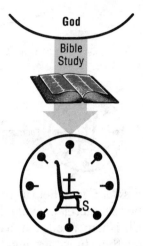

2. Jesus said, "Man shall not live by bread alone." How did He say we should live and be nourished (Matthew 4:4)?

How have you applied this to your life? Describe how it has nourished your spiritual life.

3. List the two characteristics of the workman God approves, according to 2 Timothy 2:15.

What steps have you taken to make these characteristics true in your life?

4. What did Jesus say about those who read and believe God's Word (John 8:31,32)?

What does this mean to your way of life?

5. When does the man who is spiritually mature meditate on the Word of God (Psalm 1:2,3)?

How can you do this in our hectic, pull-apart world?

6. In what specific ways do you expect God's Word to affect you?

Principle Two: We Must Pray

Read Matthew 26:31–75.

Have you ever considered that you have immediate access to the most powerful Person in the universe? Whatever you need, whatever the time, you can call upon Him. His calendar is cleared to be with you; His schedule is open for your appointment; His full attention is devoted to you.

Prayer is the inspiring experience of conversing with and praising God as our loving, heavenly Father. Few experiences can equal prayer in empowering us and lifting us above our problems. But prayer is not just an "escape hatch" for us to get out of trouble, please ourselves, or gain our selfish ends.

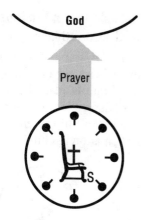

Rather, it is inviting Him to talk to us as we talk to Him. There is more to prayer, but this is basic to true prayer.

Study the above passage and answer the following questions:

1. What was Jesus' command in Matthew 26:41?

   Why did He command it?

2. Why did Peter fail to resist temptation?

3. What was the most serious result of Peter's prayerlessness?

   Think about your own prayer life. What has been the result of prayerlessness in your life?

4. How did Christ experience inner power to face the severest test of His life?

5. How often are we to pray (1 Thessalonians 5:17)?

   Prayer without ceasing involves conversing with our heavenly Father in a simple and free way throughout the day. Our prayer life should be such that we come to know the Lord Jesus in an intimate, personal way. Our prayer life becomes effective as our relationship with Christ becomes more intimate.

> I will do whatever you ask in my name, so that the Son may bring glory to the Father. You may ask me for anything in my name, and I will do it (John 14:13,14).

List ways you can increase the amount of time you spend in prayer.

Principle Three: We Must Fellowship With Other Christians

Read 1 Corinthians 12:12–27.

Fellowship is spending time and doing things with others who love Christ. Several logs burn brightly together, but the fire goes out if one is placed alone on the cold hearth. In the same way, Christians need to work together or the fire of enthusiasm will go out. Fellowship is vital for Christian growth. That is why active participation in church is so important.

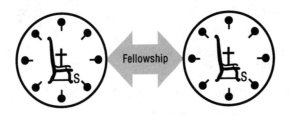

1. As God's children, what should we not neglect (Hebrews 10:23–25)?

2. According to the above verses, what should we do for one another?

    In what ways have you done them recently and for whom?

3. The new believers in Acts 2:42 continued steadfastly in what four things?

    Why is each one so vital to spiritual growth?

4. In what ways do you profit from Christian fellowship? Be specific.

5. Why is it important that a Christian be part of a small group with other Christians sharing the Word of God?

    Why is it so necessary to work out conflicts with members of your Christian circle?

    What can happen if you don't?

    What steps can you take to resolve conflict with others? (Read 1 Peter 3:8–11.)

Principle Four: We Must Witness for Christ

Read Acts 26:12–29.

A witness is a person who tells what he has seen and heard. He shares his own personal experience. Anyone who has a vital personal relationship with Christ can be a witness for Him. Witnessing is the overflow of the Christian life. A vital Christian life is contagious. As our lives are filled with the presence of the Lord Jesus, we cannot help but share Him with those with whom we come in contact.

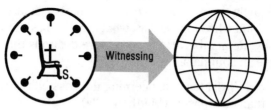

1. In Romans 1:14–16, Paul tells us his own attitude about sharing the gospel with others. Using his three "I am's" as the keys to the passage, describe his attitude in your own words.

2. Compare your own attitude concerning witnessing with Paul's (Colossians 1:28).

3. What did Peter tell us we should always be ready to do (1 Peter 3:15)?

   Where and when can you do this?

4. What was Jesus' promise in Acts 1:8?

   How is His promise shown in your life today?

5. Name at least three people to whom you are impressed to witness in the power of Christ.

   Prayerfully ask God to show you ways to share your faith in Christ with each one.

It is the privilege and responsibility of every Christian to reach his world with the message of Christ. If you would like to receive more information on how to witness effectively for Christ, write to Campus Crusade for Christ, 100 Sunport Lane, Dept. 21-00, Orlando, FL 32809. Ask for specially prepared materials to help you witness for Christ.

Principle Five: We Must Obey God

Read Romans 6:14–23.

The key to rapid growth in the Christian life is obedience to the will of God. Knowing the principles of growth is of no value unless we actually apply them to our lives. To be disobedient to the one who loves us and who alone knows what is really best for us would be sheer folly. Remember, He is even more desirous than you are that you have an abundant life.

1. What did Christ teach concerning the possibility of serving more than one master (Matthew 6:24)?

2. How much should you love the Lord (Matthew 22:37)?

3. How can you prove that you love Him (John 14:21)?

   How have you done this today?

   This week?

4. What will be the result of keeping Christ's commandments (John 15:10,11)?

5. What is God's standard of life for those who say they are abiding in Christ (1 John 2:6)?

6. Where do we get the power to obey God (Philippians 2:13)?

   What happens if we try to obey God's commands in our own effort?

7. In light of Luke 6:46–49, why do you think obedience to Christ is imperative for your life?

LIFE APPLICATION

On this chart, list the five key principles of Christian growth, a key verse relating to each one, why it is essential to spiritual maturity, and at least one way you can apply each principle to your own life.

PRINCIPLE	KEY VERSE	WHY IT IS ESSENTIAL	HOW TO APPLY

❖ ❖ ❖

The Christian's Authority

Before I became a believer in Jesus Christ, God's Word did not make sense to me. I occasionally tried to read it during my high school and college days, but found it boring. Finally, I concluded that no really intelligent person could believe the Bible.

Then I became a Christian.

My life was transformed, and my attitudes concerning the Scriptures changed. I realized the Bible was truly the holy, inspired, and eternally authoritative Word of God.

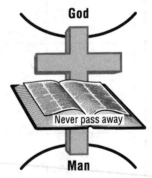

God

Never pass away

Man

❖

Objective: To understand the role and the power of the Bible in our daily Christian lives

Read: Psalm 119:97–104

Memorize: 1 Thessalonians 2:13

Not only is God's Word divinely inspired, but it is also the basis of our belief as Christians. It gives us God's perspective on how we should live and how we can be fruitful witnesses for our Lord Jesus Christ.

The Bible is God's love letter to man. From Genesis to Revelation, it tells of God's great compassion for us and of His desire to fellowship with us.

Furthermore, the Bible reveals God's attributes. It tells us that He is holy, sovereign, righteous and just; that He is loving, merciful and kind; that He is gracious, patient and faithful; that He is powerful, wise, and constantly available to His children.

And the more we read and meditate upon His precious Word—and allow His Holy Spirit to control our lives—the more fruitful we become for our Lord. Because God's Word is truth and "sharper than a two-edged sword," it is impregnated with the power of the Holy Spirit to speak to today's world and our own personal needs and circumstances.

Ultimately our views of the authority of the Bible and of the incarnation of Christ are related. In John 10:34–36, for example, Jesus taught that the Old Testament was totally accurate. In Matthew 4:4–7,10, He quoted it as being authoritative.

In addition, He taught His followers that He was speaking God's own words (John 3:34), and that His words would not pass away but would be eternally authoritative (Matthew 24:35).

He even told us that the Holy Spirit would bring to mind what He said so that the disciples would preach and write accurately, not depending upon only memory or human understanding (John 16:12–15).

A high view of inspiration should be related to personal Bible study and meditation. As you study this lesson, I urge you to apply the principles that you will learn about God's inspired Word to your life. Let God speak to you and invite the Holy Spirit to transform you into a joyful and fruitful Christian.

❖

Bible Study

Biblical Claims of Authority

1. What were the attitudes of the following prophets concerning their writings?

Isaiah 43:1–12

Jeremiah 23:1–8

Ezekiel 36:32–38

2. What were the attitudes of the following authors toward other writers of Scripture?

Paul (Romans 3:1,2)

Peter (2 Peter 1:19–21)

The writer of Hebrews (1:1)

3. If these writers had this high regard for Scripture, how should we view the Bible?

What part should God's Word have in our lives and in the way we evaluate and react to circumstances and events?

Purpose of Personal Bible Study

1. Name some practical results of a thorough study of the Word of God (2 Timothy 3:15–17).

What changes have you seen in your life from your study of the Bible?

2. In Acts 20:32, Paul says that the Word of God is able to do what two things?

3. What should be the effect of reading the Bible on your own life (James 1:22–25)?

Think of a difficult circumstance in your life. In what ways is reading and meditating on God's Word helping you cope with the situation?

How are you applying God's Word to your problem?

Preparations for Personal Bible Study

1. Set aside a definite time.

When did Moses meet with God (Exodus 34:2–4)?

When did Christ meet with God (Mark 1:35)?

When is the best time for you?

2. Find a definite place.

Where did Christ pray (Mark 1:35)?

What is the value of being alone?

3. Employ these tools:

   ◆ Modern translation of the Bible
   ◆ Notebook and pen
   ◆ Dictionary

   How can you use these tools in your Bible study?

Procedure for Personal Bible Study

Using Psalm 119:57–104, go through these three major steps of methodical Bible study:

1. *Observation:* What does the passage say? Read quickly for content.

   Read again carefully, underlining key words and phrases.

2. *Interpretation:* What does the passage mean? Ask God to give you understanding of the passage. Consult a dictionary or modern translation for the precise meaning of words.

   Ask: Who? What? When? Where? Why? How?

3. *Application:* Ask yourself, *What does the passage mean to me and how can I apply it to my life?*

   Make a list of the following:

   ◆ Attitudes to be changed
   ◆ Actions to take or avoid
   ◆ Promises to claim
   ◆ Sins to confess and forsake
   ◆ Examples to follow
   ◆ Other personal applications

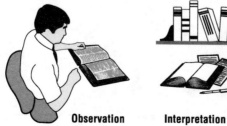 

Observation   **Interpretation**   **Application**

LIFE APPLICATION

1 Study Luke 19:1–10 and apply the Bible study method you have just learned.

What does the passage say?

What does it mean?

How does this apply to you?

How effective will this method of Bible study be for you now with other Scripture passages?

2 What changes in your life do you expect as you proceed with more in-depth Bible study?

3 Plan your Bible study time for the next four weeks. Write down the time, the place, and the passages to be studied.

❖ ❖ ❖

Learning to Pray

ommunication is a vital element in any successful relationship, including our relationship with God. He wants us to communicate with Him about our cares and concerns. He desires that we talk to Him about every area of our lives. This communication with God is called prayer.

Prayer is much more than words. It is an expression of the heart toward God. It is an experience, a relationship—not an activity.

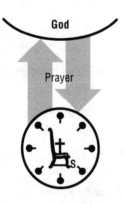

As a child of God, you are invited to come boldly before His throne. In Hebrews 4:14–16, the writer records, "Since we have a great High Priest who has gone through the heavens, Jesus the Son of God, let us...then approach the throne of grace with confidence, so that we may receive mercy and find grace to help us in time of need."

Because the one to whom you pray is the King of kings and Lord of lords, the Creator of heaven and earth, you come into His pre-

❖

Objective: To learn how to develop a personal prayer life

Read: Philippians 4:6; Psalm 62:8; Acts 4:23–33

Memorize: Mark 11:24

sence with reverence. But He is also your loving, heavenly Father who cares for you. Therefore, you can enter into His presence with a relaxed, joyful heart, knowing that God loves you more than anyone else has ever loved you or will ever love you.

❖

Bible Study

What Is Prayer?

Since prayer is communication between two persons, it can also be described as a dialogue. Write a sentence about the part each of these have in the dialogue between the believer and God.

1. Prayer is the privilege of believers (John 3:22,23).

2. We relate to God like children to a father (Ephesians 2:4,5,8; 1 Peter 5:7).

3. God wants to hear what we say (Psalms 62:8; 65:2; Proverbs 15:8).

4. God delights in and longs for our fellowship (Psalm 27:8; John 4:23; Proverbs 15:8).

5. We can talk to God about anything (Matthew 7:7; John 16:24).

6. Prayer can keep us from sin (Matthew 26:41).

How to Pray

1. What part does the Holy Spirit play in prayer (Romans 8:26,27)?

2. What do these verses teach about how to pray?
   Psalm 145:18
   Matthew 6:5–7
   Matthew 21:22
   Philippians 4:6

3. What vital elements of prayer are found in Acts 4:24–30?

4. What vital elements of prayer did Christ include in His prayer in John 17?

5. What are some of the promises Christ makes to you when you pray?

   Matthew 6:6

   Matthew 18:20

   Luke 11:9–13

   John 14:13,14

Steps to Having an Effective Prayer Life

Read the following verses and explain why each step is necessary to pray effectively.

1. Abide (John 15:7)

2. Ask (James 4:2,3)

3. Believe (Matthew 21:22)

4. Receive (1 John 5:14,15)

LIFE APPLICATION

1 Set a time and place for your daily prayer time.

Time _____   Place _____

2 Use a small notebook to help you pray effectively.

- ◆ On page one, make a list of people whom you want to remember daily in prayer.

- ◆ On page two, write a list of things for which you will praise and thank God. Update this list daily.

- ◆ On page three, write the date, prayer requests, and Scripture verses relating to requests. Leave room to write down the answer and date for each request.

- ◆ Each day, repeat the first two points, checking for answered prayers to record on earlier days.

- ◆ Keep this notebook with your Bible so you can refer to it during the day to pray for and record concerns, needs, praises, or thanks that come to mind.

❖ ❖ ❖

The Importance of the Church

A young mother once asked her child if he knew what a church was. With a big smile on his face, he said, "Yes, Mommy, that's where God lives."

Of course, the child's perception that God lives in a single, physical place is incorrect. Nevertheless his statement is profound: God does live in the church—the company of all who believe in Jesus Christ and have received Him as their Savior and Lord.

In a broad biblical sense, the church is the body of Christ—the collection of Christian believers from all over the world and from all times who are bound together by the shed blood of Christ and His resurrected presence.

In our local congregations, we play an important part of the body of Christ. God wants us to work together so that the church body can minister to others more effectively.

The church also is a unity of the Holy Spirit. Although doctrinal differences often separate Christian groups, they are united in the fact that Jesus paid the penalty for our sins by dying on the cross, and He rose from the dead that through Him we can be reconciled to God.

❖

Objective: To emphasize the importance of involvement in a local church

Read: Acts 2:41–47

Memorize: Colossians 1:18

85

The outreach of the church is world-wide. When our Lord's earthly ministry was completed, He commanded the church to carry His good news to the world. By sharing our faith in Christ, we are helping to fulfill this Great Commission.

I am convinced that a proper understanding of the church and how it is to function as a local body is important if we are to be fruitful disciples for Christ.

Some time ago I struck up a conversation with the passenger sitting next to me on a plane flight. As we talked, he was very cordial and pleasant.

Then I asked, "Where are you on your spiritual journey?"

Suddenly, he became defensive. "I had my fill of the church when I was a young boy. Can you believe that I was forced to attend services at least three times a week? Every Sunday morning and evening and every Wednesday night. Years ago I determined that when I became an adult I would never attend church again as long as I live."

"How would you like to live in a community where there was no church?" I inquired.

He dropped his head and was silent for a few moments. Then he replied, "I wouldn't like that."

Looking him firmly in the eye, I said forcefully, "You are a parasite!"

Immediately he became flustered and said impatiently, "What do you mean by that?"

"Simple. You want all the benefits of the church without any of the responsibility."

He smiled slowly, returned my direct gaze, then announced, "For the first time in twenty-five years, I'll be in church on Sunday!"

Before I became a Christian, I used to believe that the church was filled with hypocrites. Now I recognize that many people go to church—not because they are perfect—but because they need help. The church then, in the vernacular of the business world, is a repair shop, not a retail store. The church is not perfect, but it is the institution that offers hope and healing in any community or culture. It is how God reaches out to others with His love and forgiveness.

I urge you to study this lesson prayerfully and carefully. As you continue in your study of the Bible, search out passages that describe the church and its ministry on earth. Keep a diary of your studies for future reference.

❖

Bible Study

Composition of the Church

1. What did the early Christians do that we should do also?

Acts 2:41,42

Acts 4:31

Acts 5:41,42; 8:4

List several ways you can apply these in your Christian walk.

2. As God's children, how do we obey the instruction given in Hebrews 10:25?

3. The entire church is compared to a _____ of which Christ is the _____ and the individual believers are the _____ (Colossians 1;18; 1 Corinthians 12:27).

4. Read 1 Thessalonians 1:1–10, then list here some qualities God desires in members of any church.

In what ways do you demonstrate these qualities?

Ordinances of the Church

1. What do you believe baptism accomplishes (Matthew 28:19)?

Who is eligible for baptism?

What was the significance of your baptism?

   2. What is the meaning of the communion service
(1 Corinthians 11:23–26)?

   How do you prepare yourself to observe the Lord's Supper?

Purposes of the Church

   1. What should be one of the basic purposes of a church
(2 Timothy 4:2)?

   How does the church you attend fulfill the purposes given
in this verse?

   2. List several of your own reasons for joining a church.

   3. What should the church believe about Christ's:

   Birth (Matthew 1:23)?

   Deity (John 1:14)?

   Death (1 Peter 2:24)?

   Resurrection (1 Corinthians 15:3,4)?

   Second coming (1 Thessalonians 4:16,17)?

   Where does your church stand on these truths? It may be
helpful to obtain a doctrinal statement from your church
and research these areas.

   4. What abilities does God give (besides that of serving as a
prophet or apostle) to strengthen the church members
(Ephesians 4:11–13)?

   Which of these roles do you fill?

   Which would you like to be involved in?

   Why?

   How are you preparing yourself for that ministry?

LIFE APPLICATION

1 If you are not already active in a local church, prayer-fully list two or three that you will visit in the next month, with the purpose of attending one regularly.

Before you attend the first service, list the qualities you feel are essential for spiritual growth and fellowship. Ask God to show you which church He is leading you to join.

2 The following are suggestions for making your church worship more meaningful:

◆ Bow for silent prayer before the service begins. Pray for yourself, for the minister, for those taking part in the service and for those worshiping, that Christ will be very real to all, and that those who do not know Christ may come to know Him.

◆ Always take your Bible. Underline portions that are made especially meaningful by the sermons.

◆ Take notes on the sermon and apply them to your life.

Can you list some other ways?

3 If you are a part of a local church, ask God to show you ways you can be more used by Him in the church. List the ways of service that He reveals to you.

❖ ❖ ❖

Recap

The following questions will help you review this Step. If necessary, reread the appropriate lesson(s).

1. Assurance of salvation:

Suppose you have just made the great discovery of knowing Jesus Christ personally. In your enthusiasm, you tell someone close to you that you have become a Christian and have eternal life. He replies, "That's mere presumption on your part. No one can be sure that he has eternal life."

How would you answer him?

What verse(s) would you use as your authority?

2. Name some of the qualities of a Christ-controlled life.

How are they evident in your life?

3. List the five principles of growth.

Summarize briefly how each of these principles is helping you grow spiritually. How do they interact in your life?

Reread: John 3:1–20; 1 John 5:9–15; Romans 6:14–23

Review: Verses memorized

4. What are the three major steps in methodical Bible study? How have these helped you in your study?

   List at least three ways Scripture can be applied to your life.

5. Describe the role that the Bible has played in your life in the past week.

   How can you rely more fully on its power next week?

   How has using the steps to an effective prayer life changed the way you pray?

   How has having a daily prayer time helped your attitudes and actions?

6. Name some characteristics of a New Testament church.

   How does your church compare?

7. What are the two ordinances of the local church?

8. Whom does God give to the church to strengthen its members?

   Which of these roles would you like to fill?

   How are you preparing yourself for ministry?

LIFE APPLICATION

1 In what specific ways is your life different now than when you began this study about the Christian adventure?

2 In what areas do you need to obey the Scripture more?

3 Explain to several Christian friends the excitement you feel about Jesus and how your Christian life is an adventure. Use examples of how God has worked in your life and how He has answered your prayers.

❖ ❖ ❖

The Christian and the Abundant Life

Focusing on New Priorities

STEP 2

What Is the Christian Life?

The Christian life begins with receiving the Lord Jesus Christ—the gift of God's love and forgiveness—by faith. It results in a threefold commitment to a person, the person of the Lord Jesus Christ. It is a commitment to Him of your intellect, emotions, and will.

The Christian life is a personal, intimate relationship between you and Christ. This life begins in faith (Ephesians 2:8,9) and can only be lived by faith. Faith is another word for trust. We trust our lives to Christ's keeping because He has proven Himself trustworthy by His life, His death, His resurrection, and His abiding presence—His unconditional love.

❖

Objective: To understand our new life in Christ and how to begin growing

Read: John 1–3

Memorize: 2 Corinthians 5:17

As you walk in faith and obedience to God as an act of your will and allow Him to change your life, you will gain increasing assurance of your relationship with Him. You will experience God's work in your life as He enables you to do what you cannot do on your own.

❖

Bible Study

A New Creation

1. On the basis of 2 Corinthians 5:17, what has happened to you?

What are some evidences in your life of new things having come, and old things having passed away?

NEW THINGS THAT HAVE COME	OLD THINGS THAT HAVE PASSED AWAY

2. To what does the Bible compare this experience of newness (John 3:3)?

Compare the experience of physical birth with spiritual birth. What are the similarities?

3. How was your new birth accomplished (John 3:16; 1:12,13)?

4. According to Ephesians 2:8,9, what did you do to merit this gift?

Why is this so important to our spiritual well-being?

5. Colossians 1:13,14 speaks of two kingdoms. Describe the nature of each kingdom in relation to your life before and after you received Christ.

A New Relationship With God

1. What are you called (1 Peter 2:2)?

What should be your desire?

2. What is your new relationship with God (John 1:12)?

3. What does it mean to you to be a partaker of the divine nature (2 Peter 1:4)?

4. How do you know that you are God's child (Galatians 4:6; Romans 8:16)?

A New Motivation

1. How does the love of Christ motivate you (2 Corinthians 5:14,15)?

2. What has replaced self as the most important factor (verse 15)?

3. What two things have happened in your life to give you new motivation, according to Colossians 3:1–4?

   What has happened to your old life according to verse 3?

   What will motivate you to seek those things that are above, according to verse 1?

   What is the promise we are given (verse 4)? How does it affect your motivation?

A New Relationship With Mankind

1. What is new about your relationship with people (1 John 3:11,14)?

2. How can you show that you are a follower of Christ (John 13:35)?

   In what ways are you doing this in your everyday life?

3. Read 2 Corinthians 5:18–21. Describe the ministry that has been given to you.

   We are called _____ for Christ (verse 20).

   In what ways are you fulfilling your call?

4. As a follower of Christ, what is the greatest thing you can do (Matthew 4:19)?

   Name at least three ways you can do that in your own life.

5. How can your friends benefit from the message you deliver to them (1 John 1:3,4)?

LIFE APPLICATION

1 What is the greatest change you have seen in your life since you became a new creation in Christ Jesus?

2 In your new relationship with God, what now can be your response toward problems, disappointments, and frustrations (1 Peter 5:7; Romans 8:28)?

3 How will you change your goals as a result of your new motivation?

4 What is your responsibility now to other men and women? How will you carry it out?

5 List two changes you would like to see in your life now that you are a Christian. Ask God to bring about those changes.

❖ ❖ ❖

Appraising Your Spiritual Life

The two circles in the diagram below represent two kinds of lives: the self-directed life and the Christ-directed life.

The one on the left illustrates a life with self in control, and depicts a stressful, chaotic life.

The circle on the right represents a life with Jesus Christ in control, balanced and orderly, with the potential for rich, productive experiences.

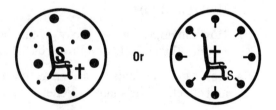

Or

Which circle best represents you?

Objective: To evaluate your relationship with Christ

Which circle would you like to have represent your life?

Read: John 4–6

Memorize: Galatians 6:7

Meditate on each question in this lesson as well as on the answer. Make this a personal appraisal of your spiritual condition.

❖

Bible Study

Types of Soil

Read the parable of the sower in Matthew 13:1–23; Mark 4:3–20; Luke 8:4–15.

1. To what does the seed refer (Mark 4:14)?

2. What are the four kinds of soil referred to in Matthew 13:4–8?

Making Soil Productive

1. What does each kind of soil represent? Compare Matthew 13:4 with 18,19.

Compare verses 5,6 with 20,21.

Compare verse 7 with 22.

Compare verse 8 with 23.

2. What must happen for the roadside soil to be changed (Hebrews 3:15)?

3. How can unproductive, rocky ground be made productive (1 Corinthians 10:13 and Proverbs 29:25)?

4. How can individuals described as thorny soil become vital and effective Christians (1 Peter 5:7; Matthew 6:19–21)?

Result of Dwelling in Good Soil

1. What condition in a Christian results in abundance of fruit (Mark 4:20; Luke 8:15)?

2. What type of soil do most of the professing Christians you know represent?

3. What type of soil would you say your life now represents?

4. What type of soil do you want your life to represent?

LIFE APPLICATION

1 How must the soil of your life be changed to become good ground or to increase in its fruitfulness?

2 List several problem areas that need changing.

3 What must you trust Christ to do?

❖ ❖ ❖

Living Abundantly

Imagine coming home one day to find a stain in your brand new living room carpet. You try everything possible to take out the discoloration. Nothing seems to work. Then someone gives you a special formula guaranteed to remove even the worst of stains. The spot remover is so powerful that it not only takes out the blotch, but it also protects the carpet from ever being blemished again.

This is what God does with our sins. Christ's excruciating death on the cross forever blotted out our unrighteousness. No sin is too deep, no stain too dark, that God cannot cleanse us to a brilliant white through the precious blood of Jesus Christ.

Christ's sacrifice for us on the cross is complete. He saved us from the penalty of sin (John 3:18; Ephesians 2:8). We are being saved from the power of sin (Jude 24,25; 2 Thessalonians 3:3). And we will be saved from the presence of sin (1 John 3:2; Philippians 3:21; 1 Corinthians 15:51,52).

You have trusted God for the payment of your penalty for sin and for eternal life. Why not trust Him now for power over sin? Remember that as you received Christ by faith, so you should walk in faith and receive the abundant life that He has promised you.

Objective: To learn the steps to abundant life

Read: John 7–9

Memorize: John 10:10

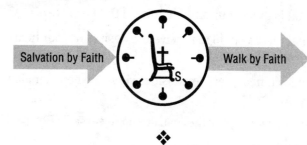

❖

Bible Study

The Basis of Abundant Living
Read Romans 6:1–23.

1. What do you know happened to you when you became a Christian (verse 6)?

2. According to verse 11, what must you do?

3. According to verse 13, what is your responsibility?

4. According to verse 16, man is a servant either of sin or of righteousness. What determines his allegiance?

   Review Romans 6:6,11,13,16 and note the progression:

   ◆ *Know* that you have been crucified with Christ.

   ◆ *Count* yourself dead to sin and alive to Jesus Christ.

   ◆ *Offer* yourself unto God.

   ◆ *Obey* God.

   (See Directory of Terms on the following page.)

   Using these four steps, dedicate yourself to serving God rather than sin.

5. Describe the benefits you have already seen from righteous living.

The Practice of Abundant Living
Read Psalm 37:1–7,34.

1. What wrong attitudes are given in verse 1?

2. What is to be your attitude toward the Lord (verse 3)?

3. What must you do to receive the desires of your heart (verse 4)?

4. Why is it necessary to consider verse 5 when you plan your future?

5. How can you apply the instruction in verse 7? Be specific.

6. What does verse 34 mean to you?

Now, review the above references and note the progression:

◆ Do not *fret.*
◆ *Trust* in the Lord.
◆ *Delight* yourself in the Lord.
◆ *Commit* your way to the Lord.
◆ *Be still* before the Lord.
◆ *Wait* on the Lord.

(See Directory of Terms below.)

The secret of the abundant life is contained in these key words: *know, count, offer, obey, fret not, trust, delight, commit, be still,* and *wait.* (Underline these words in Romans 6 and Psalm 37 in your Bible.)

Directory of Terms

Know—to be fully assured of a fact

Count—to act upon a fact, to consider it, to depend upon it instead of upon feelings

Offer—to give up, to surrender, to submit

Obey—to put instructions into effect, to comply with, to trust

Fret not—to give up worry and anxiety

Trust—to rely on wholeheartedly

Delight—to take great pleasure or joy

Commit—to place in trust or charge, to entrust

Be still—to completely listen

Wait—to anticipate with confident expectancy

LIFE APPLICATION

1 In the chart below, indicate which key words of the abundant life you are now applying, and which you need to begin to apply, through the power of Christ.

KEY WORDS	APPLYING NOW (✓)	NEED TO APPLY (✓)
KNOW		
COUNT		
OFFER		
OBEY		
FRET NOT		
TRUST		
DELIGHT		
COMMIT		
BE STILL		
WAIT		

2 How do you plan to apply these? Be specific.

❖ ❖ ❖

The Abiding Life

Alex was distressed over his constant failure to live the Christian life victoriously.

"I'm always failing," he said. "I know what is right, but I'm simply not able to keep the many commitments, resolutions, and rededications that I make to the Lord almost daily.

"What's wrong with me? Why do I constantly fail? How can I push that magic button that will change my life and make me the kind of person God wants me to be, and the kind of person I want to be?"

All of us experience this conflict when we walk in our own strength. But the victory is ours as we learn to abide in Christ.

Jesus said, "I am the vine, you are the branches. He who abides in Me, and I in him, bears much fruit; for without Me you can do nothing" (John 15:5, NKJ). The reality of abiding in Christ and Christ abiding in us is made possible through a supernatural enabling of the Holy Spirit.

Abiding in Christ means to be one with Him by faith. It is to live in conscious dependence upon Him, recognizing that it is His life, His power, His wisdom, His strength, and His ability operating through us that enable us to live according to His will. We do this by

❖

Objective: To understand and begin abiding in Christ

Read: John 10–12

Memorize: John 15:7,16

surrendering the throne of our lives to Him, and by faith drawing upon His resources to live a supernatural, holy fruitful life.

The "abiding life"—we in Christ, He in us—enables us to live a victorious and fruitful life. Millions of Christians throughout the world profess their love for Christ each week by attending church services, singing songs, studying their Bibles, and attending prayer meetings. Yet, all the talk in the world will never convince anyone that you or I truly love the Lord unless we obey Him, and this includes bearing fruit for Him. The only way we can demonstrate that we are truly abiding in Him is to produce fruit, which involves introducing others to our Savior as well as living holy lives.

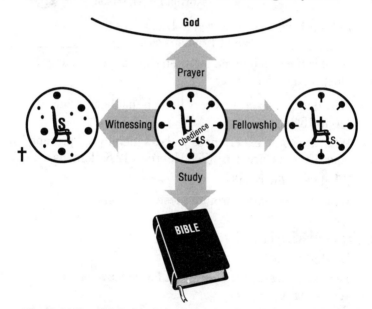

The "abiding life" also brings lasting joy. "I have told you this," Jesus said, "so that my joy may be in you and that your joy may be complete."

To live this joyful, abundant life, we must learn to live in Christ, constantly yielding total control of our lives to Him.

Is the abiding presence of Jesus Christ a reality in your life? As an expression of your will, in prayer, surrender the throne of your life to Him, and by faith invite Him to endow you with supernatural life and enable you to bear much fruit for His glory.

❖

Bible Study

The Abiding Life

"Abiding is the key to
Christian experience by
which the divine attributes are
transplanted into human soil, to the
transforming of character and conduct."
—Norman B. Harrison

1. In John 15:5, Jesus referred to Himself as the
   _____ and Christians as the _____.

   What is the relationship between Christ and you, as
   illustrated in that verse?

2. Why does Jesus prune every branch that bears fruit
   (John 15:2)?

   What are some experiences you can identify as "pruning" in
   your life as a Christian? (See Hebrews 12:6; Romans 5:3–5.)

   What were the results?

   What did you learn through these situations?

Results of Abiding in Christ

1. Read John 15:7–11.

   List two necessary qualifications for effective prayer
   according to verse 7.

2. Jesus glorified God. How can you glorify God (verse 8)?

3. Christ commands us to continue in His love. How great
   do you believe this love to be (verse 9)?

   How are we to abide in Christ's love (verse 10)?

   How do you think the result promised in verse 11 will be
   revealed in your life today?

4. What has Christ chosen us to do (John 15:16)?

What is meant by "fruit"? (See Matthew 4:19; Galatians 5:22,23; Ephesians 5:9; Philippians 1:11.)

5. Why do you think Jesus chose this particular way to illustrate our abiding in Him?

6. Will you be able to do what Christ expects of you? How do you know?

LIFE APPLICATION

 Write briefly what you need to do to begin abiding in Christ more consistently.

2 What do you think He will do as a result?

3 How do you think that will affect your life?

❖ ❖ ❖

The Cleansed Life

If the Holy Spirit was sent to give me power to live a victorious life, why do I feel so powerless, so defeated?

We often yearn for spiritual power and do not have it because of impure motives, selfish desires, or unconfessed sin. God does not fill a dirty vessel with His power and love. The vessel of our lives must be cleansed by the blood of our Lord before it can be filled with the Spirit of God.

The psalmist wrote, "Search me, O God, and know my heart; test me and know my anxious thoughts. See if there is any offensive way in me, and lead me in the way everlasting" (Psalm 139:23,24).

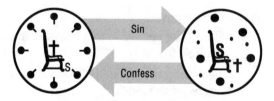

❖

Objective: To learn the importance and means of living a cleansed life, moment by moment

Read: John 13–15

Memorize: 1 John 1:9

I believe that this prayer is an essential discipline of the Christian's inner life. It expresses to God our desire for purity, our longing to make His ways our ways. Asking Him to reveal to us any unconfessed sin enables us to keep our accounts short with

Him. Confession results in cleansing. God's Word promises, "If we confess our sins, he is faithful and just and will forgive us our sins and purify us from all unrighteousness (1 John 1:9).

The Holy Spirit longs to fill us with His power and love. In this lesson, you will learn how your life can have this power. The first step is to be cleansed from sin and filled with the Spirit of God.

❖

Bible Study

Living "Out of Fellowship" With God
Study the preceding diagram.

1. What characterizes a person who is not in fellowship with God (James 1:8)?

   Think back on your life. How has this verse characterized you?

   In what way(s) has this changed since you came to know Jesus Christ?

2. Read Isaiah 59:2. What is the result of sin in one's life?

3. Do you think sin in your life has affected your relationship with God? How?

How to be Cleansed

1. What is the condition for cleansing and forgiveness (1 John 1:9)?

   The word confess means "to say the same thing as another—to agree with God."

   Confession involves three things:

   ◆ Agreeing that you have sinned (be specific)

   ◆ Agreeing that Christ's death on the cross paid the penalty for that sin

   ◆ Repentance—changing your attitude toward that sin, which will result in a change of action toward that sin

When God brings to your attention the fact that something you have done is sin, you are to confess—say the same thing God says about that specific sin. Do not just say, "I have sinned," but state what the sin was and agree with God, looking at it from His viewpoint. Then determine to put it out of your life and not do it again.

2. What two things did the psalmist do about his sin in Psalm 32:5?

Read Proverbs 28:13. What is the result of not admitting sin? Of admitting sin?

3. In what situations has each of these results been true in your life?

Living "In Fellowship" With God

1. Notice in the diagram at the beginning of this lesson that, when we confess our sins, God restores us to fellowship. Walking in fellowship with the Father and the Son is referred to as "walking in the light."

Read 1 John 1:7 and list two results promised.

Give an example of how you have experienced each in your life.

2. When we are in fellowship with God, specific things are happening within us. According to Philippians 2:13 and 4:13, what are they?

Describe how the verses can help you overcome specific temptations or weaknesses you face.

3. What is this power within us and what is its result (Romans 8:9; Galatians 5:22,23)?

List several ways the qualities found in Galatians 5:22,23 are at work in your life.

4. What should be our attitude when tempted (Romans 6:11–14)?

Why (Colossians 3:3)?

Identify ways you can obey the instructions given in Romans 6:11–14.

LIFE APPLICATION

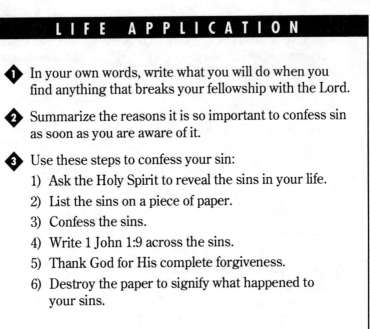

1 In your own words, write what you will do when you find anything that breaks your fellowship with the Lord.

2 Summarize the reasons it is so important to confess sin as soon as you are aware of it.

3 Use these steps to confess your sin:

1) Ask the Holy Spirit to reveal the sins in your life.

2) List the sins on a piece of paper.

3) Confess the sins.

4) Write 1 John 1:9 across the sins.

5) Thank God for His complete forgiveness.

6) Destroy the paper to signify what happened to your sins.

❖ ❖ ❖

Victorious in Spiritual Warfare

Picture with me for a moment a British soldier in the Revolutionary War. Along with his fellow soldiers, he fought against the Colonial forces, who were brilliantly led by General George Washington. As the small Colonial army fought against the overwhelming, superior troops of England, they were miraculously victorious. Even so, there were several British soldiers who refused to surrender. They refused to admit their defeat, and they continued with guerrilla activity.

This is the portrait of the Christian life. We read in Colossians 1:13,14 that God has rescued us out of the darkness and gloom of Satan's kingdom. The Christian flag of victory has been raised; Satan has been defeated. Yet the spiritual guerrilla warfare continues.

If we are to walk in the control and fullness of the Holy Spirit, we must be prepared for spiritual conflict.

I am sure there are dozens of times every day—at home, at the office, at the grocery store, while driving on the freeway—that you face temptations to compromise your Christian convictions. None of us in this life have gotten to the point of perfection. I can tell you

❖

Objective: To learn of spiritual warfare and how to use the things God has provided for the battle

Read: John 16–18

Memorize: Ephesians 6:10–12

115

that even after almost fifty years of walking with our wonderful Lord, I face such guerrilla warfare daily.

Ephesians 6:10–18 exhorts us to "put on all of God's armor so that you will be able to stand safe against all the strategies and tricks of Satan."

There are ways you can deal with the "guerrillas" in your life. Let me list just a few:

1. *Confess all known sin in your life.* Sin is the result of disobedience, and it gives Satan a stronghold in our lives.

2. *Center your affections on Christ and surrender to His Lordship.* The apostle Paul records in Romans 12:2, "Don't copy the behavior and customs of this world, but be a new and different person with a fresh newness in all you do and think" (TLB).

3. *Know that as an act of your will by faith, you can be free in Christ.* Romans 6:16 says: "Don't you realize that you can choose your own master? You can choose sin [with death] or else obedience [with acquittal]" (TLB).

4. *Be filled with the Spirit.* You are filled with the Spirit in the same way you became a Christian—by faith (Ephesians 5:18).

5. *Study God's holy, inspired Word daily.* Prayerfully apply its truths to your life.

6. *Experience daily the power of prayer.* As a child of God you are invited to come boldly before His throne to receive His mercy and find grace in your time of need (Hebrews 4:14–16).

7. *Live by faith.* Everything you receive from God, from the moment of your spiritual birth until you die, is by faith. It is impossible to please God without faith (Hebrews 11:6).

Christ died to win the victory over all the guerrillas in our lives. I encourage you to begin applying these principles to your life today, and He will help you to be strong in Him.

❖

Bible Study

Describe in your own words the picture
depicted in Paul's command given
in Ephesians 6:10–18.

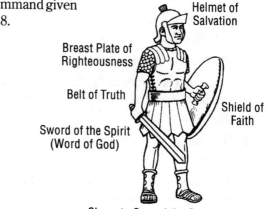

Helmet of
Salvation

Breast Plate of
Righteousness

Belt of Truth

Shield of
Faith

Sword of the Spirit
(Word of God)

Shoes to Spread the Gospel of Peace

We Are On the Battlefield

1. What two things will putting on the whole armor of God
help you to do (verses 10,11)?

How are we to defend ourselves against our enemies
(verses 10–13)?

2. Who are the enemies?

James 4:4

Galatians 5:16,17

1 Peter 5:8

3. Name the six protective pieces of armor that God provides
and expects you to wear (Ephesians 6:14–17).

4. How can you employ the sword of God's Word (verse 17)
for defense against temptation (Psalm 119:9,11)?

5. List some ways the sword of God's Word can be used in an
offensive action (2 Timothy 3:16,17).

6. How can you stay alert and always be prepared
   (Ephesians 6:18; Colossians 4:2)?

We Are More Than Conquerors Through Christ!

1. How should you respond to these enemies?

   Romans 12:2

   Galatians 5:16

   James 4:7

2. When you consider the pieces of armor and weapons
   provided, who can you conclude is really fighting the battle
   (Ephesians 6:10)?

3. Why can you always expect God to be the winner
   (1 John 4:4)?

4. How does Romans 8:31 affect your attitude toward
   adversity and temptation?

5. How do these principles help you to live a more
   abundant life?

LIFE APPLICATION

1 Describe a specific situation in your life right now in which you need to employ a spiritual "weapon."

2 Which weapon(s) will you use and how?

3 What results do you expect?

❖ ❖ ❖

LESSON 7

Attitude Makes the Difference

Your son has just been rushed into the emergency room at the hospital. He was severely injured in a traffic accident, and is not expected to live...

You've just discovered that your teenage daughter is pregnant...

The house payment is past due; the dentist is threatening to turn your bill over to collection. Your telephone has been shut off, and you're facing a layoff at the plant...

Your husband is a hopeless alcoholic. He becomes violent when he is drunk...

Crisis is part of life. We cannot escape difficulty. Jesus said, "In this world you will have trouble" (John 16:33). In short, life is a battleground. But it is not the crisis that creates the problem; it is how we react to it. The pain of trouble can be eased by the attitude we take toward it.

When two Christians face the same tragedy, one may become depressed and defeated while the other draws closer to God. What do you think is the reason for this?

Sometimes Christians believe that God has let them down when they find themselves without money, health, or prestige, or in severe straits. Such an attitude leads to cold-

❖

Objective: To begin looking at life consistently from God's perspective

Read: John 19–21

Memorize: 2 Corinthians 1:3,4

120

ness of heart, prayerlessness, distrust, worry, and selfish living.

In this study you will learn about unrecognized blessings and how attitude makes the difference between a defeated outlook and a victorious one.

❖

Bible Study

God's People in Trouble

In Exodus 14:1–4, the Israelites experienced an unrecognized blessing. As you read, notice the human viewpoint of the people and God's viewpoint as seen in Moses.

1. How did the Israelites react to apparent danger (Exodus 14:10–12)?

2. Notice how Moses reacted. Why do you think he commanded the people as he did (Exodus 14:13,14)?

3. What did God accomplish in their hearts and minds through this experience (Exodus 14:31)?

4. Think back to a crisis in your life. How did those around you respond?

How did you react?

How could you have improved your attitude?

List ways God has worked through difficulties in your life, and has shown these difficulties really to be blessings.

Taking the Proper Attitude

1. List some things the Bible guarantees when you are tempted or tested (1 Corinthians 10:13).

2. How can the Bible's guarantee in Romans 8:28 be true that everything will work out for good to those who love God?

When have you ever doubted God's work in your life? Why?

3. What response to tribulation does God expect from you,
according to Romans 5:3–5?

What are the results of tribulations? (See also James 1:3.)

4. What is the purpose of unrecognized blessings according to:

2 Corinthians 1:3,4

Hebrews 12:5–11

5. Read 1 Thessalonians 5:18 and Hebrews 13:15.

What response does God command in *all* situations?

How can you rejoice and give thanks when sorrow and
tragedy come?

Contrast this with the attitude of the Israelites in
Exodus 14:1–12.

LIFE APPLICATION

 List the methods by which an attitude of trust can become a reality for you. (See Ephesians 5:18; Galatians 5:16; 1 Thessalonians 5:17; Romans 10:17.)

 With what trial in your life do you need to trust God right now?

❸ What do you think the unrecognized blessings in that trial could be?

❹ How can you receive those blessings?

❖ ❖ ❖

Recap

The following questions will help you review this Step. If necessary, reread the appropriate lesson(s).

1. In your own words, what does the abundant Christian life involve?

2. Envision and describe the abundant life you desire for yourself.

What part does bearing fruit have?

What part does spiritual warfare play?

3. How do you know your picture of the abundant life is consistent with God's view?

❖

Reread: Luke 8:4–5;
Romans 6:1–16; John
15:1–17; 1 John 1:1–9

Review: Verses
memorized

LIFE APPLICATION

1 What specific steps do you still need to take to make the abundant life a reality for you?

2 List verses from Lesson 6 that can help you deal with temptations you face. Each week, update this list to include additional temptations and the verses to help you deal with them.

TEMPTATION	VERSE

❖ ❖ ❖

The
Christian
and the Holy Spirit

Moving
Beyond
Discouragement
& Defeat

STEP 3

Who Is the Holy Spirit and Why Did He Come?

While there is a degree of divine mystery to the nature of the Holy Spirit, He definitely is not a bundle of warm feelings or good memories. Neither is He a vague cosmic force. In this lesson, you will study biblical evidence proving that the Holy Spirit is a real person who loves and cares for you. You also will discover why He came and how He can make a difference in your life.

❖

Bible Study

Who Is the Holy Spirit?

The Holy Spirit is a person, the third person of the Trinity: Father, Son, and Holy Spirit. He is not a vague, ethereal shadow, nor an impersonal force. He is a person equal in

❖

Objective: To become acquainted with the Holy Spirit and to understand His mission

Read: John 3:1–8; Romans 8

Memorize: John 16:13,14

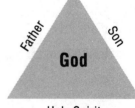

Father
Son
God
Holy Spirit

every way with the Father and the Son. All the divine attributes ascribed to the Father and the Son are equally ascribed to the Holy Spirit.

1. Personality (a person) is composed of intellect, emotions, and will. In 1 Corinthians 2:11, what indicates that the Holy Spirit has intellect?

   What evidence do you observe in Romans 15:30 that the Holy Spirit has emotion?

   How does the Holy Spirit exercise His will as recorded in 1 Corinthians 12:11?

2. Find the one word that describes the nature of the Holy Spirit in each of the following references.

   Romans 8:2

   John 16:13

   Hebrews 10:29

   Romans 1:4

3. What is His function or role?

   John 14:16,26

   1 Corinthians 3:16

   John 16:13,14

   Acts 1:8

4. What specific actions does the Holy Spirit perform?

   Acts 13:2

   Acts 8:29

   Romans 8:14

   John 16:7,8

   Romans 8:26

   2 Thessalonians 2:13

5. What are His attributes?

   Hebrews 9:14

   Psalm 139:7

   1 Corinthians 2:10,11

Why Did He Come?

1. What is the chief reason the Holy Spirit came (John 16:14)?

2. What will be a logical result when the Holy Spirit controls your life?

3. How does the following diagram compare with your life?

- Love
- Joy
- Peace
- Patience
- Kindness
- Faithfulness
- Goodness

- Life is Christ-centered
- Empowered by Holy Spirit
- Introduces others to Christ
- Has effective prayer life
- Understands God's Word
- Trusts God
- Obeys God

LIFE APPLICATION

1 Write one new insight you have gained from this lesson concerning the Holy Spirit.

2 In what area of your life do you believe the Holy Spirit needs to be more in control?

3 What will be the result when He is in control?

❖ ❖ ❖

The Holy Spirit's Relationship With You

The moment you receive Christ, you are regenerated, indwelt, sealed, baptized, and filled with the Holy Spirit. As a result, you have the potential to live a life of victory over sin and witness in the power of the Holy Spirit. This potential is released by faith as you surrender control of your life to Him.

In this lesson, you will see how the Holy Spirit can work in your life and the results you can expect as you yield yourself to His control.

Objective: To understand the work of the Holy Spirit in your life

Read: Romans 12:1–8; 1 Corinthians 2

Memorize: Ephesians 5:18

❖

Bible Study

The Work of the Holy Spirit

1. When you became a Christian (that is, at the time of your spiritual birth), the Holy Spirit did a number of things for and in you. What are they?

1 Corinthians 3:16

Ephesians 4:30

1 Corinthians 12:13

2 Corinthians 5:5

2. Explain in your own words what the Holy Spirit does for the Christian according to the following verses:

Romans 8:16

Romans 8:26,27

The Results of Being Filled With the Holy Spirit

1. Can a person be a Christian and not have the Holy Spirit dwelling in Him (Romans 8:9)? Explain.

2. What is the main reason to be filled with the Spirit (Acts 1:8; 4:29,31)?

3. What work of the Holy Spirit is necessary for successful Christian living and service (Ephesians 5:18)?

LIFE APPLICATION

1 Complete the chart below:

HOW I VIEWED THE HOLY SPIRIT IN THE PAST	HOW I VIEW HIM NOW

2 Are you filled with the Holy Spirit?

How do you know?

If not, what makes you think you are not filled?

3 Do you really desire to be filled with the Holy Spirit?

Why?

❖ ❖ ❖

Why So Few Christians Are Filled With the Holy Spirit

Through the centuries, many of Christ's followers have been ordinary people. Nothing spectacular ever happened to them or through them. Then, as happened to Peter on the day of Pentecost when he was filled with the Holy Spirit, their lives were dramatically changed.

No longer ordinary or average, they became men and women of God—bold in faith and instruments of God's power.

Today, that same Holy Spirit—with His life-changing power—is available to each of us. Yet, tragically, multitudes of Christians go through life without ever experiencing the abundant and fruitful life that Christ promised to all who trust Him.

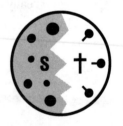

❖

Objective: To understand and deal with the barriers to a Spirit-filled life

Read: Galatians 5 and 6; Acts 5:1–11

Memorize: 1 John 2:1–6, 15–17

In this lesson, you will examine the reasons so few Christians have experienced the infilling of the Spirit. And you will have the opportunity to consider any barriers you may have erected between yourself and God. I urge you to meditate and reflect on how they may apply to your own life.

Bible Study

The Heart's Battlefield

1. How does Paul describe himself in Romans 7:19–24?

How does this description make you feel?

2. In your own words, explain why so many Christians are unhappy, according to Galatians 5:16,17.

Why the Battle Is Often Lost

1. According to each of the following verses, give one reason so few Christians are filled with the Holy Spirit.

Psalm 119:105

Proverbs 16:18

Proverbs 29:25

Luke 9:26

2. What else can create a barrier between you and the Lord that keeps you from being filled with the Spirit (Psalm 66:18)?

What else can divert you from being filled with the Spirit (1 John 2:15–17)?

- Legalistic attitude
- Impure thoughts
- Jealousy
- Guilt
- Worry
- Discouragement
- Critical spirit
- Frustration
- Aimlessness
- Fear

- Ignorance of his spiritual heritage
- Unbelief
- Disobedience
- Loss of love for God and for others
- Poor prayer life
- No desire for Bible study

3. Lack of trust in God also will keep you from being filled with the Holy Spirit. Read John 3:16, Romans 8:32, and 1 John 3:16. Describe how these verses help you trust God fully.

Basically, the reason most Christians are not filled with the Holy Spirit is that they are unwilling to surrender their wills to God.

LIFE APPLICATION

1 Examine the diagram on page 137, and write in your notebook any of those or other barriers you are aware of between yourself and God.

2 Prayerfully consider, then answer this question: "Am I willing to surrender my will to God?"

3 If you are, pray this prayer with all of your heart to turn your life over to God.

> *Dear Father, I need You. I acknowledge that I have been directing my own life and that, as a result, I have sinned against You. I thank You that You have forgiven my sins through Christ's death on the cross for me. I now invite Christ to again take His place on the throne of my life. Fill me with the Holy Spirit as you commanded me to be filled. I pray this in the name of Jesus. As an expression of my faith, I now thank You for taking control of my life and for filling me with the Holy Spirit. Amen.*

❖   ❖   ❖

How You Can Be Filled With the Holy Spirit

Learning how to be filled (controlled and empowered) by the Holy Spirit by faith can be the most important discovery of your life.

We are filled with the Spirit by faith, just as we received Christ by faith. Everything we receive from God, from the moment of our spiritual birth until we die, is by faith.

Do you want to be filled with the Holy Spirit? You can be filled right now, by faith. This lesson will show you how.

❖

Bible Study

Objective: To personally ask for the filling of the Holy Spirit by faith

Read: Acts 6:8–7:60

Memorize: Romans 12:1,2; Ephesians 5:18; 1 John 5:14,15

What You Must Know

1. What is the *command* found in Ephesians 5:18?

2. What is the *promise* found in 1 John 5:14,15?

3. According to these Scriptures, why do you need to be filled with the Spirit?

   Galatians 5:22,23

   Acts 1:8

The fruit of the Spirit is never an end in itself, but only a means to the end. We win men and women to Christ, which in turn brings glory and honor to Him (John 15:8).

What You Must Feel

1. What is one prerequisite to being filled with the Spirit, according to Matthew 5:6?

2. How are you applying this to your life?

What You Must Do

1. If your desire to be filled with the Spirit is sincere, what will you do now (Romans 12:1,2)?

This means there can be no unconfessed sin in your life. The Holy Spirit cannot fill an unclean vessel. He waits to fill you with His power.

2. How then are you filled with the Holy Spirit (Matthew 7:7–11; John 7:37–39)?

3. Will the Holy Spirit fill you if you ask Him? How do you know (1 John 5:14,15)?

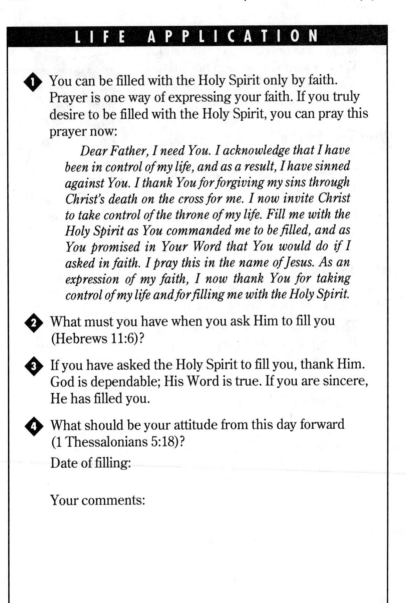

LIFE APPLICATION

1 You can be filled with the Holy Spirit only by faith. Prayer is one way of expressing your faith. If you truly desire to be filled with the Holy Spirit, you can pray this prayer now:

> *Dear Father, I need You. I acknowledge that I have been in control of my life, and as a result, I have sinned against You. I thank You for forgiving my sins through Christ's death on the cross for me. I now invite Christ to take control of the throne of my life. Fill me with the Holy Spirit as You commanded me to be filled, and as You promised in Your Word that You would do if I asked in faith. I pray this in the name of Jesus. As an expression of my faith, I now thank You for taking control of my life and for filling me with the Holy Spirit.*

2 What must you have when you ask Him to fill you (Hebrews 11:6)?

3 If you have asked the Holy Spirit to fill you, thank Him. God is dependable; His Word is true. If you are sincere, He has filled you.

4 What should be your attitude from this day forward (1 Thessalonians 5:18)?

Date of filling:

Your comments:

❖ ❖ ❖

How You Can Know When You Are Filled With the Holy Spirit

Did you sincerely follow the steps outlined in Lesson 4? Did you ask the Holy Spirit to fill you? If you did not, Lessons 5 and 6 will not mean much to you. Go back to Lesson 4 and ask God to work in your heart. If He has filled you, you will be anxious to proceed with these next two lessons.

❖

Bible Study

Results of the Spirit-filled Life

1. What will the Holy Spirit demonstrate in and through your life as a result of His filling you (Galatians 5:22,23)?

Which specific fruit of the Spirit are you most in need of?

Objective: To experience assurance of the filling of the Holy Spirit

Read: Galatians 5:16–26

Memorize: Galatians 5:22,23

2. Read Acts 1:8. How do you see this power at work in your life?

How does John 15:16 apply to you today?

3. How do you identify with 1 Corinthians 12:1–11 and Ephesians 4:11?

4. What mannerisms, language, activities, and inconsistencies in your life do you think are hindering the Holy Spirit from developing His fruit, power, and gifts in you?

5. What happens as we are occupied with Christ and allow the Holy Spirit to work in us (2 Corinthians 3:18)?

Fact, Faith, and Feelings

1. *Fact:* Why should we be filled with the Holy Spirit (Ephesians 5:18)?

2. *Faith:* What is our assurance that we have been filled with the Spirit (1 John 5:14,15)?

3. *Feelings:* When you were filled with the Spirit, did you feel any different?

Do not depend upon feelings. The promise of God's Word, not our feelings, is our authority. The Christian lives by faith in the trustworthiness of God Himself and His Word.

This train diagram illustrates the relationship among fact [God and His Word], faith [our trust in God and His Word], and feeling [the result of our faith and obedience] (John 14:21).

The train will run with or without the caboose. However, it would be futile to attempt to pull the train by the caboose. In the same way, we do not depend upon feelings or emotions, but we place our faith (trust) in the trustworthiness of God and the promise of His Word.

Though you may not be aware of a change immediately, with the passing of time you will see some evidence of your being filled with the Spirit. If there is no change, the Holy Spirit is not in charge.

1 Do you think a person can be filled with the Holy Spirit and not be aware of it? Explain.

2 Ask yourself these questions:

◆ Do you have a greater love for Christ?

◆ Do you have a greater love for God's Word?

◆ Is prayer more important to you?

◆ Are you more concerned for those who do not know Christ as Savior?

◆ Are you experiencing a greater boldness, liberty, and power in witnessing?

If you can answer yes truthfully to these questions, you undoubtedly are filled with the Spirit.

3 What does that assurance mean to you now?

4 If your answer was no to any of those five questions, what do you suppose that indicates?

5 What will you do to change your attitude or actions?

❖ ❖ ❖

How You Can Continue to Be Filled With the Holy Spirit

❖

Objective: To experience the Spirit-filled life as a moment-by-moment reality

Read: Acts 10

Memorize: John 14:21 or John 15:10

If you are a Christian, the Holy Spirit already dwells within you. When you purchase a mechanical item that runs on battery power, frequently the notice "Batteries Not Included" is printed on the box. The Holy Spirit—your Source of power for living—is "included" when you receive Jesus Christ as your Savior and Lord. Therefore, you do not need to invite Him to come into your life. He came to live within you when you became a Christian, and Jesus promised that He will never leave you.

The moment you received Christ, the Holy Spirit not only came to indwell you, but He imparted to you spiritual life, causing you to be born anew as a child of God. The Holy Spirit also baptized you into the body of Christ. In 1 Corinthians 12:13, Paul explains, "We were all baptized by one Spirit into one body."

There is but one indwelling of the Holy Spirit, one rebirth of the Holy Spirit, and one baptism of the Holy Spirit—all of which occur when you receive Christ.

Being filled with the Holy Spirit, however, is not a once-for-all experience. There are many fillings, as is made clear in Ephesians 5:18.

Bible Study

How to Be Filled Continually

Read Ephesians 5:18. In the original Greek, "be filled" means "keep on being filled constantly and continually." Living a godly life is a vital part of this process.

1. What characterizes the life of a Christian who is "being filled" constantly and continually (John 15:1–11; Galatians 5:16–25)?

2. Which two commandments do you think are most important to living the Spirit-filled life (Matthew 22:36–40)? Why?

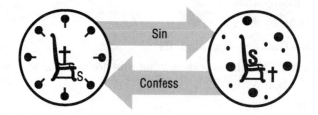

3. To be filled continually with the Holy Spirit, you must confess any known sin in your life and abide in Christ. Read John 15:1–11.

How can you abide in Christ (John 14:21; John 15:10)?

What does the example of the vine and branches in verses 1–8 mean to you in your Christian life?

4. Do not grieve the Holy Spirit.

Read Ephesians 4:25–32. How do you grieve the Holy Spirit?

Which commandment in that list do you need to pay special attention to?

How can you get rid of sin in your life (1 John 1:9)?

According to Romans 8:13, what does the Holy Spirit want to do for you?

5. Spend time daily in prayer and Bible study.

What do these verses teach about the role of prayer in the life of the Spirit-filled believer?

Hebrews 4:15,16

James 5:16

1 Samuel 12:23

James 1:5

Acts 4:31

What do these verses tell us about the role of God's Word in the Spirit-filled life?

Romans 1:16

Hebrews 4:12

2 Timothy 2:15

2 Timothy 3:16,17

6. Obey God's commandments.

According to these verses, what role does obedience have in the Spirit-filled life?

John 14:15

John 14:23–26

7. Witness for Christ.

According to Acts 1:8, for what purpose was the Holy Spirit given?

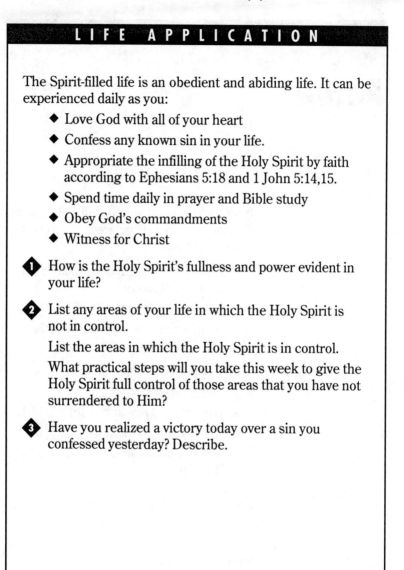

LIFE APPLICATION

The Spirit-filled life is an obedient and abiding life. It can be experienced daily as you:

- ◆ Love God with all of your heart
- ◆ Confess any known sin in your life.
- ◆ Appropriate the infilling of the Holy Spirit by faith according to Ephesians 5:18 and 1 John 5:14,15.
- ◆ Spend time daily in prayer and Bible study
- ◆ Obey God's commandments
- ◆ Witness for Christ

1 How is the Holy Spirit's fullness and power evident in your life?

2 List any areas of your life in which the Holy Spirit is not in control.

List the areas in which the Holy Spirit is in control.

What practical steps will you take this week to give the Holy Spirit full control of those areas that you have not surrendered to Him?

3 Have you realized a victory today over a sin you confessed yesterday? Describe.

❖ ❖ ❖

Recap

The following questions will help you review this Step. If necessary, reread the appropriate lesson(s).

1. Is the Holy Spirit a personality or an impersonal force?

   How do you know?

   What is the chief reason the Holy Spirit has come?

2. What is the *command* of Ephesians 5:18?

3. What is the *promise* of 1 John 5:14,15?

4. Name as many reasons as you can that Christians are not filled with the Holy Spirit.

❖

Reread: John 14:16–26; John 16:7–15

Review: Verses memorized

LIFE APPLICATION

1 What should be your motives for being filled with
the Spirit?

2 How can you be filled with the Spirit?

3 How do you know you are filled with the Holy Spirit?

4 How can you continue to be filled with and walk in
the Spirit?

❖   ❖   ❖

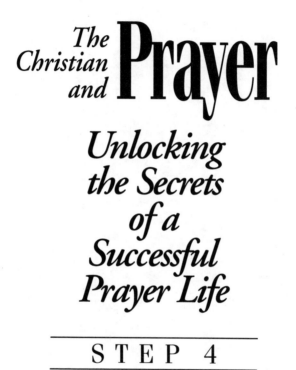

The Christian and Prayer

Unlocking the Secrets of a Successful Prayer Life

STEP 4

The Purpose of Prayer

Jesus set the perfect example of obedience in prayer. Although His day was filled from morning to night with many pressures and responsibilities—addressing crowds, healing the sick, granting private interviews, traveling, and training His disciples—He made prayer a top priority. If Jesus was so dependent upon this fellowship in prayer alone with His Father, how much more you and I should spend time alone with God.

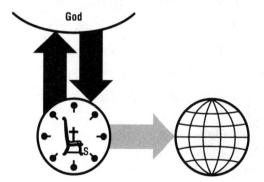

❖

Objective: To understand the importance of prayer to your Christian life

Read: Acts 3 and 4

Memorize: 1 John 5:14,15

The lives of the disciples and other Christians who have been mightily used of God through the centuries to reach their world for Christ all testify to the necessity of prayer. They too are examples of obedience to our Lord's command to pray.

Someone has wisely said, "Satan laughs at our toiling, mocks at our wisdom, but trembles when he sees the weakest saint on his knees." Prayer is God's appointed way of doing God's work.

This lesson will help you understand why prayer is so important to our Christian life. Study the lesson carefully, taking time to meditate and apply the principles you will learn.

❖

Bible Study

Why Prayer Is Important
Read John 14:13, 1 Thessalonians 5:17, Acts 4:23–33, and Matthew 9:38.

Identify at least three reasons for prayer.

The Apostles' Motive
Read Acts 4.

    1. What problem did the apostles face?

    2. Why did they not ask God to remove the persecution?

    3. For what did they pray (verse 29)?
       Why is this significant?

    4. What was their real motive (John 14:13)?

Your Motives for Praying
On the basis of your personal experience, list at least four reasons you pray.

God's Motives In Teaching Us About Prayer
Read John 3:5–8 and John 4:23,24.

    1. In what form does God exist?

       What must happen to us before we can have fellowship with Him?

What kind of worship does He desire?

What is His delight (Proverbs 15:8)?

2. List some purposes of prayer from each of the following Bible references:

Matthew 7:7

Matthew 26:41

Luke 18:1

3. From your understanding of these passages, what do you think God wants you to realize about Him?

Prayer Meets the Heart's Needs

1. According to 2 Corinthians 3:5, what is the source of the Christian's sufficiency?

How do you tap into that source?

2. Read Psalm 63. Note the elements of worship and write below the word or phrase that describes how we should worship God; include references (for example, "My soul thirsts for you—Psalm 63:1").

HOW WE SHOULD WORSHIP GOD	VERSE

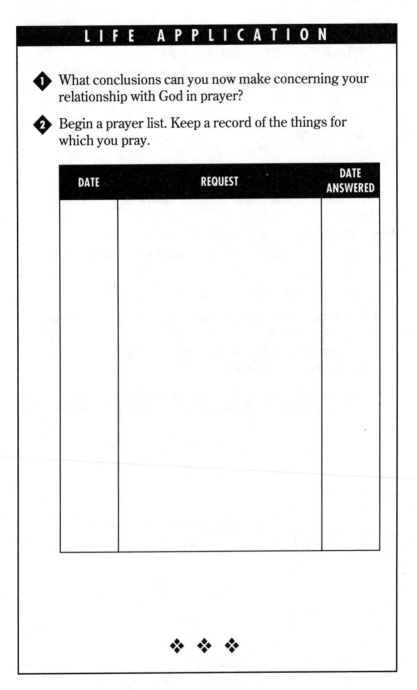

LIFE APPLICATION

1 What conclusions can you now make concerning your relationship with God in prayer?

2 Begin a prayer list. Keep a record of the things for which you pray.

DATE	REQUEST	DATE ANSWERED

❖   ❖   ❖

To Whom Should We Pray?

Because the Father, Son, and Holy Spirit work in perfect unity and harmony, each has a specific role in our prayers. The writer of the Book of Hebrews said, "Let us then approach the throne of grace with confidence [boldness], so that we may receive mercy and find grace to help us in our time of need" (Hebrews 4:16).

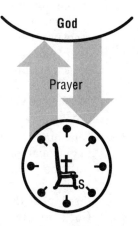

But how do we approach the most powerful Presence in the universe? Do we pray directly to Him? Do we pray to Jesus Christ and ask Him to present our needs to the Father? How can we even approach such a holy God with boldness?

In this lesson you will learn why all three persons of the Godhead are active in our prayers and why each person performs a separate but interconnecting role.

❖

Objective: To understand the roles of the Father, Son, and Holy Spirit in prayer

Read: Acts 5 and 6

Memorize: Philippians 4:6,7

❖

Bible Study

To Whom Do We Pray?

1. According to Matthew 6:6, to whom should we pray?

2. From the following passages, give several reasons for your answer:

1 Chronicles 29:11,12

Matthew 6:9

John 16:23

3. Meditate on the principles contained in the following excerpt from *How to Pray* by R. A. Torrey:

> But some will say, "Is not all prayer unto God?" No. Very much so-called prayer, both public and private, is not unto God. In order that a prayer should be really unto God, there must a definite and conscious approach to God when we pray; we must have a definite and vivid realization that God is bending over us and listening as we pray.
>
> In much of our prayer there is little thought of God. Our mind is not taken up with the thought of the mighty and loving Father. We are occupied neither with the need nor with the one to whom we are praying but our mind is wandering here and there throughout the world. When we really come into God's presence, really meet Him face to face in the place of prayer, really seek the things that we desire from Him, then there is power.

How do you approach God when you pray?

How can you better focus your attention on Him?

Think about a time when you particularly sensed God's presence when you prayed. What made this time of prayer different than others?

Why?

Through Whom Do We Pray?

Read John 14:6 and 1 Timothy 2:5.

1. How many mediators are there between God and man? Who is this mediator?

2. On the basis of Hebrews 4:14–16, describe the qualifications of our great high priest.

3. What are the requirements for a prayer relationship according to 1 John 3:21–23?

4. What does unconfessed sin in our lives do to our prayer fellowship with God (Psalm 66:18)?

5. God's Word promises in 1 John 1:9 that if we confess our sins He will forgive us. The word "confess" means to "agree with." This involves naming our sins to God, acknowledging that He has already forgiven us through Christ's death on the cross, and repenting of our sins (turning away from or changing our attitude toward them).

Follow these steps for confessing your sins:

◆ Ask the Holy Spirit to reveal any sin in your life.

◆ Write it down on a sheet of paper.

◆ Confess the sin to God and ask Him to forgive you.

◆ Receive His forgiveness by faith according to 1 John 1:9.

◆ Write the verse across the sin.

◆ Throw away the paper.

6. God honors those who truly pray in His Son's name. What is the promise recorded in John 15:16 and 16:23?

What did Jesus promise in John 14:12–14?

7. The name of Jesus means everything to God. He lifted Jesus to the highest place in the heavenly sphere and elevated His name far above all others in heaven and on earth.

From the following passages, describe the significance and standing given to the name of Jesus:

John 20:31

Acts 2:38

Acts 3:6,16; 4:10,30

Acts 19:17

Acts 4:12

Mark 9:37

Philippians 2:5–11

8. Improperly used, the name of Jesus does not bring results. To many people, the name of Jesus has become a powerless incantation, a run-together phrase, leaving them bewildered over unanswered prayer.

According to the following verses, how can we use Jesus' name properly and receive our answer from God?

1 John 5:13–15

Ephesians 5:20

Colossians 3:17

John 15:16,17

James 4:3; John 14:13

By Whom Do We Pray?

Read Ephesians 6:18 and Jude 20.

Andrew Murray, noted author and authority on prayer, wrote:

> We all admit the place the Father and the Son have in our prayer. It is to the Father we pray, and from whom we expect the answer. It is in the merit, and name, and life of the Son, abiding in Him and He in us, that we trust to be heard.
>
> But have we understood that in the Holy Trinity all the Three Persons have an equal place in prayer, and that the faith in the Holy Spirit of intercession as praying in us is as indispensable as the faith in the Father and the Son? How clearly we have this in the words, "Through Christ we have access by one Spirit to the Father."
>
> As much as prayer must be to the Father, and through the Son, it must be by the Spirit. And the Spirit can pray in no other way in us than as He lives in us. It is only as

we give ourselves to the Spirit living and praying in us, that the glory of the prayer-hearing God, and the ever-blessed and most effectual mediation of the Son, can be known by us in their power.[1]

1. According to Romans 8:26,27, why does the Holy Spirit need to help us pray?

How does He help us pray?

Why does God answer the prayers of the Holy Spirit?

2. What, then, should be our relationship with the Holy Spirit (Ephesians 5:18)?

3. As we exercise the privilege of prayer, what does God do about our anxiety (Philippians 4:6,7)?

Give an example of how this has worked in your life.

4. Why should we cast our troubles on Him (1 Peter 5:7)?

Think back to a time when you did this. How did He answer your prayer?

What did the answer mean to you?

---

[1] Andrew Murray, *The Ministry of Intercession: A Plea for More Prayer* (Fleming H. Revell Company, 1898), pp. 119,120.

LIFE APPLICATION

1 List any new insights into prayer that you have gained from this lesson.

Describe how you will use these insights to have a more well-rounded prayer life.

2 Write down at least one new way in which you want to apply prayer in your life right now.

❖ ❖ ❖

A Guide to Effective Daily Prayer

Effective prayer cannot be reduced to a magic formula. God does not respond to our requests because we have the right ritual. He is more interested in our hearts than in our words. John Bunyan, author of *Pilgrim's Progress,* said, "In prayer it is better to have a heart without words than words without a heart."

God's Word does, however, give us certain basic elements that, when included in our communication with God, will enable us to receive His answers to our prayers.

In this lesson we will consider a simple guide that you can use in your daily devotional time:

> Adoration
> Confession
> Thanksgiving
> Supplication

The guide can easily be remembered by the first letter of each word: **ACTS.**

❖

Objective: To apply a simple guide to your daily prayer time

Read: Acts 7 and 8

Memorize: 1 Corinthians 14:40

God

Adoration
Confession
Thanksgiving
Supplication

❖

Bible Study

Adoration

1. Why should we praise God?

Jeremiah 32:17

1 John 4:10

Philippians 1:6

2. What is the best way for you to show your gratitude toward God, and your faith and trust in Him in all circumstances (Philippians 4:6)?

What would you conclude that God expects of us (1 Thessalonians 5:16–18)?

If you sometimes find it hard to praise God, read some of the Psalms (Psalms 146–150 in particular).

3. How do you communicate your adoration to God?

Confession

Read Isaiah 59:1,2.

1. What will hinder fellowship with God?

2. Psalm 51 was David's prayer after he had fallen out of fellowship with God. What did David conclude that God wanted of him (Psalm 51:6,16,17)?

3. Read Psalm 32:1–7.

What was David's observation about confession?

What was his observation about not confessing his sin (verses 3,4)?

4. What should you do when you find that your fellowship with God is broken (1 John 1:9)?

What sin in your life is keeping you from fellowship with God?

How will you deal with that sin?

Thanksgiving

Let us never be guilty of being ungrateful to God.

1. How often should we give thanks (Hebrews 13:15)?

For what should we praise Him (Ephesians 5:20)?

Why (1 Thessalonians 5:18)?

2. What about a situation that seems adverse (Romans 5:3,4)?

3. How do you practice thankfulness when you pray?

As you go about your daily life?

4. Make a list of each problem, disappointment, heartache, or adversity that concerns you.

Begin to thank God for each one. Doing so demonstrates your trust in Him.

Supplication

1. Intercession.

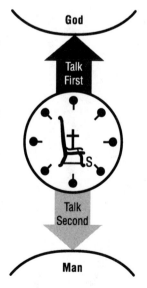

An example of intercession is provided in Colossians 1:3. What was Paul's prayer for the Christians of Colosse?

Many times our efforts in leading people to Christ are fruitless because we forget the necessary preparation for witnessing. The divine order is to first talk to God about men, and then talk to men about God.

If we follow this order, we will see results. Prayer is really the place where people are won to Christ; witnessing is just gathering in the results of prayer.

As you meditate on the above, list the requests you can make to God for Christians and non-Christians.

2. Petition.

Why should we expect God to answer our prayers (Matthew 7:9–11; Romans 8:32)?

According to Psalm 84:11,12, what has God promised to do?

What part does belief have in our prayers (Mark 11:24; James 1:6,7)?

Faith is necessary for answered prayers. What else is required (Matthew 6:9,10; 1 John 5:14,15)?

Why will God not answer some prayers (James 4:3)?

How does this relate to your prayer life?

3. Explain 2 Corinthians 12:7–10 in light of Romans 8:28.

What does this passage teach us about apparently unanswered prayer?

LIFE APPLICATION

1 Add other requests to the prayer list you began at the end of Lesson 1.

2 Begin using the ACTS system for prayer during your daily time alone with God. After several days, record how your prayers have changed.

3 List daily situations in which you could use praise and thanksgiving to help you react in a godly manner.

Now follow through by applying praise and thanksgiving in these circumstances.

❖ ❖ ❖

How to Pray With Power

Jonathan Goforth was a man of powerful prayer. It is said of him that once he felt assured of God's will in prayer, he would continue in the power of prayer until the thing was accomplished.

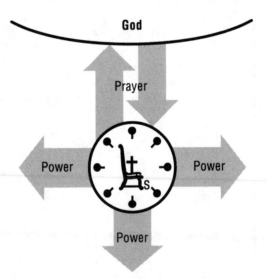

❖

Objective: To learn how to claim by faith the great power available through prayer

Read: Acts 9 and 10

Memorize: James 5:16

Andrew Murray, too, was a great prayer warrior. He wrote in *The Praying Christian:*

The Christian needs strength. This we all know. The Christian has no strength of his own. This is also true.

Where may strength be obtained? Notice the answer: "Be strong in the Lord, and in the power of His might" (Ephesians 6:10, NKJ).

Paul had spoken of this power in the earlier part of his epistle to the Ephesians (1:18–20). He had prayed to God to give them the Spirit that they might know the exceeding greatness of His power according to the working of His mighty power, which He wrought in Christ when He raised Him from the dead.

This is the literal truth: The greatness of His power, which raised Christ from the dead, works in every believer. In me and in you, my reader. We hardly believe it, and still less do we experience it.

That is why Paul prays, and we must pray with him, that God through His Spirit would teach us to believe in His almighty power. Pray with all your heart: "Father, grant me the Spirit of wisdom, that I may experience this power in my life."

Pray for God's Spirit to enlighten your eyes. Believe in the divine power working within you. Pray that the Holy Spirit may reveal it to you, and appropriate the promise that God will manifest His power in your heart, supplying all your needs.

Do you not begin to realize that time is needed—much time in fellowship with the Father and the Son, if you would experience the power of God within you?

❖

Bible Study

Power for Answered Prayer
Read Acts 12:5–18.

1. How did Peter's fellow Christians respond to his imprisonment (verse 5)?

What was God's answer to their prayer (verses 6–11)?

What was their response to God's answer (verses 13–16)?

How does seeing God answer your prayers in a powerful way change your feelings about prayer?

2. What do the following Bible references tell you about the qualities God demands in a person for powerful prayer?

Hebrews 11:1,6

Romans 12:1,2

Mark 11:25

1 John 3:22

Ephesians 5:18

Conditions to Answered Prayer

1. Why is it necessary to ask in accordance with the will of God (1 John 5:14,15)?

2. Write out John 15:7 in your own words and state what it teaches about conditions to answered prayer.

3. What is the value of several Christians praying for something as opposed to just one (Matthew 18:19)?

Prevailing Prayer

During his lifetime, George Mueller recorded more than 50,000 answers to prayer. He prayed for two men daily for more than 60 years. One of these men was converted shortly before Mueller's death and the other about a year later. As in Mueller's experience, we do not always see the answer to our prayers. We must leave the results to God.

One of the great needs of today is for men and women who will begin to pray for things and then pray repeatedly until they obtain what they seek from the Lord.

1. How long do you think we should pray for someone or something (Luke 18:1–8)?

Why do you think God honors prevailing prayer?

What part do our feelings play in prevailing prayer?

2. What did the following men accomplish through prayer?

Moses (Exodus 15:22–25)

Samson (Judges 16:28–30)

Peter (Acts 9:36–41)

Elijah (James 5:17,18)

3. How do these examples help you gain greater confidence to pray?

4. Give an example of what God has done for you or someone you know as the result of prevailing prayer.

LIFE APPLICATION

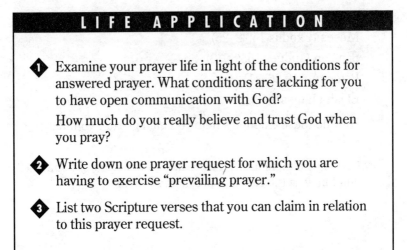

1. Examine your prayer life in light of the conditions for answered prayer. What conditions are lacking for you to have open communication with God?

   How much do you really believe and trust God when you pray?

2. Write down one prayer request for which you are having to exercise "prevailing prayer."

3. List two Scripture verses that you can claim in relation to this prayer request.

God's Promises About Prayer

It is estimated that there are more than 5,000 personal promises in the Bible. However, these promises mean little or nothing to many Christians because they do not claim them by faith (Hebrews 4:2).

Faith is a word signifying action. For example, bags of cement sitting in a warehouse will never become concrete until they are mixed with sand, gravel, and water. Likewise, God's promises will never become concrete unless they are mixed with faith and action. You must make them yours by believing them and putting your faith to work.

Objective: To claim God's promises about prayer

Read: Acts 11 and 12

Memorize: Jeremiah 33:3

This lesson will show you some of God's conditions and promises concerning prayer and His provision for your needs.

175

❖

Bible Study

What God Has Promised Concerning Prayer

Look up the following verses and identify the condition and promise in each.

1. Jeremiah 33:3

2. Matthew 21:22

3. 1 John 5:14,15

4. John 14:14

5. Which promise do you need most to apply to your own prayer life right now and why?

What God Will Provide Through Prayer

In the following verses, identify God's promises concerning:

1. Material needs
   Philippians 4:19
   Psalm 84:11

2. Guidance
   Proverbs 3:5,6
   Psalm 32:8

3. Spiritual needs
   Ephesians 1:3
   Philippians 4:13

Why God Is Dependable

1. List reasons you can trust Him to keep His promises.
   Psalm 9:10
   Psalm 115:11

Isaiah 26:4

Nahum 1:7

2 Samuel 7:28

2. In what particular circumstance of your life do you presently need to trust Him more and for what?

These promises are real—believe them; claim them; live by them.

LIFE APPLICATION

List on this chart at least three things you need to pray for, and a verse for each that promises God's provision.

NEED	PROMISE

❖   ❖   ❖

Planning Your Daily Devotional Time

Down through the years, godly men who have done great things for God have testified to the necessity of having a devotional time.

John Wesley, who shook the world for God and founded the Methodist Church, is representative of such great spiritual leaders. He thought prayer, more than anything else, to be his business.

Just as a child needs food to grow physically, so we need food to grow spiritually. We can miss a meal and not feel any ill effects, but if we don't eat for a week we begin to weaken physically. So it is in our spiritual lives.

The study of the Word of God and the practice of prayer are vitally important for spiritual growth. We may miss a day without feeding on the Word of God or praying and not feel any apparent ill effects in our lives, but if we continue this practice, we will lose the power to live the victorious Christian life.

The Christian life might be compared to a soldier in battle. He is out on the front lines but is connected with his commanding officer by radio. He calls and tells of the conditions and problems he is facing. Then his

❖

Objective: To establish a consistent and effective daily prayer life

Read: Acts 1 and 2

Memorize: Isaiah 40:31

179

commanding officer, who from his vantage point can see the entire battle area, relays instructions. Similarly, the Christian shares his joys and sorrows, his victories and defeats, and his needs as God instructs and guides him through His Word.

It is our heavenly Father who directs us in the adventure of life. He knows the steps we should take. We must take time to seek Him for guidance.

❖

Bible Study

Establish a Definite Time

A daily devotional time should be set aside for personal worship and meditation in which we seek fellowship with the Lord Jesus Christ. Once begun, this fellowship can be continued throughout the day (Psalm 119:97; 1 Thessalonians 5:17).

1. In obedience to Christ's command, what did His disciples do after His ascension (Acts 1:13,14)?

2. Although different individuals' schedules will vary, many people prefer the morning hours, before the responsibilities of the day begin.

David was called a man after God's own heart. What time did he set aside to communicate with God (Psalm 5:3)?

Name two characteristics of the devotional life of Jesus (Mark 1:35).

3. When is your best devotional time?

None of us can say that we do not have time for prayer and Bible study. We all can make time for things that we really want to do. Whether the period is long or short, set aside some time.

4. Make your devotional time unhurried. Don't think about your next responsibility. Concentrate on your fellowship with the Lord. A definite time every day will do much to help. A brief period with concentration is better than a long devotional time with your mind on many things.

How many minutes can you set aside daily for your time with God?

Choose a Definite Place

Avoid distraction by finding a quiet, private place of worship. If privacy is impossible, you will need to learn to concentrate. If you cannot have a devotional time in your own home or room, perhaps one of the following places will be suitable:

◆ A nearby chapel

◆ A corner of the school library

◆ Your office (before or after hours)

Name three other places you might find appropriate for your private prayer and Bible study.

Goal and Content of the Devotional Time

1. We should have a reason for everything we do. "Aim at nothing and you will surely hit it." Our purpose for prayer should be to establish personal fellowship with God and to fulfill our own spiritual needs.

A brief time of meeting with God in the early morning and walking in vital union with Him throughout the day, "practicing the presence of God," is more meaningful than spending an hour or more in a legalistic way and forgetting Him for the rest of the day.

During our devotional time, we should be concerned with learning where we have failed and with rededicating ourselves to the task before us. We should use the time to regroup our forces after the battles of the previous day and plan for the next day's attack.

What particular spiritual need do you feel today?

What battles did you have yesterday?

2. The devotional time should include Bible study, prayer, personal worship, and quiet meditation. These aspects of the devotional time are so closely related that you can actually engage in all at the same time.

For example, begin by reading a psalm of thanksgiving or praise. As you read, your heart will respond and you will continue to praise and worship God from a grateful heart.

Turn now to another portion of Scripture, such as Romans 8. Interrupt your reading to thank God for each truth that applies to you as a Christian. You will be amazed at how much you have to praise and thank God for, once you get started.

After you have read and prayed for a while, remain in an attitude of quiet, listening for instructions from God. Write down any thoughts that come to mind and pray about these.

Supplementary activity may include memorizing Scripture or reading from a devotional book or hymnal.

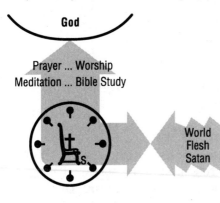

3. Study Matthew 6:9–13. Paraphrase this prayer in your own words, using expressions meaningful to you.

For additional information on prayer, see my Transferable Concept, *How You Can Pray With Confidence.*

LIFE APPLICATION

Complete these statements in your notebook:

 I have set aside the following definite time in the day for daily devotional time:

 I have decided on the following place:

3 My purpose for setting aside a definite time and place for my devotions is to:

4 I will include the following activities during my devotional time:

❖ ❖ ❖

Recap

The following questions will help you review this Step. If necessary, reread the appropriate lesson(s).

1. Why is prayer so important?

2. To be more effective in prayer, what conditions mentioned in Lessons 4 and 5 are you now meeting that you weren't meeting before?

3. Fill in the words to complete the suggested guide for prayer content:

    A

    C

    T

    S

❖

Reread: Acts 13 and 14

Review: Verses memorized

L I F E   A P P L I C A T I O N

1 Are you presently following the ACTS guide? (Remember, a guide is not mandatory, it is just helpful.)

If you use another system, what is it?

2 How has your understanding of power and promises in prayer been broadened?

3 What specific time and place have you set aside for daily prayer and devotions?

Time:

Place:

What adjustments do you need to make for it to be more effective (more or less time, different place, etc.)?

4 Memorize and remember:

> Effective praying is simply asking God to work according to His will and leaving the results to Him.

❖ ❖ ❖

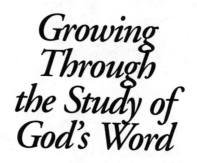

The *Christian* *and the* **Bible**

Growing Through the Study of God's Word

STEP 5

The Book of Books

The Bible is God's holy, inspired Word. It is the most powerful and most quoted book in the world. Some of the greatest men in modern history have had a deep respect for the Bible:

> *Abraham Lincoln:* "I believe the Bible is the best gift God has ever given to man. All the good from the Savior of the world is communicated to us through this Book."

> *Immanuel Kant:* "The existence of the Bible, as a book for people, is the greatest benefit which the human race has ever experienced. Every attempt to belittle it is a crime against humanity."

> *Robert E. Lee:* "In all my perplexities and distresses, the Bible has never failed to give me light and strength."

> *Daniel Webster:* "If there is anything in my thought or style to commend, the credit is due to my parents for instilling in me early love for the Scriptures."

Hundreds of millions of people have read its sacred pages, making it the best-selling book of all time.

The composition of the Bible is indeed amazing. A library of sixty-six books, it was

Objective: To recognize the unparalleled composition of the Bible and become familiar with its structure

Read: Acts 15 and 16

Memorize: 2 Timothy 3:16,17

written by forty different human authors under the divine inspiration of the Holy Spirit. These writers wrote independently, knowing almost nothing of the others' part. None had anything in common, and their literary qualifications were diverse. Moses, for example, was a man of learning, trained in the best universities of Egypt. Peter, on the other hand, was a fisherman without claim to formal education. Yet each wrote the wisdom of God with powerful force.

It took the Old and New Testament writers fifteen centuries to complete the Bible, which was written in three languages (Hebrew, Aramaic, and Greek) on three continents. Indeed, this collection of books is really one, not sixty-six, for it is coherent in content and progressive in truth.

The Bible is composed of 1189 chapters (929 in the Old Testament and 260 in the New Testament) and utilizes 773,746 words to convey its life-changing message. This literary masterpiece contains history, laws, poetry, prophecy, biography, dramatic stories, letters, and revelations. In the words of Sir Isaac Newton:

> There are more sure marks of authenticity in the Bible than in any profane history.

Christian Church leaders of the fifth century A.D. decided upon the list of books to be included in the Bible. This collection of accepted writings came to be known by scholars as the "canon," and were considered inspired and authoritative.

In this lesson you will study the various names of the Bible, survey the construction of the Old and New Testaments, and gain insights that will make your own Bible study more meaningful.

❖

Bible Study

Various Names of the Bible

List the various names the Bible is called according to the following references:

> 1 Corinthians 15:3,4
>
> Ephesians 6:17

Construction of the Bible

1. To become familiar with your own Bible, leaf through it and look at these divisions and books as you progress through the lesson. If possible, use a Bible with headlines to help you answer the questions.

The Bible is composed of two main sections: the Old Testament, containing 39 books, and the New Testament, containing 27 books.

2. Read Genesis 1 and Revelation 22. From these two chapters, summarize the scope of the contents of the Bible.

Divisions of the Old Testament

The Old Testament can be divided into five parts:

1. *Pentateuch.* The first five historical books, written by Moses, also are called the books of the Law. List these books.

Identify at least four major events recorded in these books.

2. *Historical Books.* The next twelve books tell of the establishment of the kingdom of Israel, of Israel's repeated turning from God to sin, and finally of the Assyrian and Babylonian exile—God's punishment. List these twelve books as follows and identify a main character in each section:

First three (pre-kingdom era)

Next six (duration of the kingdom)

Last three (exile and post-exile period)

3. *Poetry.* Of the next five books, Psalms—the Hebrew hymn book—is probably the best known. List the five books of poetry.

    Describe how God has used one of these books to comfort and strengthen you in a difficult situation.

4. *Major Prophets.* Written shortly before Israel was taken into captivity and during the exile, these books prophesy the coming Messiah and other world events. They also contain warnings of impending disaster if Israel did not turn from her wicked ways. List the five books of the Major Prophets.

    Identify at least one major prophecy in each.

5. *Minor Prophets.* These last twelve books of the Old Testament are called minor only because they are shorter, not because they are less important. They mainly concern Israel and the coming Messiah. List all twelve in your notebook.

    Read one of the books and summarize its main points.

Divisions of the New Testament

The New Testament can also be divided into five parts.

1. *Gospels.* The first four books of the New Testament tell of Christ's life and ministry. List them.

    What was Jesus' last command to His disciples (Matthew 28:19,20)?

    How does this apply today?

2. *Acts.* This history of the early church, which also describes the ministries of Peter and Paul, consists of only one book. For practice, write it in your notebook.

    What is its significance for us today?

3. *Pauline Epistles and Hebrews.* Thirteen of the epistles (letters) were written by Paul, and were named for the church or individual to whom they were sent. Although the author of Hebrews is not identified, many believe Paul also wrote that fourteenth epistle. List all fourteen.

Write down your favorite verse in each book and describe why it is meaningful to you.

4. *General Epistles.* There are seven general epistles, and they are named not for the recipients but for the authors. List them in your notebook.

Identify one major truth in each book, and tell how you will apply each truth to your life.

5. *Revelation.* The last book of the New Testament is one of prophecy. It describes the end times and the triumph of Christ in His second coming. Write the name of it.

Describe the central message of the book (Revelation 22:12–17).

What are its promises to those who overcome (chapters 2,3)?

What warning does the writer of this book give (22:18,19)?

LIFE APPLICATION

1 What new insight about the composition of the Bible have you gained from this study?

How will this help you in your daily life?

2 To know the Bible well and to be able to find Scripture references quickly, you should memorize the names of the books in the order in which they appear. Master one group, and then go on to the next.

Focus on one division each week until you have memorized all the books of the Bible. Review these frequently until they are fixed in your mind.

Today, commit to memory the books of the first division, the Pentateuch, and write them again in your notebook.

❖ ❖ ❖

The Central Person of the Bible

J esus is the most remarkable and fascinating person in history. He has inspired more hope, taught more compassion, and shown more love than any other man who has ever lived.

Jesus is the central figure of the Bible. His birth as the Jewish Messiah and Savior of the world was prophesied by Old Testament authors. Their writings contain more than three hundred separate references to the coming of Jesus, with many unique details. Christ fulfilled 100 percent of all the Old Testament predictions of the birth, life, death, and resurrection of the Messiah.

❖

Objective: To recognize the entire Bible as God's revelation of Jesus Christ to us

Read: Acts 17 and 18

Memorize: 1 Corinthians 15:3,4

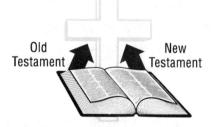

Old Testament   New Testament

The New Testament makes an even more revolutionary claim: that Jesus Christ is the center of all biblical prophecy. The Scripture proclaims:

> Long ago God spoke in many different ways to our
> fathers through the prophets [in visions, dreams, and
> even face to face], telling them little by little about his
> plans. But now in these days he has spoken to us through
> his Son to whom he has given everything, and through
> whom he made the world and everything there is
> (Hebrews 1:1,2).

And the Book of Ephesians declares:

> God has told us his secret reason for sending Christ,
> a plan he decided on in mercy long ago; and this was his
> purpose: that when the time is ripe he will gather us all
> together from wherever we are—in heaven or on earth—
> to be with him in Christ, forever (Ephesians 1:9,10).

The precise fulfillment of the immense body of biblical prophecy
is found in one unique and revolutionary Man—Jesus of Nazareth.
Claiming that He was the predicted One of old, Jesus stepped into
time. And the pieces of the prophetic puzzle slipped into place. We
can clearly see that He was the center of God's revelation to man.

❖

Bible Study

What Christ Said About Himself and the Old Testament

1. What did Christ say of the Scriptures in John 5:39?

2. Read Luke 24:25–27, 44–48.

What was Christ's claim concerning the Old Testament
teaching about Himself?

What parts of the Old Testament did Christ say referred to
Him (verse 44)?

What do you think Christ wants you to understand about
the Old Testament from verse 26?

From verses 46, 47?

What the Apostles Said About Christ and the Old Testament

1. What does Peter conclude in Acts 3:18?

2. Keeping in mind that the New Testament had not yet been written, how did the apostle Paul use the Old Testament to show that it contained the "good news" of Christ (Acts 17:1–3)?

3. What three things occurred in Christ's life that Paul said were taught in the Old Testament (1 Corinthians 15:3,4)?

4. What does Paul conclude in Romans 15:8,9 about the ministry of Christ?

Old Testament Prophecies Concerning Christ Fulfilled in the New Testament

All of the more than 300 Old Testament prophecies about the first coming of the Messiah were fulfilled in the life of Christ. Here are a few of them.

1. Compare these Scripture references and record the prophecies fulfilled.

COMPARE	WITH	FULFILLMENT
1 Samuel 16:19 Isaiah 11:1	Luke 1:31–33	
Genesis 3:15	Galatians 4:4 Hebrews 2:14	
Numbers 24:17	Matthew 2:2,9	
Isaiah 9:6	Matthew 1:23	
Isaiah 40:3	Matthew 3:1–3	
Zechariah 9:9	Matthew 21:1–11	

COMPARE	WITH	FULFILLMENT
Psalm 69:21	Matthew 27:34	
Psalm 34:20	John 19:33,36	
Job 19:25–27	Galatians 3:13 1 John 3:2	

2. What is your impression after seeing these Old Testament prophecies and their New Testament fulfillment?

Christ, the Central Person of the New Testament

1. The four Gospels are the history books of Christ's ministry. (Read Matthew 1:1; Mark 1:1; Luke 1:1–4; John 20:30,31.)

In what ways did the disciples know Jesus (1 John 1:3)?

Do the four Gospels purport to record all that Jesus did (John 20:30)?

Why were the historical facts and teachings of Jesus Christ written (John 20:31)?

2. The Book of Acts is a historical account of the acts of the Holy Spirit through the apostles.

Who wrote it (Luke 1:1–4 and Acts 1:1)?

How do you think the passage in Luke applies to the Book of Acts?

3. The Epistles are letters written to show the church the practical outworking of the life of Christ in the lives of those who wrote them. By example, they teach us regarding our membership in the body of Christ, and about our privileges, responsibilities, and destiny.

Read Colossians 2:6–8.

What are Christians to do?

How are we to do it?

Of what are we to beware?

What would you say our greatest responsibility is?

4. The Book of Revelation is the only New Testament book of prophecy. Read Revelation 1:1–3.

This book is the revelation of whom?

What is its purpose?

Who gave such knowledge?

How was this knowledge given, and to whom?

How will studying the Book of Revelation affect your life and under what conditions?

LIFE APPLICATION

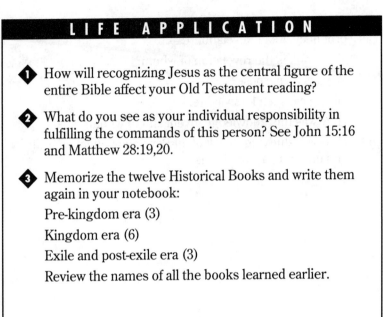

1 How will recognizing Jesus as the central figure of the entire Bible affect your Old Testament reading?

2 What do you see as your individual responsibility in fulfilling the commands of this person? See John 15:16 and Matthew 28:19,20.

3 Memorize the twelve Historical Books and write them again in your notebook:

Pre-kingdom era (3)

Kingdom era (6)

Exile and post-exile era (3)

Review the names of all the books learned earlier.

❖ ❖ ❖

Authority of the Old Testament

Researchers in Israel recently subjected the first five books of the Old Testament to exhaustive computer analysis. They came to a different conclusion than expected.

Skeptics had long assumed that the Torah, or Books of Moses, was the work of multiple authors. But Scripture scholar Moshe Katz and computer expert Menachem Wiener of the Israel Institute of Technology refuted this belief. They discovered an intricate pattern of significant words concealed in the canon, spelled by letters separated at fixed intervals.

According to Katz, the statistical possibility of such patterns happening by chance would be one in three million. The material, he said, suggests a single, inspired author—in fact, it could not have been put together by human capabilities at all. "So we need a nonrational explanation," he said. "And ours is that the Torah was written by God through the hand of Moses."

The Old Testament was considered by its writers to be the inspired and authoritative Word of God. Our Lord Himself, the New Testament writers, and the early church also affirmed its authenticity.

Objective: To gain confidence in the trustworthiness of the Bible by examining the authority of the Old Testament

Read: Acts 19 and 20

Memorize: 2 Peter 1:20,21

Of Moses it is said, "Moses then wrote down everything the Lord had said" (Exodus 24:4). David said, "The Spirit of the Lord spoke through me; his word was on my tongue" (2 Samuel 23:2). The prophet Jeremiah said, "The word of the Lord came to me, saying..." (Jeremiah 1:4). Ezekiel, Daniel, and Amos made it perfectly clear that their messages were absolutely and wholly from God.

Jesus frequently referred to Old Testament Scriptures during His earthly ministry. In confronting the unbelief of the Jews, Jesus affirmed that the "Scripture cannot be broken" (John 10:35). During His Sermon on the Mount, Jesus said, "I tell you the truth, until heaven and earth disappear, not the smallest letter, not the least stroke of a pen, will by any means disappear from the Law until everything is accomplished" (Matthew 5:18).

"Thus saith the Lord"
2,000 times in Old Testament

While teaching in the temple courts, Jesus cited Psalm 110:1 and declared that David spoke by the Holy Spirit (Mark 12:35,36). After His resurrection, Jesus said to His disciples, "This is what I told you while I was still with you: Everything must be fulfilled that is written about me in the Law of Moses, the Prophets and the Psalms." Then Luke notes, "He opened their minds so they could understand the Scriptures" (Luke 24:44,45). The Jews used the expression, "The Law, the Prophets, and the Psalms" to represent the entire Old Testament.

Concerning the birth of Christ, Matthew records, "All this took place to fulfill what the Lord had said through the prophet" (Matthew 1:22). In quoting the song of Zechariah (the father of John Baptist) concerning the birth of Jesus, Luke included the affirmation, "as he said through his holy prophets of long ago" (Luke 1:70). And the writer of Acts records Peter's speech concerning the fate of Judas who betrayed Jesus, "Brothers, the Scripture had to be fulfilled which the Holy Spirit spoke long ago through the mouth of David" (Acts 1:16).

Many other passages testify to the authority of the Old Testament, often with the words, "that the Scripture might be fulfilled" (John 19:24,36) or "for this is what the prophet has written" (Matthew 2:5). Peter affirmed, "No prophecy of Scripture came about by the prophet's own interpretation. For prophecy never had its origin in the will of man, but men spoke from God as they were carried along by the Holy Spirit" (2 Peter 1:20,21).

As the early church grew, differences in doctrines surfaced. But no matter how much the church fathers differed in their teachings, they were unanimous in one thing: that in the entire Old Testament, God and Christ, the incarnate Word of God, spoke by the Holy Spirit through men. They affirmed the writing of Paul to Timothy, "All Scripture is God-breathed and is useful for teaching, rebuking, correcting and training in righteousness" (2 Timothy 3:16). Unlike other doctrines, the authority of the Scripture was undebatable.

Belief in the absolute authority of the Scripture is foundational to your faith. I encourage you to study this lesson carefully and prayerfully so you will be able to assure others of the divine authorship and sureness of God's holy Word.

❖

Bible Study

Testimony of Its Writers

The phrase, "thus saith the Lord," or its equivalent, occurs more than 2,000 times in the Old Testament.

1. Write out the statements concerning inspiration made by the following writers:

   David (2 Samuel 23:2)

   Isaiah (Isaiah 8:1,5,11)

   Jeremiah (Jeremiah 1:9)

   Ezekiel (Ezekiel 3:4)

   What is different about each? What is the same?

2. What two statements of Moses in Exodus 31:18 and 32:16 show that God actually wrote the Ten Commandments?

3. What statement made by David shows that the pattern for the temple was dictated by God (1 Chronicles 28:19)?

Testimony of Christ

The New Testament had not been written during Christ's earthly ministry, and His references to the Scriptures refer to the Old Testament writings. He never once denied or made light of Old Testament Scriptures; He related Himself to them as their fulfillment. He said:

> These are the Scriptures that testify about me (John 5:39).

1. How did Christ describe those who did not believe the Old Testament prophecies (Luke 24:25)?

2. What is the result of not believing in the Old Testament (John 5:46,47)?

3. What did Christ think of His responsibility concerning Old Testament prophecy (Matthew 5:17,18)?

4. What was Christ's view of the story of man's creation as recorded in Genesis (Matthew 19:4–6)?

5. What authority did Christ use to answer:

   Satan (Matthew 4:4,7,10)?

   Men (Matthew 22:29–32,43–46)?

6. Summarize Christ's attitude and view of the Old Testament.

Testimony of the Apostles

It is evident from their inspired writing that the apostles of Christ considered the Old Testament Scriptures prophetic and inseparable from the authority, power, and ministry of Christ.

1. *Peter.* From whom did the apostle Peter say the writings of the Old Testament came (2 Peter 1:21; Acts 1:16)?

   How did Peter feel about the Old Testament historical account he recorded in 1 Peter 3:20?

   Who did Peter say were inspired by God (Acts 3:20,21)?

2. *Paul.* How much of the Old Testament is inspired by God, according to Paul in 2 Timothy 3:16?

What did Paul believe the Old Testament to be (Romans 3:2)?

3. *James.* Acceptance of the Old Testament writing is evidenced in the Book of James by references to whom?

2:21

2:25

5:11

5:17

4. *John.* One of the many evidences that John believed the Old Testament is his acceptance of which story (1 John 3:12)?

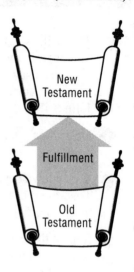

LIFE APPLICATION

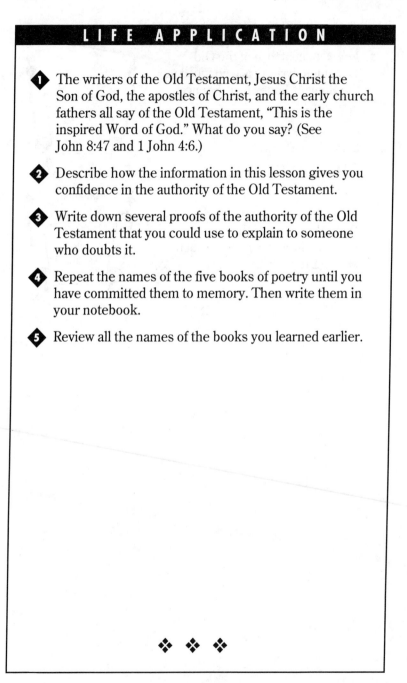

1 The writers of the Old Testament, Jesus Christ the Son of God, the apostles of Christ, and the early church fathers all say of the Old Testament, "This is the inspired Word of God." What do you say? (See John 8:47 and 1 John 4:6.)

2 Describe how the information in this lesson gives you confidence in the authority of the Old Testament.

3 Write down several proofs of the authority of the Old Testament that you could use to explain to someone who doubts it.

4 Repeat the names of the five books of poetry until you have committed them to memory. Then write them in your notebook.

5 Review all the names of the books you learned earlier.

❖ ❖ ❖

Authority of the New Testament

As you prepare to start this lesson, pick up your Bible and thumb through the pages of the New Testament. Have you ever thought about its origin and how its twenty-seven books were collected together into one volume?

Since the first of the books was probably not written until about A.D. 50, the church did not have a "New Testament" for the first twenty years following our Lord's ascension. Instead, the early Christians relied on the Old Testament and the eye-witness accounts of His disciples.

Christianity began with the preaching of Jesus but was spread word-of-mouth by the faithful witness of His followers. Eventually the oral gospel and the writings of the apostles to the churches were preserved for us in the books of the New Testament.

❖

Objective: To gain confidence in the Bible's authority by looking at the reliability of the New Testament

Read: Acts 21 and 22

Memorize: Matthew 24:35

The New Testament grew book by book, beginning with the writings of Paul. As Paul established churches in new communities, he kept in touch with them by letter. Beginning with the letters to the Thessalonians, Paul corresponded with his churches until his death. His letters were copied, compiled, and circulated among the churches until they became known throughout the Christian communities.

As the years passed and the number of living eye-witnesses became fewer, the Gospels were written to preserve their accounts. Mark wrote his Gospel first, followed by Matthew, Luke, and John.

In addition to Paul's letters and the Gospels, other epistles, the Book of Acts, and the Book of Revelation soon appeared until the church had in its possession all the books of our New Testament by the close of the first century.

These twenty-seven books, however, represent only a few of the numerous writings produced by the early Christians, many of which attempted to reinterpret the sayings and teachings of Christ. For more than two hundred years, the church fathers could not decide which of those works should be considered written under the guidance and inspiration of the Holy Spirit and thus be approved for reading in the public services of the church. The need for unity in belief and practice among Christians eventually led the fathers to separate the writings that were in harmony with the teachings of Jesus from those that were not.

The authoritative list of books developed slowly and gradually under the influence of the Holy Spirit until by the year 400 most Christians had accepted the twenty-seven books that now compose our New Testament. Today almost all of Christianity— Catholics and Protestant groups of many kinds—have placed their approval upon them.

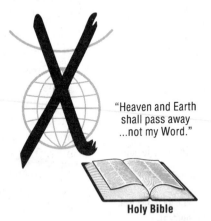

"Heaven and Earth shall pass away ...not my Word."

Holy Bible

In 1874 the Scriptures were under severe attack by critics, and John W. Haley published a defense entitled *Alleged Discrepancies of the Bible*. In the preface he wrote:

> Finally, let it be remembered that the Bible is neither dependent upon nor affected by the success or failure of

any book. Whatever may become of the latter, whatever may be the verdict passed upon it by an intelligent public, the Bible will stand. In the ages yet to be, when its present assailants and defenders are moldering in the dust, and when our very names are forgotten, (God's Word) will be, as it has been during the centuries past, the guide and solace of millions.

Bible Study

Authority Given the Apostles by Christ

1. What four things did Christ say the Holy Spirit would do for the apostles (John 16:12–15)?

Why do you think the apostles could not know all the truth at that time?

How would they in the future?

2. What authority did Christ give the apostles (John 17:18; 20:21)?

3. On what basis did Christ select the apostles to bear witness of Him (John 15:26,27; Luke 24:46–48)?

How did Paul fit in according to Acts 9:3–6; Acts 26:13–15, and 1 Corinthians 15:7–9?

4. What authority did Christ give Paul (Acts 26:15–18)?

How do we fit into this as witnesses?

The Apostles Wrote Under Christ's Authority

1. *Paul.* What does he call himself at the beginning of the book of Romans?

From whom did Paul receive what he preached (1 Corinthians 11:23; Galatians 1:11,12)?

What was Paul's authority and purpose (2 Corinthians 5:20)?

Read 2 Peter 3:15,16. What did Peter think about
Paul's writings?

What did he think about those who misuse the
New Testament?

2. *Writer of Hebrews.* Where did the writer of Hebrews get his
authority (Hebrews 1:1,2)?

3. *James.* What did this half-brother of Jesus (Jesus's Father
is God) call himself (James 1:1)?

4. *John.* What does John claim as the authority for writing his
epistles (1 John 1:1–3)?

How was Revelation written (Revelation 1:1)?

5. *Jude.* What does this other half-brother of Jesus call himself
in Jude 1?

What do you think Paul, James, and Jude meant by saying
they were bondservants of Christ?

6. *Peter.* What does he call himself (1 Peter 1:1)?

What does Peter make known (2 Peter 1:16)?

7. On whose writings is the foundation of the church of
Jesus Christ established (Ephesians 2:20)?

8. What is the gospel of Christ, according to the apostles
(Romans 1:16)?

9. Why were the apostles confident that they wrote correctly
about Christ (2 Corinthians 4:5,6)?

LIFE APPLICATION

1 God has miraculously preserved His Word for us. Although the above study should convince us that the New Testament is the Word of God, what is your greatest assurance that it is God's Word (John 16:13; 8:47; 18:37)?

2 How does the information in this lesson help you trust the Bible more than you may have in the past?

How will you use the deeper trust in:

Witnessing?

Praying?

Daily living?

3 Commit to memory the names of the five books of the Major Prophets. Then write them in your notebook.

4 Review the names of all the other books you have previously learned.

❖ ❖ ❖

The Power of God's Word

I believe a knowledge of the Bible without a college education is more valuable than a college education without the Bible.

—William Lyon Phelps, former professor at Yale University

Lila and her husband were expecting their fourth child and were looking forward to the new baby's arrival with eager anticipation. Then, unexpectedly, their dreams were shattered by a miscarriage.

Not only was Lila grieved by the loss of the child, it soon became apparent that her life was in grave danger. Serious complications suddenly became evident, and she was rushed by ambulance to the hospital.

Lila was vaguely aware of her surroundings as she slipped in and out of consciousness. Her family was at her side encouraging her, and many friends and loved ones were praying fervently.

During the crisis, she found it nearly impossible to focus her mind on anything except for one clear impression that persisted in her mind. "I can endure…I can survive…I can withstand…all things through Christ who strengthens me."

❖

Objective: To experience the power of God's Word in our daily lives

Read: Acts 21 and 24

Memorize: Hebrews 4:12

Somehow, in spite of the loss of blood and the close proximity of death, she was aware that she was not remembering the words just right. Yet intuitively she understood that God was promising to see her through.

Two weeks later, she returned home weakened but alive. While reading her Bible, she suddenly remembered the exact Scripture.

> I can do all things through Christ who strengthens me (Philippians 4:13, NKJ).

How she praised God for His Word, which had penetrated the fog of unconsciousness with a powerful promise of strength and provision!

In the Epistle to the Hebrews, Paul records:

> The word of God is living and active. Sharper than any double-edged sword, it penetrates even to dividing soul and spirit, joints and marrow; it judges the thoughts and attitudes of the heart (Hebrews 4:12).

God's holy, inspired Word has several characteristics that guarantee powerful results.

First, *it is infused with the power of the Holy Spirit.* It has been said that a Bible that is falling apart usually belongs to a person who isn't. That is because God's Word is energetic and active, speaking to today's world and our own personal needs and circumstances.

Second, *God's Word is truth.* It awakens our conscience. With the power to reach into the private corners of our hearts, the Word bares our motives and secret feelings and reveals our hidden longings.

Third, *God's Word discerns our true character.* It exposes the weaknesses in our attitudes and conduct, enabling us to correct ourselves by the power of His Holy Spirit.

As you study this lesson, I urge you to begin hiding the Word of God in your heart, drawing upon its wisdom for your life. Remember that God's Word will never return to Him void, but will most certainly accomplish what it was sent to do. Share the Word with a friend, bearing witness to the faithfulness of our wonderful Lord and the power and authority of His Holy Spirit.

❖

Bible Study

The Word of God

Tell what God's Word is or what it does, or both, according to the following Scripture references (use dictionary for definition of key words if needed).

1. What it is:

Hebrews 5:12–14

Philippians 2:16

Ephesians 6:17

2. What it does:

1 John 2:5

John 12:48

Romans 10:17

John 15:3

3. Both:

1 Peter 1:23

John 8:31,32

John 17:17

1 Peter 2:2

Hebrews 4:12 (5 things)

How to Understand the Word of God

1. Read 1 Corinthians 2:14.

   No one can understand the Word of God by his own ability. Why?

2. Describe in your own words a natural man's reaction to spiritual things.

3. Explain in your own words how one must come to understand the Word of God. See 1 Corinthians 2:7–12 and Romans 8:5–9.

   Why do some individuals deny the authority of Scripture, the deity of Christ, the inspiration of the Bible, and other basic teachings in the Word of God?

   What should be our response to them?

LIFE APPLICATION

1 When we approach the Word of God, what is the first thing we should understand (2 Peter 1:20,21)?

2 What is one way the power of the Bible manifests itself, according to 2 Timothy 3:15?

3 How have you experienced that power in your life recently?

4 The twelve books of the Minor Prophets are probably the most difficult of all to learn and remember. Give extra diligence to memorizing this division, then write the names in your notebook.

❖ ❖ ❖

The Need for God's Word

❖

Objective: To gain spiritual dependence on God's Word for daily Christian living

Read: Acts 25 and 26

Memorize: Psalm 119:105

Before I became a believer in Jesus Christ, God's Word didn't make any sense to me. I tried to read it occasionally during my high school and college days, but found it boring. Finally, I concluded that no really intelligent person could believe the Bible.

But when I became a Christian, my life was transformed, and my attitudes concerning the Scriptures changed. I realized that the Bible was truly the holy, inspired Word of God. For almost fifty years it has been more important to me than the thousands of books in my library combined.

Why is the Bible so important to the Christian? Let me share five basic reasons.

First, *the Word of God is divinely inspired.* The apostle Paul wrote, "All Scripture is God-breathed and is useful for teaching, rebuking, correcting and training in righteousness, so that the man of God may be thoroughly equipped for every good work" (2 Timothy 3:16).

Second, *the Scripture is the basis of our belief.* As the divinely-inspired Word, the Bible gives us God's perspective on how we should live. It offers His pardon for our sins, reveals His purpose for our lives, shows us

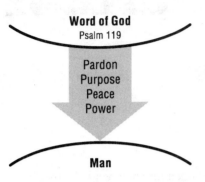

Word of God
Psalm 119

Pardon
Purpose
Peace
Power

Man

how to live peacefully in a world of turmoil, and commands us to appropriate His power so we can be fruitful witnesses for our Lord Jesus Christ.

Many years ago, while I was a student at Fuller Theological Seminary, two gifted young evangelists came to speak during our chapel program. Both believed and preached the Word of God without questioning its authority. Later, however, they began to doubt that the Bible was truly inspired in every word.

One of these men finally rejected the integrity of the Scripture altogether. As a result, he had no moorings on which to base his life and ministry. He is now a skeptic and an outspoken opponent of the Christian faith.

The other young evangelist chose to believe that the Bible is truly the authoritative, inspired Word of God, and what he could not understand he entrusted to God and believed by faith.

Few remember the name of the first man. But the second is Billy Graham, whom God has used to touch the lives of millions around the world.

Third, *the Bible is God's love letter to man.* From Genesis to Revelation, it tells of God's great compassion for us and of His desire to have fellowship with us. John 3:16, perhaps the most beloved passage in the Bible, summarizes the depth of His love for us:

> God so loved the world that he gave his one and only
> Son, that whoever believes in him shall not perish but
> have eternal life.

Fourth, *the Bible reveals God's attributes.* It tells us that He is holy, sovereign, righteous, and just; that He is loving, merciful, and kind; that He is gracious, patient, and faithful. We have no trouble trusting Him if we really understand who He is and how holy, loving, and wonderful His purposes are for us.

Fifth, *God's Word teaches us how to live holy lives and to be fruitful witnesses for our Lord.* The more we read and meditate on His precious Word—and let His Holy Spirit control our lives—the more fruitful we become.

Are you spending time meditating on God's Word daily? If not, let me encourage you to begin today. As you study this lesson, ask God to reveal Himself to you in a fresh, new way and let Him speak to your heart of His will for you. I encourage you to depend on God's Word for your daily Christian living.

Bible Study

What We Should Know About the Bible

Read Psalm 119.

1. What does the psalmist call God's Word in the following verses of Psalm 119?

   Verse 1

   Verse 2

   Verse 4

   Verse 5

   Verse 6

   Verse 7

   Verse 43

   Verse 72

   Verse 105

   Verse 123

2. What does this tell you of the importance of knowing God's Word?

3. When does God discipline His children (Psalm 119:126)?

4. What value does the Word have for us (Psalm 119:72)?

5. What is necessary in order to learn the Word (Psalm 119:73)?

How God's Word Affects Our Feelings

1. According to these verses in Psalm 119, what does the psalmist recognize is accomplished by respecting and learning God's Word?

Verse 7

Verse 8

Verse 9

2. From Psalm 119:10–16, list at least three attitudes of the psalmist that show his love for the Word of God.

3. Why is adversity sometimes good for us (Psalm 119:67 and 71)?

4. From these verses in Psalm 119, what is the reaction of those who love Christ when His Word is not kept?

Verse 136

Verse 158

5. How can we have great peace (Psalm 119:165)?

Results of Appropriating God's Word

1. Read these verses in Psalm 119, and write what affect the Word has on us when we do the following:

Know and memorize the Word (verse 98)

Meditate on it (verse 99)

Obey it (verse 100)

Follow it (verse 105)

What does the Word give us (verse 130)?

2. According to Psalm 119, what should we do as a result of appropriating the Word?

Verse 11

Verse 32

Verse 63

Verse 74

Verse 157

Verse 176

L I F E   A P P L I C A T I O N

 What impresses you most about Psalm 119?

2 List three ways in which you recognize your personal need for God's Word today.

3 Many people can recite the four books of the Gospels. Can you? Add the one book of New Testament history, and write all five books in your notebook.

Since this division is quite easy, go ahead to the next division, the Pauline epistles and Hebrews. That division is harder to learn so you should get started on it now.

❖ ❖ ❖

Private Bible Study Methods

Martin Luther said he studied his Bible in the same way he gathered apples. He encourages us to:

> Search the Bible as a whole, shaking the whole tree. Read it rapidly, as you would any other book. Then shake every limb—study book after book.

> Then shake every branch, giving attention to the chapters when they do not break the sense. Then shake each twig by a careful study of the paragraphs and sentences. And you will be rewarded if you will look under each leaf by searching the meaning of the words.

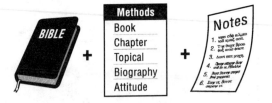

❖

Objective: To establish good habits of regular, systematic study of the Bible

Read: Acts 27 and 28

Memorize: Colossians 3:16,17

The *Thompson Chain Reference Bible* gives this suggestion:

> Study the Bible as a traveler who seeks to obtain a thorough and experimental knowledge of a new country.

> Go over its vast fields to truth; descend into its valleys; climb its mountains

of vision; follow its streams of inspiration; enter its halls of instruction; visit its wondrous portrait galleries.

Remember that many doctrinal errors have grown out of a lack of spiritual perspective, or a narrow view of scriptural truth. The Savior says, "Ye do err, not knowing the Scriptures, nor the power of God."

Seek to understand the deep things of God. Study "The Word" as a miner digs for gold, or as a diver plunges into the depths of the sea for pearls.

Most great truths do not lie upon the surface. They must be brought up into the light by patient toil.

Every time you and I read and study God's Word carefully, we are building up our storehouse of faith. When we memorize the Word, our faith is being increased.

Reading the Bible is vital for every Christian. How can we learn about God or grow spiritually if we do not spend time studying the Book in which He has made Himself known to us?

Taking a few minutes each day to read a chapter is a good way to start. But we should also block out extended periods of time for exploring God's Word and reflecting on what He is saying to us.

❖

Bible Study

Proper Attitude for Bible Study

When you personally received Christ as your Savior and Lord, you began a great adventure. That great adventure is mapped out in the pages of the Holy Scriptures. As you read and study the Bible in the power of the Holy Spirit, you will receive meaning, strength, direction, and power for your life. You will learn and claim the many great promises God has reserved for His own.

Approach the Bible in prayer; with reverence, awe, and expectancy; with a willing mind; and with a thirst for truth, righteousness, and fullness in the Lord Jesus Christ. When you come with a humble and contrite heart, you can trust God the Holy Spirit to reveal God's truth to you, and you will experience the cleansing power of His eternal Word.

Above all, as you study God's Word, be eager to obey all that He commands, and rejoice in the knowledge that you are an ambassador for Christ, seeking men in His name to be reconciled to God.

1. How do you feel about Bible study?

2. What do you see at this point as your main purpose in studying God's Word?

3. Have you established a definite goal regarding Bible study?

Tools Needed

First, obtain at least two translations of the Bible. Study the various translations. You would not expect to learn much about the physical laws of our universe without diligent and persistent study. Should you expect to acquire much knowledge of God and the unsearchable riches of His Word without studying with equal diligence and persistence?

As funds are available, you will want to secure a topical Bible, a concordance, and a Bible dictionary. Additional Bible study books are helpful and can be added as convenient. However, always remember, Bible study involves just that—studying the Bible. The other items are merely tools to assist you in getting the rich truths God has for you in His Word.

As you consider each study of the Scriptures, may I suggest you record God's Word to you in a journal. This will not only result in a deeper, more serious study, it will also give you a written record of how God speaks to you and of your response to Him.

1. List the tools you now have.

2. List the additional tools you desire in the order in which you plan to obtain them.

Suggested Methods

1. *Book study.* The Bible contains many books. Yet the divine plan of God to redeem men in Christ Jesus runs through the whole of it. Be careful to consider each book as a part of the

whole. Read it through. Following these suggestions will help make your study more meaningful:

◆ *Mark and underline* as God speaks to you through His Word.

◆ *Outline* it.

◆ *List* the names of the principal characters; tell who they are and their significance.

◆ *Select* from each chapter key verses to memorize and copy them on a card to carry with you.

◆ *List* teachings to obey and promises to claim.

◆ *Consider* the characteristics revealed of God the Father, God the Son, and God the Holy Spirit.

Which book would you particularly like to study using this method? (It is best to start with one of the shorter ones.)

2. *Chapter study.* To get a grasp of the chapter, answer the following questions:

◆ What is the principal subject of the chapter?

◆ What is the leading lesson?

◆ What is the key verse? (Memorize it.)

◆ Who are the principal characters?

◆ What does it teach about God the Father?

◆ What does it teach about Jesus Christ?

◆ What does it teach about the Holy Spirit?

◆ Is there any example for me to follow?

◆ Is there any error for me to avoid?

◆ Is there any duty for me to perform?

◆ Is there any promise for me to claim?

◆ Is there any prayer for me to echo?

Chose a chapter from the book, and apply these questions.

3. *Topical study.* Take an important subject—such as grace, truth, prayer, faith, assurance, justification, regeneration, or peace—and, using a topical Bible and a concordance, study the scope of the topic throughout the Bible.

You will find it necessary to divide each topic into sub-topics as you accumulate material; for example, forms of prayer, prayer promises, examples of prayer in Scripture, Christ's teaching on prayer, Christ's ministry as we pray, the ministry of the Holy Spirit in prayer.

What topic do you plan to study first?

How much time have you scheduled for it?

4. *Biographical study.* There are 2,930 people mentioned in the Bible. The lives of many of these make extremely interesting biographical studies. Why is it important to study the characters of the Bible (1 Corinthians 10:11; Romans 15:4)?

Using a concordance, topical Bible, or the proper name index in your Bible, look up every reference in the Bible of someone you would like to study.

Name the person you would like to study.

State your reason for choosing that particular person.

Answer the following questions:

◆ What was the social and political atmosphere in which he (or she) lived?

◆ How did that affect his life?

◆ What do we know of his family?

◆ What kind of training did he have in his youth?

◆ What was accomplished by him during his life?

◆ Was there a great crisis in his life? If so, how did he face it?

◆ What were his outstanding character traits?

◆ Who were his friends? What kind of people were they?

◆ What influence did they have on him?

◆ What influence did he have on them?

◆ Does his life show any development of character?

◆ What was his experience with God? Notice his prayer life, faith, service to God, knowledge of God's Word, courage in witnessing, and attitude toward the worship of God.

◆ Were any particular faults evident in his life?

◆ Was there any outstanding sin in his life?

◆ Under what circumstances did he commit this sin?

◆ What was its nature and its effect on his future life?

◆ What were his children like?

◆ Was there some lesson in this person's life that will help to enrich your life?

By the time you complete the studies outlined in this *Handbook*, you will have been introduced to each of these four methods. You already have taken the first step in the book study method by reading the Book of Acts. Lessons 2 and 4 of *Step 2: The Christian and the Abundant Life* were chapter studies. You will soon be ready to apply these as well as the other two methods to more advanced work in your own individual Bible study.

LIFE APPLICATION

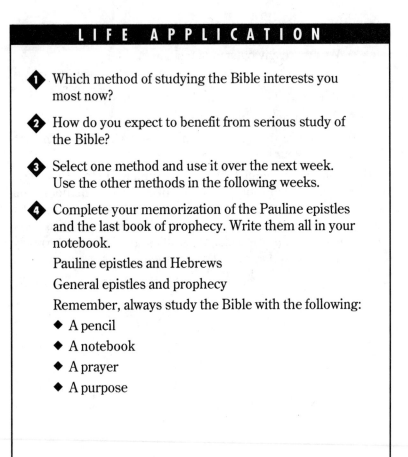

1 Which method of studying the Bible interests you most now?

2 How do you expect to benefit from serious study of the Bible?

3 Select one method and use it over the next week. Use the other methods in the following weeks.

4 Complete your memorization of the Pauline epistles and the last book of prophecy. Write them all in your notebook.

Pauline epistles and Hebrews

General epistles and prophecy

Remember, always study the Bible with the following:

◆ A pencil

◆ A notebook

◆ A prayer

◆ A purpose

❖ ❖ ❖

Recap

The following questions will help you review this Step. If necessary, reread the appropriate lesson(s).

1. In your notebook, write the divisions of the books of the Bible and the names of each book in each division. Review any division you do not know well.

2. How would you explain the statement, "Christ is the central person of the Bible?"

3. Who do you think is the real source of the authority of the Scripture?

   Describe how this is evident in biblical history.

4. Name at least three things the Word of God accomplishes that indicate its supernatural power.

   Write down several changes that the Bible has made in your life. Be specific.

5. Why do you need the Word of God?

Reread: Acts 15–28

Review: Verses memorized

6. What steps do you still need to take to be fully prepared for serious study of the Bible?

7. Review the names of the books of the Bible and write them one final time. Be sure the spelling is correct.

L I F E   A P P L I C A T I O N

1 Begin a journal of what you are learning through your Bible study. Buy a small notebook and record:

- ◆ The portion of Scripture you are studying
- ◆ The method you are using

For each day of study, record the following:

- ◆ Date
- ◆ Lesson that is important to you
- ◆ How you can apply it to your life
- ◆ Results of previous lessons you have applied to your daily situations

Also, write down prayer requests and answers as well as verses you have memorized.

When you finish the study, begin again with another portion of Scripture.

2 Periodically review your journal to see how you are growing spiritually and to remind yourself of important lessons you have learned.

The Christian and Obedience

Living Daily in God's Grace

STEP 6

Obedience—The Key to Knowing God's Will

Have you ever wondered what God's will is for your life? Have you needed to make a difficult decision and wondered what God wanted you to do in that situation?

We all struggle with questions about our future. Questions like: How can I know God's plan for my life? Which job should I take? Is this the person God wants me to marry? Is this a good investment to make? Should I share the gospel with my boss? You probably have questions you could add to that list.

The greatest discovery I have ever made concerning how to know the will of God involves the following:

- ◆ Fully surrendering my life to the Lordship of Christ

- ◆ Living a life of obedience in the power of the Holy Spirit

- ◆ Maintaining my first love for our Lord

Many Christians are trying so hard to discover the will of God that they lose the joy of the Lord and leave their first love for Him.

❖

Objective: To desire to follow God's will above all else

Read: Romans 1 and 2

Memorize: John 14:21

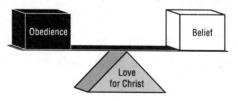

235

But all we need to do is abide in Christ, maintain our first love for Him, and walk in the power of the Holy Spirit, and we will be in the will of God. So as you continue to walk in the Spirit, He will guide you in making the most important decisions of life. He will also guide you in the daily, moment-by-moment decisions and actions of your life.

Speaking of the Holy Spirit, Jesus says, "When he, the Spirit of truth, comes, he will guide you into all truth...and he will tell you what is yet to come" (John 16:13). So the key to knowing God's will is to be obedient to the guidance of the Holy Spirit of truth. If you are willing to trust and obey God and live a holy life, God will reveal Himself to you and direct your steps as a way of life.

Satan is the enemy of our soul. His mission is to keep us from being effective and fruitful in our witness. But although he wields great power, Satan can never defeat us if we are completely yielded and obedient to Christ.

Some people are reluctant to trust God completely with their lives, fearing that He may want to make a change in their plans. Yes, He *will* change our plans. His plans are infinitely better than the very best we could ever conceive.

Is it not logical that the One who created us knows better than we the purpose for which we were created? And since He loves us enough to die for us, is it not logical to believe that His way is best (Romans 8:32)?

Obedience is the true test of our love for Christ and the secret to discovering God's will for our life.

❖

Bible Study

Disobedience of King Saul
Read 1 Samuel 15.

1. What was God's command to Saul through Samuel?

2. Describe how Saul rationalized his actions (15:7–9).

3. Was Saul's repentance sincere?

4. The main principle illustrated is stated in verse 22. What is it?

5. What are some ways Christians rationalize disobedience today?

Obedience of Paul
Read Acts 9:1–22.

1. What was God's command to Paul (here called Saul)?

2. How did he comply?

3. Why was Paul's obedience so important at this particular time?

4. How do you think Paul's obedience illustrates the truth of the principle in 1 Samuel 15:22?

Obedience of Ananias
Read Acts 9:10–22.

1. What was God's command to Ananias?

2. What was Ananias' reaction?

3. How did he finally respond?

4. Why was his obedience so essential at this particular time?

5. How does his obedience indirectly influence you?

LIFE APPLICATION

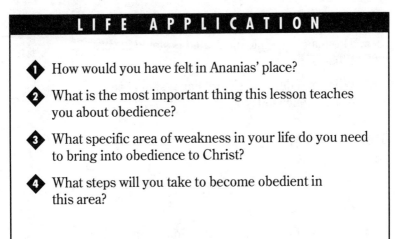

1 How would you have felt in Ananias' place?

2 What is the most important thing this lesson teaches you about obedience?

3 What specific area of weakness in your life do you need to bring into obedience to Christ?

4 What steps will you take to become obedient in this area?

❖ ❖ ❖

Insincere Obedience

At a high school graduation recently, one student was heard to make these remarks: "Yeah, I finally made it. It's a good thing, too. If I had blown it, my parents would have killed me!"

In contrast, during the ceremony one of the student speakers, an oriental girl who was a foreign exchange student declared through her tears, "I want to express my deepest appreciation to my parents for loving me and for giving me the opportunity to get an education in this great land. I want to do

❖

Objective: To recognize obedience that is external only, and become obedient from the heart

Read: Romans 11–13

Memorize: Colossians 3:23

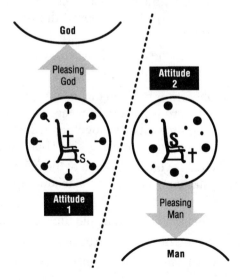

everything I can to show them how much I love them and to make them proud of me."

What a difference in motivation between these students. The first obviously lived in fear of his parents, while the second understood and appreciated what her parents had done for her.

The epitaph of Amaziah, a king of Israel, reads, "He did what was right in the sight of the Lord, but not with a loyal heart" (2 Chronicles 25:2, NKJ). Obedience involves attitude, not merely outward actions. What is your motivation when you obey Christ? Do you serve Christ out of fear and self-serving ambition? Or from a loyal heart because you understand and appreciate God's love and what He has done for you?

❖

Bible Study

An Example of Insincere Obedience
Read Acts 4:32—5:11.

1. At one time, Jerusalem Christians held goods as common property. Each Christian put his funds into a common treasury, which then supplied the needs of the Christian community.

   What made them willing to give up personal possessions (verse 32)?

2. One writer has said that many today view the local church as if it were a restaurant where all kinds of people meet for a short time, sit down together in the same room, then part, not knowing or caring anything about each other.

   What is your estimation of the fellowship in our churches today compared with the fellowship of the Jerusalem Christians?

   What kind of attitude did the early Christians display?

   Do you think this is true in your church?

   What can you do to improve the fellowship in your church?

3. When Barnabas sold his land, which was probably valuable, and gave the money to the church, no doubt other Christians praised his devotion.

   How do you think Barnabas' action might have influenced Ananias and Sapphira?

4. What do you suppose motivated Ananias and Sapphira to sell their possessions and give money to the church?

5. How did their motive differ from Barnabas' motive?

Importance of Our Christian Testimony

1. How can it be possible to study the Bible, share Christ with others, or attend Christian meetings, and yet be committing sin when you think you are pleasing God?

2. What did Christ say was wrong with the people of His day (Mark 7:6)?

3. Why is your heart attitude just as important to God as your outward action?

Attitude in Giving and Prayer

Read Matthew 6:1–8.

1. Each of us has a tendency to do things for the approval of our friends. When this desire becomes our sole motivation, our attitude is wrong. Think of a person you know who has a godly attitude toward giving. How do his actions differ from those described in Matthew 6?

2. List some ways you can help keep your giving sincere.

3. Public prayer is not wrong in itself. When you pray aloud with others, to whom are you talking?

4. How can you make your public prayers a testimony to how much you love God?

LIFE APPLICATION

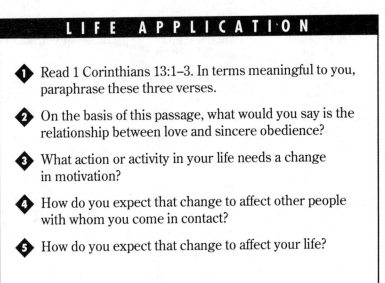

1 Read 1 Corinthians 13:1–3. In terms meaningful to you, paraphrase these three verses.

2 On the basis of this passage, what would you say is the relationship between love and sincere obedience?

3 What action or activity in your life needs a change in motivation?

4 How do you expect that change to affect other people with whom you come in contact?

5 How do you expect that change to affect your life?

❖　❖　❖

Personal Purity

Few areas of life are more important than our relationship to the opposite sex, and few areas are so exposed to temptation.

Some time ago, my heart was grieved as I learned of a respected Christian leader who had fallen into a life of sin. He had obviously not intended to do so, but when the temptation came he gave in—and as a result his wife, his family, his friends, and fellow Christians suffered tremendous heartache.

Most tragically, his testimony and witness for the Lord Jesus Christ suffered untold damage, and the overall cause of our Lord was ridiculed and rejected by many because of his sin.

As Christians we are called to live lives that are holy. We are to set aside the evil ways of the world and honor Christ by living in faithful obedience to His commandments.

God's Word tells us, "As obedient children, do not conform to the evil desires you had when you lived in ignorance. But just as

❖

Objective: To desire a holy life

Read: Romans 3 and 4

Memorize: 1 Corinthians 6:18

he who called you is holy, so be holy in all you do; for it is written: 'Be holy, because I am holy'" (1 Peter 1:14–16).

As you study this lesson, consider these principles:

1. Immorality originates in the mind, and God must give us victory there by His Holy Spirit.

2. The Bible gives a healthy outlook on sex. God's Word teaches that the sexual relationship can be a source of enjoyment and blessing when confined to the proper area—marriage. The Bible never pictures sex as sinful, distasteful, or dirty. Just as fire may be a great boon to man but can bring havoc when used improperly, so sex is a great blessing, but can ruin a life when abusively indulged.

3. Our gracious God forgives and cleanses in this area as He does in all others, so that we need carry no unnecessary load of guilt. David repented of his sin of adultery with Bathsheba. He said, "I acknowledged my sin to you and did not cover up my iniquity. I said, 'I will confess my transgressions to the Lord'—and you forgave the guilt of my sin" (Psalm 32:5).

4. In all our conduct toward the opposite sex, we must set the highest example and give no occasion for others to doubt our testimony.

❖

Bible Study

Purity and the Mind

1. What does Christ say of impure thought (Matthew 5:27,28)?

2. List the things on which we are to think (Philippians 4:8).

   Why does the human mind not want to think on these things (Romans 8:7)?

3. What are some things in our modern life and homes that naturally lead to impure thoughts?

4. How do we gain victory over impure thoughts (Galatians 5:16)?

What can we do to avoid thinking impure thoughts (Romans 13:14)?

5. Apply these verses to the things you listed in question 3. How will you handle each area of temptation?

Note: Temptation in the thought life is not the same as sin. Evil thoughts may pass through the mind, but sin comes from dwelling on the thought.

How can we avoid some temptations (2 Timothy 2:22)?

Purity and the Opposite Sex

1. What does the Bible say about the sexual relationship in its proper place (Hebrews 13:4)?

2. When tempted by immorality, what is a Christian to do (1 Corinthians 6:18)?

Why?

3. List some things you can be certain will help you when you are tempted (1 Corinthians 10:13).

4. Write in your own words the warnings against immorality found in the following Scriptures:

Proverbs 6:26

Proverbs 6:32

1 Thessalonians 4:3–8

Purity and Forgiveness

1. Write in your own words what the following verses say about God's forgiveness:

Psalm 103:12

Isaiah 43:25

1 John 2:1,2

2. What must we do to obtain God's forgiveness (1 John 1:9)?

LIFE APPLICATION

1 What area of impurity in your life do you need to face and deal with?

2 What are you doing or have around you that increases the temptation?

3 Choose an appropriate verse or passage from this lesson, apply it to your situation, and write the result you expect to attain.

❖ ❖ ❖

No Matter What Others Think

William Carey, an impoverished English shoemaker born late in the 18th century, had to overcome great odds to obey the call of God to become a missionary in India. In opposition to his work, the Directors of the huge, influential East India Company presented this resolution to the English Parliament:

> The sending out of missionaries into one Eastern possession is the maddest, most extravagant, most costly, most indefensible project which has ever been suggested by a moonstruck fanatic.

Then in 1796, the General Assembly of the Church of Scotland passed the following resolution:

> To spread the knowledge of the gospel amongst barbarians and heathens seems to be highly preposterous.

One opposer—a speaker in the House of Commons—said he would rather see a band of devils let loose in India than a band of missionaries.

But despite all this antagonism, Carey persisted. "Why is my soul disquieted within me?" he wrote. "Things may turn out better than I expect. Everything is known to God, and God cares."

❖

Objective: To obey God regardless of popular opinion or peer pressure

Read: Romans 7 and 8

Memorize: Matthew 10:32

William Carey stood the test and became the father of modern missions.[1]

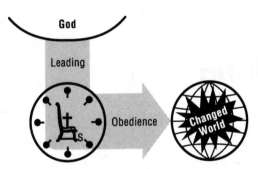

A sincere, committed Christian will always take his stand for Christ regardless of opposition, popular opinion, or peer pressure. If we yield to the fear of man, Satan may ruin our testimony substantially. If we obey the leading of the Spirit of God, men and women will be won to Christ.

I encourage you to take your stand for Christ and be a fruitful witness for Him no matter what others think.

❖

Bible Study

Peter's Renunciation

Read Matthew 26:57–75 carefully.

1. Peter knew and loved Christ in his heart, but when it came time to openly identify himself as a follower of Christ, what did he do (verse 58)?

2. Note the contrasts between Christ and Peter:

   Who accused Christ (verse 59)?

   Who accused Peter (verses 69,71)?

   How did Christ answer His accusers (verse 64)?

   How did Peter answer his accusers (verses 71–74)?

---

[1] Adapted from *The Challenge of Life* by Oswald J. Smith.

What happened to Jesus because He told the truth (verses 67,68)?

What was the result when Peter told those lies (verse 75)?

3. Some have said that Christ's teachings are only for weaklings, cowards, neurotics, and those who need some kind of crutch. As you look at the examples here of Christ and Peter, how would you evaluate such a statement?

4. Describe what Jesus' example means to you in facing your peer pressures.

Peter's Restoration

1. After Christ's resurrection, what did the angel announce to the women in Mark 16:7?

Why did the angel single out Peter's name from all the rest?

2. Upon what basis can Christ restore you even though you have denied Him?

Peter's Transformation

1. Less than two months later at Pentecost, Peter stood up from among the disciples to give a bold defense of the Christian faith to a ridiculing crowd (Acts 2:13–15).

What shocking thing did Peter fearlessly tell the crowd (Acts 2:36)?

2. What made this dramatic difference in Peter's life (Acts 1:8; 4:8)?

3. And what resulted (Acts 2:37–41)?

4. Compare the actions of the disciples during the crucifixion (Luke 22:47–62; 23:49; Matthew 26:56) and during this account in Acts. What part does Christian fellowship and unity play in standing up to peer pressure?

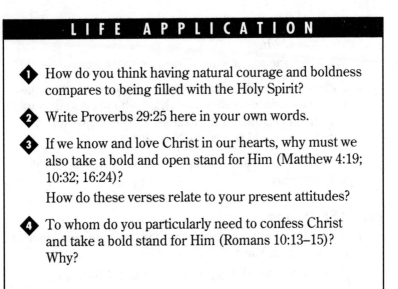

LIFE APPLICATION

1 How do you think having natural courage and boldness compares to being filled with the Holy Spirit?

2 Write Proverbs 29:25 here in your own words.

3 If we know and love Christ in our hearts, why must we also take a bold and open stand for Him (Matthew 4:19; 10:32; 16:24)?

How do these verses relate to your present attitudes?

4 To whom do you particularly need to confess Christ and take a bold stand for Him (Romans 10:13–15)? Why?

❖ ❖ ❖

Taming the Tongue

We've all met people with a sharp, critical tongue. Picture this scene. A couple from your Bible study group are having problems, and they have chosen to confide in you.

The man is big, a real outdoorsman, and works hard on a construction job. The wife is petite and frail. But she is as skilled with her tongue as David was with his slingshot against Goliath.

You're not with them long until the man bristles at his wife's verbal jabs.

"I just can't stand it when Karen puts me down in such a sarcastic way!" he complains.

"Oh, great big Mac," she digs, "can't take care of himself!"

Mac purses his lips and shakes his head. "I don't think I can take this much longer. I love my wife, but she's killing me with her tongue!"

Often the hostility in our hearts reveals itself through our words and actions. The word "tongue" is mentioned ninety-three times in the Bible, often referring to its destructive power:

The lash of the tongue (Job 5:21).

❖

Objective: To obey God in what we say

Read: Romans 9 and 10

Memorize: James 3:2

251

Your sin prompts your mouth; you adopt the tongue of the crafty (Job 15:5).

Though evil is sweet in his mouth and he hides it under his tongue (Job 20:12).

A deceitful tongue crushes the spirit (Proverbs 15:4).

Their tongue is a deadly arrow (Jeremiah 9:8).

The tongue also is a fire, a world of evil among the parts of the body. It corrupts the whole person, sets the whole course of his life on fire, and is itself set on fire by hell (James 3:6).

No man can tame the tongue. It is a restless evil, full of deadly poison (James 3:8).

Poisonous Words

James goes on to say, "With the tongue we praise our Lord and Father, and with it we curse men, who have been made in God's likeness. Out of the same mouth come praise and cursing. My brothers, this should not be" (James 3:9,10).

Few things are more self-contaminating than poisoned words that spring from the depths of a bitter heart.

If we are to please God and maintain a testimony that brings glory to our Lord, we must learn to control what we say. James says, "If anyone considers himself religious and yet does not keep a tight rein on his tongue, he deceives himself and his religion is worthless" (James 1:26). How often through an unkind word have we borne unfaithful witness to God's love and forgiveness!

A Test of Love

A test of our love for God comes in the manner of our speech. Can we say with the psalmist, "His praise was on my tongue" (Psalm 66:17), "My tongue will tell of your righteous acts all day long" (Psalm 71:24), or "May my tongue sing of your word" (Psalm 119:172)?

Will we follow the wisdom of Solomon who said, "The tongue of the wise brings healing" (Proverbs 12:18) and "The tongue that brings healing is a tree of life" (Proverbs 15:4)?

And can we say with Samuel, "His word was on my tongue" (2 Samuel 23:2)?

The words of Peter hold good advice for us today: "Whoever would love life and see good days must keep his tongue from evil and his lips from deceitful speech" (1 Peter 3:10).

This takes self-control.

Key to Self-Control

Self-control is vital to a fruitful Christian life. After counseling with thousands of people through the years, I am convinced that an undisciplined Christian cannot live a victorious, abundant life or be an effective witness.

The key to self-control is being filled with the Holy Spirit. The reason most of us fail in self-control is that we try to do it in our own strength. You and I know from experience that, apart from God, self-discipline in our tongue is impossible. But "when the Holy Spirit controls our lives he will produce this kind of fruit in us: love, joy, peace,...self-control" (Galatians 5:22, TLB).

We must develop and exercise self-control through daily dependence on the Lord Jesus Christ and the power of His Holy Spirit. I encourage you to study this lesson carefully. Prayerfully apply the principles you will learn to your everyday life, and invite the Holy Spirit to take control of your tongue that you may bring blessing to those around you and be a fruitful witness.

❖

Bible Study

Effects of the Tongue

Read James 3:1–13.

1. Though we may study our Bibles faithfully, attend Christian meetings regularly, and even talk to our friends about Christ, one thing marks us as really mature Christians. What is it?

2. When you control your tongue, what else will happen (verse 2)?

3. James compares a wicked tongue to an incorrectlyhandled steering mechanism on

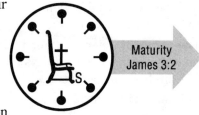

Maturity
James 3:2

a ship. What would happen if the ship were an oil tanker in rocky water?

How does this relate to the damage of "spilled" words?

4. What does it take to start a forest fire in a drought?

What does it take to put out a forest fire?

What damage can be caused by just a few words of gossip that you pass on?

5. Give an example from your own life in which you suffered from the "fire" of someone's destructive words.

How did you respond?

How would you respond today?

Why?

Sins of the Tongue

1. Name the sins of the tongue that are condemned in the following references in Proverbs:

6:16–19

11:13

15:1

17:9

27:2

Give examples of how you may have been hurt by or how you may have offended another in each of these areas.

2. Read Ephesians 4:29.

How does this apply to profanity, obscene language, off-color jokes, and so on?

What else can you name that could be included here?

What does this verse say we should do instead?

Significance of the Tongue
Read Matthew 12:33–37.

1. For what shall we give account to God?

2. What illustration does Christ use to explain good and bad words?

3. How does He apply it?

4. What, then, is the real source of an evil tongue?

5. How does this relate to attitude?

6. What is the only solution to taming the tongue for a believer (Galatians 5:16)?

LIFE APPLICATION

1 How will you obey the instructions indicated in James 1:19 in your own life?

How about James 1:26?

2 Think about the attitudes expressed through your words in the past week. Ask yourself these questions, and answer them honestly.

What attitude do I need to confess and make right with God?

To whom do I need to go and ask forgiveness because he or she has been affected by my words?

❖ ❖ ❖

The Key to Inner Security

Obedience to our Lord in every facet of our lives is the key to inner security and experiencing the presence of Christ.

I recall one wealthy and influential businessman in California who sacrificed everything he had to care for his dying wife. Eventually he spent his fortune seeking to find a cure for her disease.

By the time I learned of their situation, they had lost their entire fortune including their palatial home. They were living in modest circumstances in a little trailer on a parking lot in Hollywood.

I went to see them with fear and trembling. How in the world could I, a healthy, young Christian businessman, identify with this poverty-stricken husband? He had already lost his large fortune and was about to lose his most precious friend and mate of nearly forty years.

The trailer was neat as a pin. When I stepped into their humble home, it was as though I were entering a corner of heaven. There, sitting beside his dying wife, was this man holding her hand. Both of them had radiant faces. The joy of the Lord filled the place.

Objective: To find inner security in obedience to Christ

Read: Romans 5 and 6

Memorize: Matthew 6:33

I had come to minister to them, but they ministered to me instead. They were trusting God with their lives. Like Job, they were saying of their Lord, "Though he slay me, yet will I hope (trust) in him..." (Job 13:15).

I will always remember the peace of heart and mind that this couple enjoyed because they had learned to trust and obey the will and ways of God even in the midst of tragedy.

Many people hope to find security in their possessions when only a right relationship with God can bring abundant life. Through the years, I have be-come increasingly con-vinced that there are no unhappy obedient Christians. Further-more, I have never met a person living a dis-obedient life who can honestly say that he is happy. I have observed many Christians like 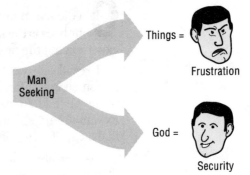 the businessman and his dying wife, however, who have found peace and blessing in tough times because they were walking with God in faith and obedience.

We can find no lasting security in a life apart from God as the Lord of our lives. God alone is the owner of all that we possess and the total source of our supply. Are you experiencing the joy of Christ in your life? His love? His peace? The sense of His direction? If not, could it be that you are not obeying His commands? When you withhold the resources that God has entrusted to you for His work, He has little with which to bless you, and your life becomes un-fruitful and unhappy.

We are not our own anymore; we have been bought with a price, the precious blood of the Lord Jesus Christ (1 Peter 1:18–20). Giving Him control of our time, talents, and treasure is our way of express-ing gratitude to our great and glorious God and Father for all that He has done to fill us with His presence.

❖

Bible Study

The Rich Fool
Read Luke 12:13–34.

1. What was foremost on the mind of the man in verse 13?

2. Why did Jesus deny his request?
In light of this, why do you think He denies some of our requests?

3. Why was the man in the parable a fool?

4. How do people today make the same mistake this man made?

5. Name some illustrations Jesus used in verses 24–28 to show the uselessness of worrying about material things.

6. Give some examples from recent events that show how true verse 34 is.

7. How does this parable help you put your priorities in order?

A Follower of Christ
Read Philippians 4:10–19.

1. How did Paul react to the lack of money?

2. Where did Paul obtain the strength to face adverse circumstances?

3. Is it easier for you to handle humble circumstances or prosperity?
Why?

4. How does having your priorities straight affect material changes in your life—whether for the better or worse?

5. Study verse 19. Why do you think God promises to supply our needs, but not necessarily our desires?

6. Read 1 Timothy 6:17–19. How do these verses compare with the world's view? Be specific.

7. Against what things did Paul warn the rich in 1 Timothy 6:17–19?

8. What did he exhort them to do?

Why?

9. How would your obedience to these verses affect relationships in the following:

Your family?

Your church?

Your neighborhood?

Christ Himself

1. In your own words, write what Jesus Christ did for us according to 2 Corinthians 8:9.

2. Read 2 Corinthians 9:7,8.

Because of what Jesus Christ has done for us, we should be willing to invest part of our income in His work. When we give toward His work, what should our attitude be (verse 7)?

3. Note the use of the words *all* and *every* in verse 8. Why can you be cheerful even though you may give sacrificially to God's work?

When you have done this, what has been the result?

L I F E   A P P L I C A T I O N

❶ Think about the circumstances of your life. What part do they play in your search for security?

❷ In which areas of your life do you feel greedy or materialistic?

How have these feelings affected your spiritual well-being?

❸ List on this chart your most important possessions. Prayerfully yield each one to God. Then write down one way you can show that it belongs to Him.

POSSESSION	ACTION

❖   ❖   ❖

Recap

The following questions will help you review this Step. If necessary, reread the appropriate lesson(s).

1. In your notebook, complete the following statements:

   True obedience to God *is not*...

   True obedience really *is*...

2. How is your obedience expressed in the following:

   Your attitude toward God's will?

   The sexual purity of your life?

   The degree of satisfaction you find in your possessions?

   Your courage in witnessing for Christ?

   Your speech?

   The true motivation for your actions?

❖

Read: Romans 14–16

Reread: 1 Samuel 15 and Acts 4:32–5:11

Review: Verses memorized

3. Describe the result of a young child's obedience to his parents. Compare it to a Christian's relationship with his heavenly Father.

   How has your obedience to God benefited your life?

LIFE APPLICATION

 List the area from this study that concerns you most.

 Review the verses that pertain to that area.

3 Write down at least three ways you can grow in that area.

4 Commit this area to the Lord, asking Him to fill you with His Holy Spirit and to help you grow in this area.

❖ ❖ ❖

The Christian and Witnessing

Bringing Words of Hope to the World Around You

STEP 7

Why We Witness

I think a man's religion is so personal we shouldn't discuss it."

"I don't like people who are dogmatic and fanatical about religion. They try to force their views on everybody they meet."

"Well, I have my own religion, and I'm happy with it."

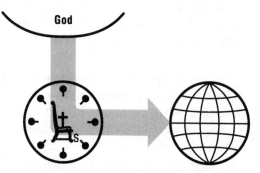

❖

Objective: To understand the reasons to witness for Christ

Read: Galatians 1 and 2

Memorize: 2 Corinthians 5:14,15

Perhaps you have heard comments like these from someone you know. Or even made them yourself before you became a believer.

During approximately fifty years of sharing Christ and training others to do the same, I have found no biblical rationale to justify fearing those responses as a reason for not witnessing.

In fact, the need for people to hear the Good News of God's love and forgiveness is a matter of life and death. The writer of Ecclesiastes observes:

> Death is the destiny of every man; the living should
> take this to heart (Ecclesiastes 7:2).

Man's self-will is characterized by an attitude of active rebellion or passive indifference. Because of sin, he is by nature degenerate and corrupt, destitute of God's love, undeserving of His forgiveness, and so destined to death—eternal separation from God. But Christ does not want anyone to perish, but wants everyone to come to repentance (2 Peter 3:9).

He placed such high value on the human soul that He personally gladly exchanged the perfection of heaven for a life of poverty, suffering, shame, and death to seek and to save what was lost (Luke 19:10).

From His earliest youth and throughout His life, Jesus clearly understood His mission and purpose. His concern for the lost was so deep that at times the flood of compassionate tears rolled down His face. Jesus, the manliest of men, wept. Similarly, Paul pleaded night and day with everyone who would listen to be reconciled to God.

Since then, people of every century and many walks of life have had a heart of compassion for those who are living apart from God. Great spiritual leaders such as John Wesley, D. L. Moody, and Billy Sunday dedicated their lives to reaching people with the message of hope.

When one young missionary who had been sent home because of illness was asked why he was so eager to get back to his people, he said, "Because I cannot sleep for thinking about them."

Our Lord has commissioned each of us to share the Good News and "seek the lost." He said, "Go and make disciples of all nations"; and, "Go into all the world and preach the good news to all creation" (Matthew 28:19; Mark 16:15). It is our greatest calling, then, to share the love and forgiveness He has given us with those who have never received Him as their Savior and Lord.

From my personal experiences and studies of God's Word, five key concepts have been made clear to me—concepts that impact the lives of every Christian.

Christ has given a clear command to every Christian.

Jesus Christ's last command to the Christian community was to make disciples. This command, which the church calls the Great Commission, was not intended merely for the eleven remaining disciples, or just for the apostles, or for those in present times who may have the gift of evangelism. This command is the responsibility of every man and woman who professes faith in Christ as Lord.

Men and women are lost without Jesus Christ.

Jesus said, "I am the way and the truth and the life. No one comes to the Father, except through me" (John 14:6). God's Word also reminds us, "There is salvation in no one else! Under all heaven there is no other name for men to call upon to save them" (Acts 4:12, TLB).

Men and women are truly lost without Jesus Christ. He is the only way to bridge the gap between man and God. Without Him, people cannot know God and have no hope of eternal life.

Rather than being "not interested," the people of the world are truly hungry for the gospel.

One of the greatest misconceptions held by Christians today is that men and women do not want to know God. But wherever I go around the world, I find ample proof that just the opposite is true. The Holy Spirit has created a hunger for God in the hearts of millions.

I have discovered that at least 25 to 50 percent of nonbelievers are ready to receive Christ in most parts of the world if properly approached, one on one, by a trained Spirit-empowered witness. And I believe that among that number may be some of your own family members, a neighbor or a co-worker, or a person you do not yet know to whom God may lead you. They are ready to hear a clear and simple presentation of the Good News of God's love and forgiveness.

Jesus said, "The fields are ripe unto harvest." Can we afford to be selfish with the gospel when such overwhelming evidence shows that so many people are hungry for God? By sharing our faith in Christ with others, we can help change our world for our Lord.

We Christians have in our possession the greatest gift available to mankind: God's gift of eternal life, which we received with Jesus Christ at our spiritual birth (John 3:16).

Christ is risen! We serve a living Savior! He not only lives within us in all His resurrection power, but He also has assured us of eternal life. He died on the cross in our place for our sin, then rose from the dead. We have direct fellowship with God through Jesus Christ. And this fellowship, this peace, this gift of eternal life, is available to all who receive Him.

The love of Jesus Christ for us, and our love for Him, compels us to share Him with others.

Jesus said, "The one who obeys me is the one who loves me..." (John 14:21, TLB). In other words, He measures our love for Him by the extent and genuineness of our obedience to Him. As we obey, He promises He will reveal Himself to us.

> Because he loves me, My Father will love him; and I
> will too, and I will reveal myself to him (John 14:21, TLB).

What are we to obey? When it comes to witnessing, we have the specific commandment from Jesus Christ to go into all the world with the Good News.

Helping to fulfill the Great Commission is both a duty and a privilege. We witness because we love Christ. We witness because He loves us. We witness because we want to honor and obey Him. We witness because He gives us a special love for others.

God wants you to witness because of the benefits He offers to those who receive Christ:

◆ They become children of God.

◆ Their bodies become temples of God.

◆ All of their sins are forgiven.

◆ They begin to experience the peace and love of God.

◆ They receive God's direction and purpose for their lives.

◆ They experience the power of God to change their lives.

◆ They have assurance of eternal life.

God also wants you to witness because of the benefits you will receive. Witnessing will stimulate your spiritual growth, lead you to pray and study God's Word, and encourage you to depend on Christ. You will experience the tremendous privilege and honor of representing Jesus to the world (2 Corinthians 5:20).

The Holy Spirit came to provide the power for you to do so (Acts 1:8). Wouldn't you like to share with someone else the most valuable thing you have?

All over the world, I have asked two questions of Christians, young and old, rich and poor, new Christians and people who have been believers for more than half a century. I have asked these questions also of some of the most famous Christians in the world. The answers are always the same, no matter who I ask.

1. What is the most important experience of your life?

"Knowing Christ as my Savior."

2. What is the most important thing you can do for another person?

"Help him or her to know Christ."

If you are a Christian, you undoubtedly would give the same answers to these questions. Yet if you are like the majority of Christians today, you have never introduced anyone to Christ. But you would like to do so, and you know in your heart that this is what God called you to do.

❖

Bible Study

What Is a Witness?

1. Describe what a witness testifies to in a courtroom.

How is that like sharing your faith in Christ?

2. What are you admonished to do in Psalm 107:2 (use *The Living Bible*)?

   Why is this hard for you to do?

3. How have you followed this admonishment today?

   This week?

   This month?

   If you have not, what is keeping you from witnessing?

The Motivation for Witnessing

1. What did Jesus command you to do (Mark 16:15; Matthew 28:19,20)?

2. Read Acts 20:24–27,31,32.

   How important would you say Paul's ministry of witnessing was to him?

   Why?

3. Read 2 Corinthians 5:14,15.

   What caused Paul to witness?

   What attitude should we have about what Jesus has done for us?

   How should that change our lives?

4. What does Jesus Christ say about the one who is ashamed of Him (Luke 9:26)?

   How should this affect your witness?

5. If you are faithful to follow Jesus, what does He promise to do (Matthew 4:19)?

   How has He helped you do this?

The Message

1. We are called Christ's ambassadors in 2 Corinthians 5:18–20. (An ambassador is one who is appointed to represent his country in a foreign land.) Reflect on the duties of an ambassador.

How do these relate to the Christian life and to witnessing about your faith in Christ?

2. Why did Jesus say He came into this world (Luke 19:10; Mark 10:45)?

3. As a representative of Christ, what would be your message to those who do not know Him personally? Write your answer in words you could use with a non-Christian.

4. How does Paul express the message in 1 Corinthians 15:3,4?

LIFE APPLICATION

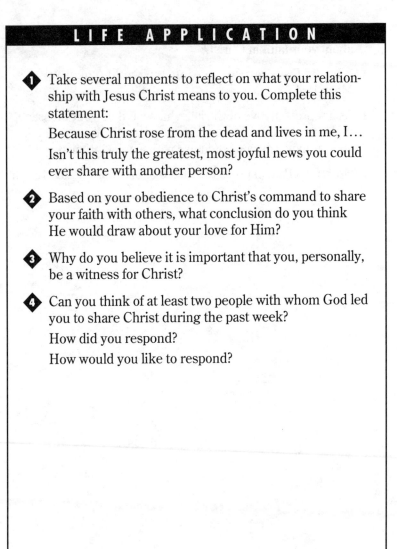

1 Take several moments to reflect on what your relationship with Jesus Christ means to you. Complete this statement:

Because Christ rose from the dead and lives in me, I...

Isn't this truly the greatest, most joyful news you could ever share with another person?

2 Based on your obedience to Christ's command to share your faith with others, what conclusion do you think He would draw about your love for Him?

3 Why do you believe it is important that you, personally, be a witness for Christ?

4 Can you think of at least two people with whom God led you to share Christ during the past week?

How did you respond?

How would you like to respond?

❖ ❖ ❖

In this lesson we will observe Christ's example in witnessing. Jesus demonstrated how to witness in the most effective manner as He talked to the woman of Samaria. Study John 4 carefully to discover new approaches and techniques of witnessing.

❖

Bible Study

Example of Jesus
Read John 4:1–42.

1. What everyday experience did Jesus use as an opportunity for witnessing?

2. What do you think is the advantage of beginning a conversation on the level of a person's immediate interest?

   Think of an occasion in which you used a person's special interest to share Christ with him. How did he respond?

3. List some of your natural opportunities to witness for Christ.

4. Why do you suppose Jesus sent all twelve of His disciples to buy provisions when two of them could have done it?

5. Who spoke first, Jesus or the woman of Samaria?

   Why is this significant when considering how to witness?

6. What did Jesus do repeatedly when the woman tried to divert His attention from her sin and her need?

Responses of the Samaritan Woman

1. How did the woman first respond to Jesus' approach?

   How does verse 15 indicate that her attitude changed?

   What do you think brought it about?

2. What did Jesus say that demonstrated His divine powers?

3. How did Jesus describe God (verse 24)?

   Why is this statement important?

4. Who was the woman looking for and why?

5. What did Jesus claim about Himself?

Effectiveness of Jesus' Witness

1. How effective was the approach Jesus used in witnessing to this woman of Samaria?

2. What was the result of His witness?

3. How did the people to whom she witnessed respond? Why?

"Sound Barriers"

Sometimes witnessing can seem like breaking a sound barrier, like when an airplane accelerates to supersonic speed. Introducing the subject of Jesus can produce much stress and nervousness.

The *first sound barrier* occurs when we first mention the name of Jesus Christ and the value of knowing Him. Once we turn the conversation from dating, fashions, politics, work, sports, or any other topic to spiritual things, we have broken the first barrier. It is sometimes hard to do, and it does not always come easily.

The *second sound barrier* comes when we present the gospel. That nervous feeling returns once again. We must blast through this one also because many people, when they understand who Jesus Christ is and what He has done for them, *will* want Him in their lives.

The *last barrier,* asking the person to receive Christ right now, is the most difficult. But this is the most important step. Often we tell the person how to become a Christian and then just leave him high and dry. Until we ask the person to trust Christ as his or her Savior and Lord, our witness is not complete.

LIFE APPLICATION

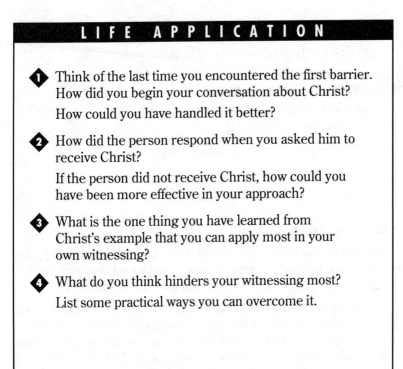

1 Think of the last time you encountered the first barrier. How did you begin your conversation about Christ?

How could you have handled it better?

2 How did the person respond when you asked him to receive Christ?

If the person did not receive Christ, how could you have been more effective in your approach?

3 What is the one thing you have learned from Christ's example that you can apply most in your own witnessing?

4 What do you think hinders your witnessing most?

List some practical ways you can overcome it.

❖ ❖ ❖

Qualifications for Witnessing

Personal preparation is the key to becoming a successful witness.

The first step is to *be sure that you yourself are a Christian.* Commit your entire person —your intellect, your emotions, your will— to Him and receive the gift of God's love and forgiveness through the Lord Jesus Christ.

The second step is to *be sure there is no unconfessed sin in your life.* If some sinful attitude or action is hindering your fellowship with God, He cannot live through you, and you will not be a joyful Christian or a fruitful witness for Christ.

The third step is to *be filled with the Holy Spirit.* To be fruitful in your witness for Christ, you must appropriate by faith the fullness of God's Spirit. Invite the Holy Spirit to control and empower you—to enable you to live a holy, godly life by faith and to make you a fruitful witness for Him.

The fourth step is to *be prepared to communicate your faith in Christ.* Keeping Christ

❖

Objective: To take spiritual inventory in preparation for witnessing

Read: Galatians 5 and 6

Memorize: Matthew 4:19

279

on the throne of your life as the Lord of your heart is the best preparation for communicating your faith.

Carefully study the eighth chapter of Acts. List the qualifications for witnessing. Ask the Holy Spirit to make these qualities real in your own life.

❖

Bible Study

Philip's Opportunity
Read Acts 8:26–40.

1. According to verses 26 and 27, why do you think God called Philip for this particular assignment?

2. To whom did Philip witness (verse 27)?

3. Who told Philip to join the chariot (verse 29)?

Does the Holy Spirit lead us in this same way today?

Describe an example from your life.

4. How did Philip respond?

5. How did Philip approach the man (verse 30)?

6. Was the man ready?

Why?

What was his response?

7. What Old Testament passage was the Ethiopian reading (verses 28,32,33)?

To whom did this refer?

8. What was Philip's message?

Philip's Qualifications

1. Philip demonstrated at least eight qualities that contributed to his effectiveness for Christ. Place the appropriate verses after the following words:

- ◆ Knowledge of the Word of God
- ◆ Boldness
- ◆ Compassion
- ◆ Humility
- ◆ Obedience
- ◆ Receptivity, sensitivity to guidance
- ◆ Tact
- ◆ Enthusiasm

2. Reflect on each of these qualities. How are they at work in your life?

Which ones do you have difficulty with?

List ways you could strengthen these areas.

Possible Hindrances to Our Witnessing

For each hindrance, describe in your notebook how it affects your witnessing.

1. *Spiritual lethargy*

If you are not excited about something, chances are you won't tell many people about it. For many Christians, the excitement of the Christian walk has been dulled by everyday distractions, materialistic pursuits, and unconfessed sin. Like the believers in Ephesus, these men and women have left their first love.

2. *Lack of preparation*

Personal dedication to Christ and understanding how to witness and what to say are imperative. Preparing your heart through prayer gives you the right attitude and opens yourself to the power of the Holy Spirit.

3. *Fear of man*

We possibly will be persecuted by unbelievers, as well as believers, but the fear of man will prove to be a snare (Proverbs 29:25). Christ said of those who feared to confess His name, "They loved the praise of men more than the praise of God."

4. *Fear of failure*

"They won't believe; they won't accept such simple truth." Certainly some will reject or neglect the gospel, but you should never believe the lie of Satan that people are not interested. Christ said, "Open your eyes and look at the fields! They are [present tense...'now'] ripe for harvest" (John 4:35).

Jesus said, "The harvest is plentiful but the workers are few. Ask the Lord...to send out workers into his harvest field" (Matthew 9:37,38).

5. *Fear that the new Christian will not go on and grow in the Lord*

Review the parable of the sower (Matthew 13:1–23). Every seed of the Word of God will fall on one of these types of soil: path, rocky, thorny, or good. Some new Christians will become disciples. Keep up the faithful search for these disciples!

6. *Lack of practical "know-how"*

As a result of thousands of surveys, we have found that the vast majority of Christians today not only believe they should share their faith, but they also really want to. However, they don't receive the practical hands-on training that will ease their fears and help them witness effectively. The result is a guilt trip: They know they should, but they hesitate because they don't know how.

LIFE APPLICATION

 Which hindrance is the greatest problem for you? Why?

What steps will you take to overcome it?

2 Have you let distractions, lethargy, materialism, or unconfessed sin rob you of your excitement in Christ? In what ways?

3 In a time of quiet prayer, ask God to reveal any unconfessed sin in your life. After reading 1 John 1:9, confess any such sin, and ask for God's cleansing and forgiveness.

4 Look back through the list of qualities in Philip's life and identify the ones you would like to have God develop in your life.

5 Spend some time in prayer, asking God for those characteristics to be developed in your life and witness.

❖ ❖ ❖

Witnessing and the Word of God

When the early Christians received the power of the Holy Spirit at Pentecost, the news spread quickly throughout Jerusalem, and a large crowd gathered, seeking the meaning of this phenomenon. Peter, under the control and in the power of the Holy Spirit, addressed the inquisitive crowd.

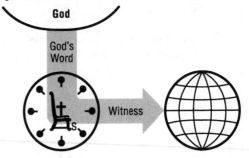

Who were these people? Some had been present at the crucifixion earlier and had cried, "Crucify Him" and, "Let his blood be on us and on our children" (Matthew 27:22, 25). Possibly some in the front row were those before whom Peter had used profanity when he denied Christ (Matthew 26:73,74).

Under these fearful circumstances, Peter's resources had to be God's Word, prayer, and the Holy Spirit. The purpose of this lesson is to demonstrate the use of the Word of God in witnessing, and its results.

Objective: To learn to use the power of God's Word in witnessing

Read: Ephesians 1 and 2

Memorize: 1 Peter 3:15

❖

Bible Study

Peter's Witness

Read Acts 2.

1. Of all the disciples, why was Peter the least qualified to witness for Christ, and yet the most qualified, as suggested above and in Acts 2?

2. How much of Peter's sermon involves quotations from the Bible (such as from Joel, David, etc.)?

   How much Scripture memorization do you suppose Peter had done in his early life?

3. What part does the Holy Spirit play...

   In those who share Christ's message (John 14:26)?

   In those who hear Christ's message (John 16:8–11)?

4. What part does prayer play (Acts 2:42–47)?

5. What did Peter say to convince them of sin (Acts 2:23,36)?

6. List some great things Peter preached about God (verses 24,34,35,38,39).

The Crowd's Response

1. How many became Christians that day?

2. List the emotions experienced by the hearers before and after conversion.

3. Why did some listeners react in anger first?

The Power of the Word

1. Summarize Isaiah 55:11.

2. According to Hebrews 4:12, how does the Word of God affect the non-Christian as you witness?

3. In Ephesians 6:17, what is the Bible called?

Why?

As you will see in more detail in Lesson 6, it is the Holy Spirit who brings men to grips with the issues as we witness.

The Value of Scripture Memorization

Committing portions of Scripture to memory is the best way to know the Word of God, and as a result, to know Christ. Also, by having the promises and commands of the Word memorized, we can apply them to any life situation at a moment's notice, especially when we want to use them in an unexpected witnessing opportunity.

1. List some things God has promised us (2 Peter 1:2–4):

2. List some ways that memorizing Scripture will help you, according to the following verses:

1 Peter 2:2,3 and Hebrews 5:12–14

Joshua 1:8 and Psalm 1:1–3

Psalm 32:8

3. List some ways, mentioned in the following references, in which God's Word will nourish your growth:

Romans 10:17

Psalm 119:11

Psalm 119:165

4. Name one thing for which God's Word was absolutely essential, according to 1 Peter 1:23.

LIFE APPLICATION

1 List specific ways in which the preceding Bible verses will help you in your witnessing.

2 Which verse do you believe you need the most?

3 Memorize that passage.

4 How will you apply it?

❖ ❖ ❖

Witnessing and Prayer

Do you want your loved ones, your friends, and neighbors to come to Christ? Begin to claim them for God as you pray. Follow the example of our Lord, our High Priest, whose prayer is recorded in John 17:20: "My prayer is not for them alone. I pray also for those who will believe in me through their message."

Just as Jesus prayed that the Holy Spirit would work in the lives of His disciples, so we can pray that the Holy Spirit will convict non-believers and give them a strong desire to know God. Paul and other writers of the New Testament were frequently requesting prayer for others as well as for themselves.

Although God wants everyone to come to repentance, He chooses to wait for the prayers of a concerned believer to release the Holy Spirit in that person's heart. In our ef-

Objective: To make prayer a vital part of witnessing

Read: Ephesians 3 and 4

Memorize: Acts 4:31

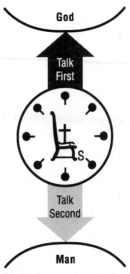

forts to lead people to Christ, we must first talk to God about men, then talk to men about God. If we follow this divine order, we will see results.

Since it is God's will that none should perish, and since God promises to answer any prayer offered in accordance with His will (1 John 5:14,15), we can know with assurance that God will answer our prayers for the salvation of souls for whom He has impressed us to pray (Philippians 2:13).

Prayer is really the place where people are won to Christ; sharing the Good News is just gathering in the fruit.

The aim of this lesson is to demonstrate that prayer played a major part in the witness of the early church.

❖

Bible Study

What the Early Christians Prayed For
Read Acts 4.

1. What problem did these Christians face?

2. What do you think would have happened to Christianity if they had stopped witnessing?

3. How important is the soul-winning witness to the cause of Christ today? Give two specific examples.

4. How did these Christians solve their dilemma:
   Before magistrates?
   In private?
   In public?

5. What protected them (Acts 4:21)?

6. For what did they pray?

The Answer to Their Prayer

The answer to their prayer was immediate and definite. They prayed, and God answered as He had promised. None could stand against them, and they were victorious in Christ.

1. How can you profit from their courage, prayer, and effective witness?

2. Successful praying is simply asking God to work according to His will and leaving the results to Him. From this statement, what part does faith play in your prayers?

3. In what ways can other people depend on your courage, prayer, and witness?

4. Someone has said, "Prayer is not an argument with God to persuade Him to move things our way, but an exercise by which we are enabled by His Spirit to move ourselves His way."

   How does this statement help us understand our role in witnessing?

   In our willingness to share our faith?

The Christian's Opposition

1. How were the witnessing Christians of the early church persecuted? (The Book of Acts gives several examples.)

2. In your opinion, who is the author of resistance to Christian witness?

   Why?

   How does knowing this help you have more courage?

God's Timing

1. Success in witnessing is simply taking the initiative to share Christ in the power of the Holy Spirit and leaving the results to God.

   How do you react when a person does not receive the gospel right away?

   How should you react?

2. God's will does not operate according to our timetable. Think of a situation when God's answer to your prayer did not come at the time you expected. How did He answer that prayer?

Relate the timing of this incident to waiting on God for His harvest.

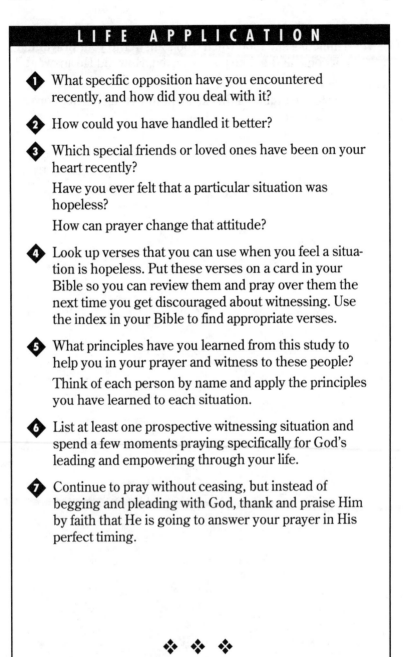

LIFE APPLICATION

1 What specific opposition have you encountered recently, and how did you deal with it?

2 How could you have handled it better?

3 Which special friends or loved ones have been on your heart recently?

Have you ever felt that a particular situation was hopeless?

How can prayer change that attitude?

4 Look up verses that you can use when you feel a situation is hopeless. Put these verses on a card in your Bible so you can review them and pray over them the next time you get discouraged about witnessing. Use the index in your Bible to find appropriate verses.

5 What principles have you learned from this study to help you in your prayer and witness to these people?

Think of each person by name and apply the principles you have learned to each situation.

6 List at least one prospective witnessing situation and spend a few moments praying specifically for God's leading and empowering through your life.

7 Continue to pray without ceasing, but instead of begging and pleading with God, thank and praise Him by faith that He is going to answer your prayer in His perfect timing.

❖ ❖ ❖

Witnessing and the Holy Spirit

When you talk about Jesus, expect God to use you. The Lord Jesus promised His supernatural resources to all who join with Him in helping to fulfill the Great Commission.

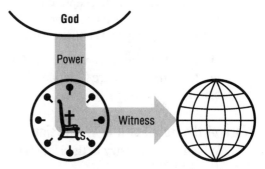

You are assured of that same resurrection power and presence today through the power of the Holy Spirit. Our Lord honors the faithful witness of all who place their trust in Him.

Self-consciousness and fear of what others will say, however, will hinder our witness. Stephen was a table waiter (Acts 6:2–5), not an apostle. He was brought before the most wicked opponents of Christianity. He could have retreated because he felt inadequate to face these people, but he yielded to the Holy Spirit's control of his life. As a result,

Objective: To understand and trust in the Holy Spirit's leading as you witness

Read: Ephesians 5 and 6

Memorize: John 15:26, 27

his faithfulness to Christ, even to accepting death by stoning, mightily moved the unbelievers and laid the basis for Saul's conversion.

❖

Bible Study

Work of the Holy Spirit in a Believer's Life

Read Acts 6 and 7, and underline every mention of the Holy Spirit.

1. What part did the Holy Spirit play in Stephen's life?

2. What spiritual indictment did Stephen pronounce upon his hearers that cut them to the heart?

3. As a Spirit-filled man, Stephen had two purposes that were his greatest concerns, as seen in his desire to witness and in his dying prayer. What were they?

4. How do these concerns show the fullness of the Holy Spirit in Stephen? (Compare Galatians 5:22,23; 2 Corinthians 5:14,15.)

Work of the Holy Spirit in Witnessing

1. What is the ministry of the Holy Spirit (John 15:26; 16:13,14)?

2. How is it accomplished in a person who witnesses of Christ (Acts 1:8; 6:10)?

   How is it being accomplished in your life?

3. What will the Holy Spirit do for the witnessing person (Acts 4:31)?

4. What will the Holy Spirit do for the person receiving the Good News (1 Corinthians 2:10–12)?

5. How does that passage compare with 2 Corinthians 4:3,4?

6. It is the Holy Spirit who brings us face to face with the facts regarding our condition and our need. This action is called "convicting, reproving, exposing, bringing to light."

If we were to witness on our own, we would accomplish nothing. But when the Holy Spirit uses our witness, He brings a person face to face with important facts, presenting them so forcefully that these facts must be considered.

What are these facts (John 16:7–11)?

7. What promise does God give us regarding His Spirit (2 Corinthians 1:21,22)?

LIFE APPLICATION

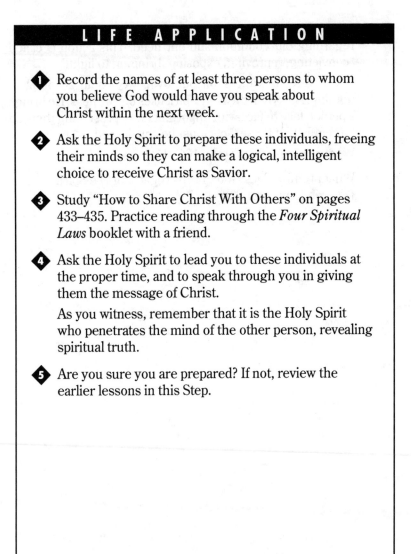

1 Record the names of at least three persons to whom you believe God would have you speak about Christ within the next week.

2 Ask the Holy Spirit to prepare these individuals, freeing their minds so they can make a logical, intelligent choice to receive Christ as Savior.

3 Study "How to Share Christ With Others" on pages 433–435. Practice reading through the *Four Spiritual Laws* booklet with a friend.

4 Ask the Holy Spirit to lead you to these individuals at the proper time, and to speak through you in giving them the message of Christ.

As you witness, remember that it is the Holy Spirit who penetrates the mind of the other person, revealing spiritual truth.

5 Are you sure you are prepared? If not, review the earlier lessons in this Step.

❖ ❖ ❖

Recap

The following questions will help you review this Step. If necessary, reread the appropriate lesson(s).

1. What is the most important reason you have learned to witness for Christ?

2. How have you overcome the problem that most hinders your witnessing?

3. What is the next most troubling hindrance for you, and how do you plan to overcome it?

4. Summarize why you think a knowledge of the Word of God is important in witnessing.

5. How will prayer specifically help you?

6. Why do you think the Holy Spirit does not speak of Himself?

❖

Reread: Galatians and Ephesians

Review: Verses memorized

LIFE APPLICATION

1 Write a three-minute testimony of your personal experience with Christ. Briefly share three things:

1) What your life was like before your decision

2) Why and how you received Christ

3) How Christ has changed your life

List benefits of knowing Christ. Explain in greater detail what it is like to be a Christian. (Attach your testimony to this lesson.)

2 Begin a prayer diary listing those whom God has laid on your heart to share your faith in Christ.

Record:

◆ Their prayer needs

◆ Their responses to your witness

◆ Their spiritual growth

3 List the opportunities God has given you to witness for Him in the past month. Then praise and thank God for them.

❖ ❖ ❖

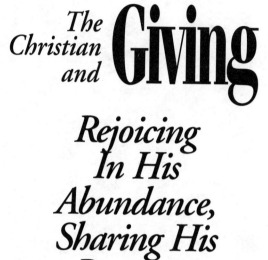

The Christian and Giving

Rejoicing In His Abundance, Sharing His Resources

STEP 8

God's Ownership Over All

As Christian stewards we must realize that in Christ "we live and move and have our being" (Acts 17:28). In this lesson, you will see the basis of God's claim on your life.

Jesus Christ created us (Colossians 1:16). He bought us with His precious blood (1 Peter 1:18,19). And God anointed Him as our Lord (Ephesians 1:20–23; Acts 10:36; Romans 10:12). Thus, the whole of our life—our personality, influence, material substance, everything—is His, even our successes.

The Bible tells us that since Christ died for us, "those who live should no longer live for themselves but for him who died for them and was raised again" (2 Corinthians 5:15).

❖

Objective: To surrender everything we have to God because we can rest in His ownership of all

Read: Genesis 1–3

Memorize: 1 Chronicles 29:11

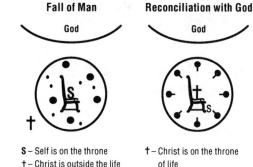

Fall of Man

God

Reconciliation with God

God

S – Self is on the throne
† – Christ is outside the life

Result: Separation from God, discord and chaos in life

† – Christ is on the throne of life

Result: Order, and stewardship evident

301

Not to acknowledge and act upon God's total ownership of everything we are, have, and will be is to rob ourselves of His blessing
and make ourselves unfit for His service (2 Timothy 2:15,16,19–21).

❖

Bible Study

Creation and Fall of Man

1. After what pattern did God create man (Genesis 1:26)?

Theologians have long debated just what it is in man that
constitutes the image of God. That image seems to include
the basic characteristics of personality: intellect, emotion, and
will. Adam and Eve had intellect (Genesis 2:19), emotion
(Genesis 3:10), and will (Genesis 3:6), just as God does.

2. What did man do to bring about separation between himself and God (Genesis 3:1–7)?

Note: This passage gives important insight into the character
of sin. Adam did not get drunk or commit immoral acts. He
and Eve merely asserted their independence from God, re-
belled against His command, and took control of their own
lives. *Sin is being independent of God and running your own
life.*

3. How did the sin of man affect his:

Intellect (2 Corinthians 4:2,4)?

Emotions (Jeremiah 17:9)?

Will (Romans 6:20)?

4. How did this act of rebellion affect the world
(Romans 5:12)?

Reconciliation

1. How did God bring us back and reconcile us to Himself (Romans 5:8–10)?

2. What has God given us to enable us to live for Him (John 14:26)?

Our Responsibility

1. God now has restored us to a position of fellowship similar to what Adam had. What does that declare about our present relationship with God (1 Corinthians 6:19,20)?

2. What, then, is to be our response to God (Romans 12:1,2)?

3. Many people attempt to compromise and give God less than full allegiance. How did Jesus regard that practice in Matthew 12:30?

4. In Revelation 3:15,16, how did Jesus describe His attitude toward those who will stand neither for nor against Him?

5. What logical choice did Elijah present to the people (1 Kings 18:21)?

If Elijah's logic is true, we must take one of two positions. If we determine that Jesus Christ is Lord and God, we must serve Him loyally. If He is not, He is an imposter and Christianity is obviously a hoax. If this were true, we should dissuade men from being Christians. It is one or the other! We must stand either with Christ or against Him, but never try to stand in between.

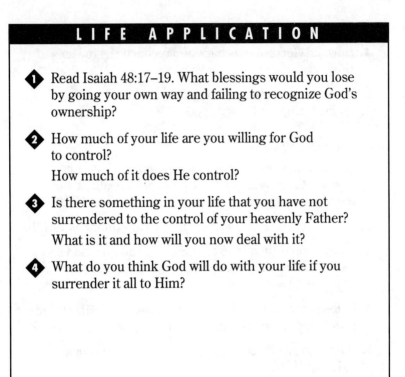

LIFE APPLICATION

1 Read Isaiah 48:17–19. What blessings would you lose by going your own way and failing to recognize God's ownership?

2 How much of your life are you willing for God to control?

How much of it does He control?

3 Is there something in your life that you have not surrendered to the control of your heavenly Father?

What is it and how will you now deal with it?

4 What do you think God will do with your life if you surrender it all to Him?

❖ ❖ ❖

Examples of Perfect Giving

Giving began with God. His supernatural expression of giving was in the sacrifice of His only begotten Son that we might receive forgiveness for our sins, become children of God, and enjoy eternal life.

God continues to give of Himself today in love, forgiveness, peace, power, and purpose. By this He enables us to live full, meaningful lives.

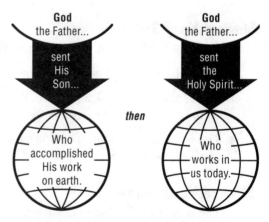

❖

Objective: To follow biblical examples of stewardship

Read: Luke 23–24; Colossians 1–2

Memorize: John 8:28

Giving was the lifestyle of our Lord Jesus. A concise description of His lifestyle appears in the Book of Acts, which records, "He went around doing good" (Acts 10:38). Jesus gave in feeding the multitudes. He gave in healing the sick. He gave in teaching His disciples.

He gave in empowering His disciples for evangelism. He gave in compassion for the poor. He gave in offering rest to the weary. He gave in dying on the cross for our sins. He gave in sending His Holy Spirit.

Giving is also an attribute of the Holy Spirit. He strengthens and encourages us (Acts 9:31), renews us (Titus 3:5), reveals things to us (Luke 2:26), and helps us (John 14:6, NASB). He leads and guides us (Luke 4:1; Acts 13:2,4; John 16:13), brings the love of God to us (Romans 5:5), teaches us (Luke 12:12; John 14:26), and empowers us (Acts 1:8; 4:31).

Nowhere can we find more perfect models of stewardship than in God the Father, God the Son, and God the Holy Spirit. As you study this lesson, prayerfully consider how you can apply their examples to your life.

❖

Bible Study

Stewardship of God the Father

1. Read John 3:16. What was God's greatest gift to mankind?

2. What else does God give us (Romans 2:4,7; 1 John 5:11)?

3. Read John 3:34, 10:10, and 14:16. What has the Father given us to enable us to live abundantly?

4. List some characteristics of God's nature that make giving a priority with Him.

Stewardship of God the Son

1. List acts of Christ that indicate perfection in His stewardship (Philippians 2:5–8).

2. What was Christ's supreme purpose in life (John 6:38; Hebrews 10:7)?

3. Read John 12:23–33.

As part of God's will for Jesus, what was involved (verses 23,27,32,33)?

In verse 24, Jesus uses the example of a grain of wheat that is planted in the earth. In what sense does a grain of wheat have to "die" to bring forth fruit?

How does that apply to us (compare verse 25)?

If, as a Christian, you are unwilling to make any sacrifice to reach others for Christ, to suffer any hardship, to face any self-denial, to suffer any persecution, but instead you want everything to be comfortable, easy, and effortless, how will this affect your fruit-bearing?

4. List some characteristics of Christ's nature that make giving a priority with Him.

Stewardship of God the Holy Spirit

1. What are some duties the Holy Spirit performs as God's steward, as revealed in the following verses?

John 16:13

Romans 5:5

Romans 8:14

Romans 8:16

Romans 8:26

John 16:7–11

In what way does this convicting ministry of the Holy Spirit help us in evangelism?

2. When the Holy Spirit controls a person, who is glorifed (John 16:14)?

3. List characteristics of the Holy Spirit's nature that make giving a priority with Him.

LIFE APPLICATION

 How does the giving nature of God the Father inspire you to give?

2 How can you best apply to your life the example that Jesus set? Be specific.

3 What does the Holy Spirit want to do in your life at this time?

4 List ways you can cooperate as suggested in Acts 4:31, Ephesians 5:18–20, and Romans 12:1,2.

❖ ❖ ❖

Stewardship of Our Time

Does the principle of tithing apply equally to our time as it does to our money?

How much of our time should we set aside for the work of the Lord each week?

How are you using the time God has given you?

Time is the heritage of every person. Whether a king or street sweeper, an astronomer or truck driver, a business tycoon or grocery clerk, each of us has the same number of hours.

Many necessities and opportunities demand much of our day. Our work takes up a large percentage of our life. Being a good husband or wife, father or mother, employer or employee requires time.

As Christians, we have spiritual priorities as well. How many hours or days in a month should we set aside for evangelism and discipleship and the ministries of our church? What about caring for the poor, the orphans, and widows as God's Word commands (James 1:27; Galatians 2:10)?

❖

Objective: To become wise stewards of all that God has created us to be individually

Read: Romans 12

Memorize: Galatians 2:20

With all these tasks competing for our time, how can we balance our responsibilities to fulfill our temporal and spiritual duties?

As a good steward, you must manage your time wisely. Let me suggest a way to accomplish this task that Christians seldom consider today—tithing your time.

Tithing reflects a thankful, obedient attitude and acknowledges God as the source and owner of all that we possess. A voluntary act of worship, tithing teaches us to put God first. A faithful steward serves because he has such a heart for God. As we has seen, everything we have is a gift from God. Every second of every minute, every minute of every hour, twenty-four hours a day belong to Him. Although God's Word does not specifically require us to tithe our time, our Lord did command us to put Him first in all things (Matthew 6:31–33). Giving back a percentage of our time enables us to give God priority and assures that we will fulfill our service to Him.

❖

Bible Study

Right Attitude About Time
Read Psalm 90:12.

1. What should be our prayer concerning the use of the time that God gives us?

2. Why is the proper use of our time today so important (James 4:13–15)?

3. What does God demand of us in the stewardship of our time (Psalm 62:8)?

   When do you find this hardest to do?

4. What does Christ admonish us to do as stewards of time until He comes again (Mark 13:33–37)?

5. If we are wise stewards and heed the commands of our Lord, how will we use our time (Ephesians 5:15,16)?

What does making use of our time have to do with wisdom? With evil days?

Right Relationship With God

1. As wise stewards concerned over the use of our time, what will we want to understand (Ephesians 5:17)?

2. What is necessary in order to know fully the will of God concerning the duties of our stewardship (Ephesians 5:18)?

3. What will the Holy Spirit give the faithful steward to enable him to perform the duties of stewardship (Acts 1:8)?

4. In whose name should the steward perform these duties (Colossians 3:17)?

5. What should be our attitude as we utilize the time over which God has made us stewards (Ephesians 5:19–21)?

6. How would you describe such a useful and joyous life (John 10:10)?

Most Important Use of Time

1. As wise stewards who know and are obedient to the will of God, what will we spend much of our time aggressively doing (Mark 16:15)?

2. What does God say about a soul winner in Proverbs 11:30?

3. Of what value is a soul according to Christ in Mark 8:36,37?

4. What is the greatest thing that has happened in your life?

5. What, then, is the greatest thing you can do for another?

6. What happens in God's presence when one repents and receives Christ (Luke 15:7,10)?

7. How did Paul feel about those whom he had won to Christ (1 Thessalonians 2:19,20)?

LIFE APPLICATION

Keeping track of how you spend your day can be of great value in evaluating the stewardship of your time. On a sheet of paper, record the number of hours spent on business, class, sleep, Christian service, recreation, etc. Place the total hours per week used in each activity on the chart below.

STEWARDSHIP OF TIME	
Study and class _____	Activities and athletics _____
Devotional life _____	Commuting _____
Christian service _____	Employment _____
Rest _____	Laundry and clean-up_____
Recreation and social life _____	Miscellaneous _____

 Determine what blocks of time are wasteful. How could you use them to serve the Lord?

❷ In your notebook, list ways to tithe your time that can be worked into your present schedule.

❖ ❖ ❖

Stewardship of Our Bodies

Some time ago, my heart grieved as I learned of a respected Christian leader who had fallen into a life of sin. He had obviously not intended to do so, but when the temptation came, he yielded. As a result, his wife, his family, his friends, and fellow Christians suffered heartache. Most tragically, his testimony and witness for the Lord Jesus has suffered untold damage. Many have ridiculed and rejected the cause of Christ because of his sin.

Since God wants us to live a holy life, the enemy seeks to entrap us in sin and defeat. One of Satan's methods is to tempt us to misuse our bodies.

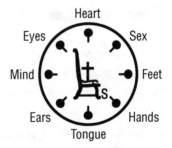

❖

Objective: To surrender our bodies to Christ, from the heart

Read: Psalm 51; Galatians 5; Ephesians 5

Memorize: Psalm 139:23,24

But God created our bodies for His glory. By surrendering them to Him, He can use us to further His kingdom and help us grow in our faith.

313

This study will help you understand the importance of giving control of your body to God. You will also discover danger areas in using your physical self and how to help further the cause of Christ with different parts of your body.

❖

Bible Study

The Spirit and the Body
Read 1 Peter 4:1,2 and Hebrews 10:1–10.

1. How did Jesus regard His body (1 Peter 4:1,2)?

2. What does Christ's sacrifice mean to us (Hebrews 10:10)?

   Look up the word *sanctified* in a Bible dictionary. How does the word relate to your stewardship?

3. What do you learn about the body of the Christian from Romans 8:8,9 and Romans 12:1?

4. Express in your own words the additional reasons given in 1 Corinthians 6:19,20 for being a good steward of your body.

   How are we to do this (Galatians 5:16; Romans 12:1; Matthew 26:41)?

Individual Parts of the Body
1. The tongue

   Why is it so important to be a good steward of the tongue (James 3:2–6; James 1:26)?

   What should you know concerning its use (Matthew 12:36)?

   List areas in which you misuse your tongue.

   How has this affected your life?

   How should you use your tongue properly (James 3:9,10; Ephesians 4:29; Proverbs 21:23; Psalm 39:1; Proverbs 4:24)?

2. The heart

What must we understand about the heart (Jeremiah 17:9)?

How can we counteract our natural tendencies (Psalm 139:23,24)?

What condition of heart does God require (Psalm 51:17)?

What kind of heart does God look for and why (2 Chronicles 16:9; Matthew 5:8; 2 Thessalonians 3:5; Psalm 15:1,2)?

3. The mind

What is your responsibility in being a steward of your mind (1 Peter 1:13)?

Whose mind should you have and which qualities should you strive for (Philippians 2:5–8; 1 Corinthians 2:12–16)?

What is the result of keeping your mind focused on God (Isaiah 26:3)?

How can you keep your mind on Him (Philippians 4:6,7; Deuteronomy 11:18)?

4. The hands

What does God think about the work of your hands (Proverbs 12:14,24)?

How did the apostles feel about the importance of what their hands had done (Acts 20:34,35; 1 Thessalonians 4:11,12)?

How can we use our hands to glorify God?

Proverbs 31:20

Ephesians 4:28

Deuteronomy 15:10,11

Ecclesiastes 9:10

5. The feet

Contrast the feet of those who do evil with those who do good (Isaiah 59:7; Romans 3:15; Isaiah 52:7; Psalm 119:101,105; 56:13).

How do Romans 10:15 and Ephesians 6:15 relate to evangelism?

6. The eyes

   What is the importance of the eyes (Matthew 6:22,23)?

   Describe what this means to you.

   What sins can we commit with our eyes?

   Proverbs 21:4

   Jeremiah 22:17

   Proverbs 27:20

   Matthew 5:28

   1 John 2:16

   What privilege did the apostles have (1 John 1:1–3)?

   How can we avoid temptation (Psalm 19:8; 119:37; 121:1,2; 123:1)?

7. The ears

   Write down ways we can misuse hearing.

   Proverbs 21:13

   2 Timothy 4:3,4

   What can listening to God give us?

   Romans 10:17

   John 5:24

   How can you apply James 1:19,22 to your daily life? Give specific examples.

Sexual Expression

1. Compare the sexual sins in 1 Corinthians 6:9,10,13–18 with marriage in 1 Corinthians 7:1–8.

2. God considered David a man after His own heart, yet what was David's great sin (2 Samuel 11:2–5,14–17,26,27)?

3. What is God's stern judgment against misusers and abusers of sex (1 Corinthians 6:9,10)?

   Why is it especially tragic if a Christian becomes involved in the misuse of sex (1 Corinthians 6:15–18)?

How serious is sexual lust, according to Christ (Matthew 5:28)?

4. How can the application of the following verses enable you to overcome sexual lust?

Philippians 4:8

Psalm 119:11

1 Corinthians 10:13

Romans 6:11–13

1 Thessalonians 4:3–5

Psalm 119:9

List things in your life that tempt you to have impure thoughts. How can you apply these verses to each?

L I F E   A P P L I C A T I O N

1 How does stewardship of each individual part of the body affect each part?

How could it affect the body as a whole?

2 How would you apply 1 Thessalonians 5:22 to the following:

The use of your tongue?

The desires of your heart?

The control of your mind?

The work of your hands?

Where you go?

What you see?

What you hear?

Your conduct with members of the opposite sex?

❖   ❖   ❖

Stewardship of Our Talents and Gifts

God created us with a great variety of talents. You may be able to run a marathon, organize a group meeting, teach, or write. Your skill may be typing, photography, or painting. Perhaps you sing or play a musical instrument. Maybe you are a carpenter, landscaper, engineer, mechanic, or bookkeeper. Each of us has a unique function to perform in life and in the Body of Christ.

Ministering
Teaching
Giving
Helping
Exhorting
Having Faith
Showing Mercy
Ruling

Objective: To recognize our talents and abilities and to surrender them to God for His use and glory

Read: 1 Corinthians 12

Memorize: 1 Peter 4:10

The Bible refers to the church as the Body of Christ with Christ as its Head (1 Corinthians 12:27; Ephesians 5:23). Just as your body has many specialized parts, each with its own function, so the church is composed of many individuals, each with his own special function to perform—and contribution to make—to the rest of the Body. I encourage you to identify your talents, and ask God to show you how to use them for His glory.

Every Christian possesses both natural talents and spiritual gifts. Our natural abilities come to us at physical birth and are developed through life. Our spiritual gifts are imparted by the Holy Spirit, enabling us to minister to others in behalf of Christ.

❖

Bible Study

Natural Gifts

1. What talents and natural abilities do you have?

2. How did you acquire them or improve on them?

3. According to 1 Corinthians 4:6,7 and Exodus 4:11, what should your attitude be about them?

4. How would you apply Colossians 3:17 to the stewardship of your natural gifts?

Spiritual Gifts

1. Major passages on spiritual gifts in the Bible are:

- ◆ Romans 12:3–8
- ◆ 1 Corinthians 12:1–31
- ◆ Ephesians 4:4–8,11–16
- ◆ 1 Peter 4:10,11

From these passages make a composite list of spiritual gifts (combine any two that might be identical). Across from each one, give your brief definition of the gift. (You may wish to consult a concordance or a Bible dictionary.)

2. What are some reasons God has given gifted people to the church (Ephesians 4:11–16)?

3. Why will two people not exercise the same gift in the same manner (1 Corinthians 12:4–6)?

4. Though some spiritual gifts seem to be of greater value than others (1 Corinthians 12:28–31), what ideas does Paul stress to keep Christians from personal pride because of those they may possess (Romans 12:4,5; 1 Corinthians 12:12–26; 1 Corinthians 13; Ephesians 4:11–16)?

5. List several principles that describe what your attitude and responsibilities should be toward your spiritual gifts (Romans 12:3–8).

LIFE APPLICATION

Follow these steps to more fully understand your part in the Body of Christ:

1 Realize that you have at least one spiritual gift, probably more (1 Corinthians 12:11).

2 Pray that God will make your gifts known to you.

3 Determine which of your activities the Lord seems to bless and inquire of other mature Christians who know you well what your spiritual gifts might be.

4 List what you believe your spiritual gifts are.

5 Seek to develop your gifts in the power of the Holy Spirit.

6 Realize that you may have other gifts of which you are not presently aware, so exercise various gifts. Be aware that you are accountable to God for stewardship of your spiritual gifts.

❖ ❖ ❖

Stewardship of Our Possessions

Objective: To surrender all our of material wealth to God, and to give with joy and gratitude

Read: 2 Corinthians 9; Matthew 6:19–34; 25:14–30; Luke 12:15–21

Memorize: Luke 16:13

One afternoon, Grandpa Clark strode into his house, pockets bulging with treats for his grandchildren. As he settled into his creaking rocker, the children clamored around him with expectant faces, each pushing and shoving to be the first to see what Grandpa had brought them.

The gray-haired man dug deep into his pockets and pulled out a fistful of candy, handing each child a favorite treat. When he finished, he leaned back in his rocker with a smile of contentment to watch them tear at the wrappings.

On his left, two jealous brothers argued over whose flavor of Lifesavers tasted better. Another child sat at his feet munching a candy bar. Suddenly, a tiny red-haired sweetheart patted her grandpa on the arm. Concern furrowed her brow.

"Would you like some of my M&Ms, Grandpa?" she asked with sad, shy eyes. "You don't have anything."

Grandpa Clark peered down at his only granddaughter and grinned. Gently, he gathered her dainty form into his lap. "Why, you haven't even opened your candy," he observed.

She stared into his eyes with a frank expression. " 'Cause I want you to have the first one."

"Why, thank you, I think I will," he smiled, carefully opening her little package. With relish, he removed a couple of colored candies and popped them into his mouth. Then he wrapped his arms tightly around her, engulfing her happy face.

This story clearly illustrates tithing—giving back to God the first part of what He has given us.

As you recall, the word *tithe* comes from a Greek term simply meaning *the tenth*. Godly principles underlay this practice. Tithing accomplishes the following:

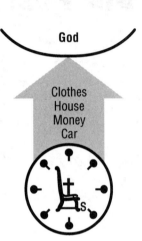

- ◆ Acknowledges God as the source and owner of all that we possess
- ◆ Is a voluntary act of worship
- ◆ Teaches us to put God first
- ◆ Is a practical guideline for systematic giving
- ◆ Provides spiritual release and blessing

Tithing performs a role entirely different from that of mere giving, which suggests that we own all that we possess. Through tithing we acknowledge that God created our increase. As stewards of what God entrusted to us, we set aside a proportion to use for the cause of Christ. We never consider any part of our possessions to be our exclusive property but prayerfully tithe on the entire amount.

"The purpose of tithing," we have learned, "is to teach you always to put God first in your lives" (Deuteronomy 14:23, TLB). God does not honor a gift that comes from leftovers. He requires the first and the best of our increase (Exodus 22:29,30; Proverbs 3:9,10). Tithing ensures this.

Ten percent, an Old Testament measure for giving, is a good beginning point for a faithful and dedicated steward. And though we are not under the Law but under grace, as Dr. J. B. Gabrell declared,

"It is unthinkable from the standpoint of the cross that anyone would give less under grace than the Jews gave under law."

Measuring their giving by the grace of the cross and not by the legalism of the Law, the early Christians did not limit themselves to the tithe. They gave much more. And they gave in the Spirit of Christ, as a demonstration of His pre-eminence in their lives, to help fulfill the Great Commission.

Bible Study

Money—The Old Testament Standard

1. What did God command those under the Law of Moses to do (Leviticus 27:30; Malachi 3:8–10)?

2. What would you say the "storehouse" is (Deuteronomy 12:5,6,11)?

3. How much is a tithe (Genesis 14:20; Hebrews 7:2)?

Money—The New Testament Standard

1. As believers in Christ, we are under grace, rather than the Old Testament Law. Whereas the Law in itself did not provide eternal life for those who attempted to keep it (Galatians 2:16), we have received life by the favor of God though we do not deserve it and could not possibly earn it.

Therefore, do we have a higher or lower motivation and standard for stewardship of our possessions than those under the Law?

2. How did Jesus regard a person's responsibility in that area (Matthew 23:23)?

3. Read 2 Corinthians 8–9.

In this passage, Paul attempts to encourage the Corinthian church to give financially to help needy Christians. He first points them to the example of the Macedonian church.

What was the attitude of the Macedonians in giving their money to God (2 Corinthians 8:2–5)?

In light of this, what do you think God is interested in?

Nevertheless, why is giving money an important part of our Christian life (2 Corinthians 8:7; 9:12,13)?

In what sense does the one who "sows" (gives) sparingly reap sparingly (2 Corinthians 9:6)?

What kind of attitude does God want you to have in giving (2 Corinthians 9:7)?

When is it hard for you to give that way?

God's Priority for Missions

1. Who is the great example of giving (2 Corinthians 8:9)?

2. In your own words, summarize the last command Jesus gave His disciples (Matthew 28:19,20).

3. Read John 14:21,23,24. Describe how this relates to fulfilling the Great Commission.

4. Oswald Smith said, "If you see ten men carrying a heavy log, nine of them on one end and one man struggling to carry the other, which end would most need your help? The end with only one man." This illustrates how inequitably the evangelized nations have been using their resources to help fulfill the Great Commission.

   What percentage of your giving is going to overseas missions?

   To home missions?

5. Prayerfully consider what kind of adjustments you feel the Lord is leading you to make in your missions giving. Record your decisions in your notebook.

Other Possessions

1. To whom do you and your possessions belong (Psalm 50:12; 1 Corinthians 6:19,20)?

2. What should be your motive in the use of whatever you possess (1 Corinthians 10:31)?

LIFE APPLICATION

1 What is your understanding about tithing? Describe your view in a short paragraph.

2 What is the difference between "giving" and "tithing"? Which one describes your practice and why?

3 Ask yourself, "Is my heart attitude one of joy and gratefulness as I give?" How do you express your attitude?

4 List some Christian groups or churches that are working to fulfill the Great Commission in which you would like to invest financially.

❖ ❖ ❖

Trusting God for Our Finances

Changing economic conditions exemplify the instability of finances throughout the world. Instead of placing their trust in the Lord who promised to meet all of their needs, most Christians trust in their investments, savings, and retirement plans to ensure security and happiness—only to find their hopes dashed when financial reverses deplete their assets. Many are wasting their lives trying to achieve financial security in a volatile world.

Our heavenly Father, on the other hand, wants us to enjoy a full, abundant life free from the cares and stresses brought by confidence in money and other material possessions. Rather than trusting in a worldly system that cannot assure our welfare or relying on our own weak capabilities to provide for our needs, He calls us to depend entirely on Him.

Permit me to suggest a plan that will help you release your faith in God and develop your trust in Him for your finances.

❖

Objective: To learn how to trust God for our finances and ask Him to supply our needs

Read: Proverbs 3:5,6; John 10:10; Matthew 6:33,34

Memorize: Psalm 12:6

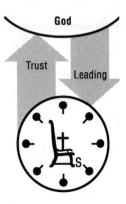

❖

Bible Study

Recognize That God is Worthy of Your Trust

1. Read Psalm 12:6. How much can we trust God?

2. What will happen if you make God's promises the foundation of your financial security (Proverbs 3:5,6)?

3. List the financial areas that are hardest for you to put into God's hands. Prayerfully dedicate them to Him.

Realize That God Wants You to Live a Full and Abundant Life

1. Read John 10:10. How does this promise apply to financial freedom?

2. Does abundant life mean having all the money or possessions you want? Why or why not?

3. Do you feel you have abundant life right now? If not, what is keeping you from it?

Substitute Faith for Fear

1. How does fear interfere with your trust in God?

2. Read 2 Timothy 1:7. Contrast the two kinds of spirits mentioned.

3. Write down the financial areas that make you fearful. Surrender these to the Lord.

Ask God to Supply Your Needs

1. What is the difference between needs and wants? Be specific.

2. Why do we lack good things (James 4:2,3; John 15:7)?

3. Faith requires action. According to 1 John 5:14,15:

a) As an act of your will, ask God to supply your needs.

b) Expect Him, as an expression of your faith, to provide for your needs.

Keep Your Heart and Motives Pure

1. What wrong motives do we sometimes display (James 4:3)? What is the result?

2. Write down the wrongful motives that you battle.

Then:

a) Confess them to God.

b) Claim the power of the Holy Spirit to help you rely on Him to supply your needs.

Take a Step of Faith

1. What is essential to your Christian walk (Hebrews 11:6)?

2. One way to enlarge your faith is to make a "faith promise"— one that is greater than you are capable of fulfilling according to your present income. It is not a pledge that must be paid. Rather, it is a voluntary "promise" based on your faith in God's ability to supply out of His resources what you cannot give out of your own. You give as God supplies.

Describe a time in which God led you to give above your means.

What was the result?

If you have never made a "faith promise," you may want to do so now after prayerfully considering various worthwhile investments you can make for God. Keep a careful record of your giving and how God supplied your needs in a special way.

LIFE APPLICATION

1 Read Luke 6:38. How does this verse apply to financial freedom?

2 Suppose a new Christian confides in you that he is afraid to give God control over his checkbook. How would you advise him?

3 Review the steps to trusting God for your finances. Which of these steps are weak areas in your life?

Why do you find them difficult?

What could you do to strengthen them?

4 Prayerfully consider the faith promise God would have you make. Write that promise in your notebook.

❖ ❖ ❖

Our Accountability to God

Many Christians miss the special blessing of God because they do not obey our Lord's command recorded in the Gospel of Matthew:

> Don't store up treasures here on earth where they can erode away or may be stolen. Store them in heaven where they will never lose their value, and are safe from thieves. If your profits are in heaven your heart will be there too (Matthew 6:19–21, TLB).

Jesus knew that by storing up treasures on earth, we would soon take on the appearance of the world. Through selfish desires, we would cease to reflect the character of God and seek our own glory. By laying up treasures in heaven, on the other hand, we would declare the glory of His kingdom.

Everything we do to bring men and women into the kingdom of God, every act of kindness, every expression of love is laying up treasure in God's storehouse. We give out of love for God and gratitude for His love and sacrifice for us through the gift of His only begotten Son, our Savior Jesus Christ.

God will hold us accountable for our motivation in giving and for our faithful obed-

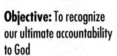

Objective: To recognize our ultimate accountability to God

Read: Luke 19:12–27; Matthew 24 and 25

Memorize: 2 Corinthians 5:10

ience to our Lord's command to help fulfill the Great Commission and so reach the world for Christ. The apostle Paul wrote:

> We will all stand before God's judgment seat. So then, each of us will give an account of himself to God (Romans 14:10,12).

Relating the parable of the shrewd manager, Jesus said:

> There was a rich man whose manager was accused of wasting his possessions. So he called him in and asked him, "What is this I hear about you? Give an account of your management…" (Luke 16:1,2).

God considers "an immortal soul beyond all price. There is no trouble too great, no humiliation too deep, no suffering too severe, no love too strong, no labor too hard, no expense too large, but that it is worth it, if it is spent in the effort to win a soul."[1]

As faithful stewards, our primary financial responsibility is to help worthy ministries reach the largest possible number of people for Christ. We are accountable to our Lord's last command before He ascended into heaven to "Go and make disciples of all nations" (Matthew 28:19).

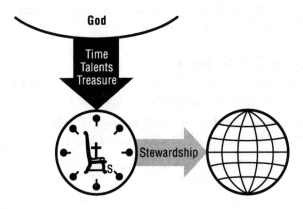

---

[1] "Junk That Missionary Barrel," *Moody Monthly* (September 1977), p.56.

❖

Bible Study

The Christian at Christ's Coming

1. According to 2 Corinthians 5:10, what will Christ do when
He comes again?

2. Notice that Paul says "we all." Who is this primarily for?

Note: Our sins have already been judged in Christ (Romans
8:1). The judgment here is of our works since the time we
became a believer.

3. Read 1 Corinthians 3:11–15.

God's judgment of our works is compared to the reaction
of certain materials to fire. According to this passage, what
is God most interested in regarding the works we do for
Him (verse 13)?

How is it then possible for us to spend long hours working
for God, but have no reward whatsoever?

A Christian's works may be rejected, but what can he
himself still be sure of (verse 15)?

The Time of Christ's Coming

1. The judgment of the Christian will take place when Christ
comes again. When will that be (Acts 1:6,7)?

2. On what should we concentrate until He comes
(Acts 1:8; Matthew 28:19,20; Mark 16:15)?

3. Why has Christ waited so long already before coming
(2 Peter 3:9)?

The Earth at Christ's Coming

Read Mark 13. This chapter foretells the world conditions as Christ's coming approaches. As we see the world today becoming more like this, we know His coming is drawing nearer.

1. What will we see happening in religion (verses 5,6,21,22)?

2. What will the world situation be (verses 7,8)?

3. What will occur in nature (verse 8)?

4. What will the attitude be toward true believers (verses 12,13)?

5. Describe in your own words what you think Christ's coming will be like (verses 26,27).

Preparing for Christ's Coming

1. As a believer, what are you to do as His coming draws near (Mark 13:33)?

2. How will obedience to that instruction affect the following:

Your employment?

Your social life?

Your worship?

Your giving?

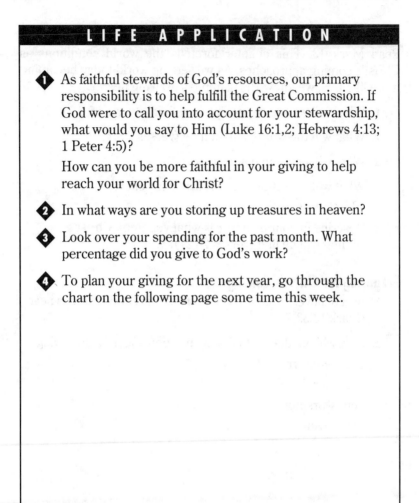

LIFE APPLICATION

1 As faithful stewards of God's resources, our primary responsibility is to help fulfill the Great Commission. If God were to call you into account for your stewardship, what would you say to Him (Luke 16:1,2; Hebrews 4:13; 1 Peter 4:5)?

How can you be more faithful in your giving to help reach your world for Christ?

2 In what ways are you storing up treasures in heaven?

3 Look over your spending for the past month. What percentage did you give to God's work?

4 To plan your giving for the next year, go through the chart on the following page some time this week.

❖ ❖ ❖

Stewardship Plan

1. Begin by asking God how much and where He wants you to invest your time, talents, possessions, and money. Write these ideas here.

2. Prayerfully develop a systematic plan for giving each month in each of these areas:
   ◆ Time
   ◆ Talents
   ◆ Possessions
   ◆ Money

3. Plan to set aside some time and resources for needs you may become aware of at your church, in your neighborhood, or other places.

4. Dedicate your plan to God. Ask Him to use your resources to bring the greatest glory to His name.

5. Begin to implement your plan with a joyful heart, expecting God to bless you through your stewardship.

Recap

The following questions will help you review this Step. If necessary, reread the appropriate lesson(s).

1. Define "Christian steward" in your own words.

2. Why are we referred to as Christian stewards?

3. Summarize your responsibilities as a steward of God as you now understand them.

Reread: Romans 12;
1 Corinthians 12; James 3:1,2

Review: Verses memorized

L I F E   A P P L I C A T I O N

 List several things over which you exercise stewardship.

 What is the most important thing for you to realize about your attitude toward stewardship?

 In which particular areas of your life have you seen a change for the better in your Christian stewardship?

❖ ❖ ❖

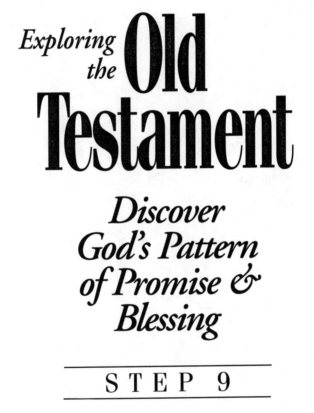

Exploring **Old**
the
Testament

Discover
God's Pattern
of Promise &
Blessing

STEP 9

The Drama Begins

Genesis gives us a picture of man's origin, his fall, and God's provision for his salvation. Because the Bible is indeed the inspired Word of God, we can depend upon Genesis being absolutely correct in every detail.

As we have seen, man was created to have fellowship with God, but because of his stubborn self-will, he chose to go his own independent way and fellowship was broken. This is what the Bible calls sin.

As a result of the fall of Adam, all mankind inherited a sin nature. The apostle Paul writes, "Sin entered the world through one man, and death through sin, and in this way death came to all men, because all sinned" (Romans 5:12).

It is this first act in the drama of mankind that sets the stage for all that is to follow. If there had been no sin, there would have been no need for redemption, and no need for a Bible to tell us of the way of redemption.

"In The Beginning"
Genesis 1–3

❖

Objective: To recognize how the book of Genesis relates to us today

Read: Genesis 1, 2, and 3

Memorize: Romans 5:12

This lesson focuses on the origins of man and sin and the results of the fall. As you study, relate the events of our earliest history to the condition of our present world and how it affects you today.

❖

Bible Study

Origin of Man

1. How did our world come into existence (Genesis 1)?

2. What was the condition of the world and everything that was in it at this time (Genesis 1:10,12,18,21,25)?

3. How did the first man come into existence (1:27)?

4. Was he an intelligent being at this time (2:20)?
How do you know?

5. How was the first woman brought into existence (2:21,22)?

Origin of Sin

1. What was man's commission from God (1:28–30)?
What was man's relationship with God at this time (1:28)?

2. How would you describe Satan's personality characteristics when he appeared as a serpent, confronting Eve (3:1–5)?
How has he used these same personality characteristics in confronting you?

3. Whose word did Satan question (3:1)?
Did Eve answer truthfully (3:2,3—look particularly at the last phrase of verse 3, then at 2:17)?

4. In light of 1 John 2:16, analyze the temptation and list the three parts of it (3:6).

5. Why was it wrong for Adam and Eve to eat of this tree (2:16,17)?

Sin's Result

1. What was the result of the sin of the man and the woman (3:7,8)?

2. What was the penalty for sin for each of the following (3:14–19):

The serpent?

The woman?

The man?

How was man's relationship with God altered (3:8–10)?

3. What did God's promise regarding Satan's destiny (3:15)?

The "seed of the woman" is the way the Bible describes the entrance of Christ into the world—conceived of the Holy Spirit, born of a woman, without a human father. (Compare Matthew 1:18–23.)

In light of this, explain the correlation between Christ's first and second coming and this verse.

L I F E   A P P L I C A T I O N

1 How does Adam's and Eve's sin affect you today (Romans 5:12)?

2 Starting with Genesis 3:15, God begins to point to the time when the penalty for sin would be paid on man's behalf by the seed of the woman. In the chart on the next page, notice the prophecies pointing to Christ and their fulfillment in Him.

These are only a few of the more than three hundred Old Testament references to the coming of the Messiah that were fulfilled in the life, ministry, death, and resurrection of Jesus.

Look up all the references listed there regarding the promises and their fulfillment and read them.

What is the overall picture they present to you?

3 Read Romans 3:23 and 6:23. Describe what Jesus' death and resurrection mean to you.

❖   ❖   ❖

God's Promised Messiah

	PROMISE	FULFILLMENT
1. Born of a virgin	Genesis 3:15; Isaiah 7:14	Matthew 1:18–23
2. From the nation of Israel	Genesis 12:3; Numbers 24:17,19	Matthew 1:1–17
3. Tribe of Judah, family of David	Genesis 49:10; Isaiah 11:1,10	Luke 1:31–33
4. Born in Bethlehem	Micah 5:2	Luke 2:4,6,7
5. Time of coming	Daniel 9:24–26	Galatians 4:4
6. Part of childhood in Egypt	Hosea 11:1	Matthew 2:14,15
7. Suffering and atonement	Isaiah 53:4–6	2 Corinthians 5:21
8. Triumphal entry	Zechariah 9:9	Matthew 21:2,4,5
9. Crucifixion	Psalm 22	Matthew 27
10. Resurrection	Psalm 16:9,10	Acts 2:31,32

Adam Through Abraham

T he fall of Adam not only affected man's relationship with God, but it eventually caused a breach in human relationships. The downward course of human nature plunged even deeper with the murder of Abel by his brother Cain.

As people began to forge a civilization without God, violence and death became constant realities of human existence. Man's wickedness became so vile that God regretted ever making a human being.

Finding only Noah and his family worthy of saving, God decided to destroy His creation by flood. Nevertheless, after the flood, man's inherent sin nature caused him to once again go his own willful way. This time, God met man's arrogance by confusing the language of evil people and scattering them over the face of the earth.

Even so, we see the redemptive heart of God at work in the stories of Abraham, Isaac, Jacob, and Joseph. The calling of Abraham brought the promise of salvation. Because Abraham obeyed God in faith and love, God

❖

Objective: To learn from biblical example the importance of obedience in the Christian life

Read: Genesis 4,6,7,12,22

Memorize: Romans 4:20,21

Adam — Abraham
Genesis 4–22

was able to give him a promise of blessing to the world. The story of Abraham shows how God developed and tested Abraham's faith in relationship to the promise.

The chosen line through Abraham and Isaac led down to the promised Messiah, Jesus Christ, who fulfilled the promise of blessing and redemption. The lineage of Christ is part of the fabric of the Book of Genesis. Those selected to be in the line were chosen because they were men of faith like Abraham. Today, we who choose Jesus by faith have our part with faithful Abraham (Romans 4:16).

❖

Bible Study

Cain and Abel

1. In Genesis 4, two sacrifices are made. Evaluate each. Why was one acceptable to God and the other was not?

2. What do you think verse 7 means?

3. Read Hebrews 11:4. What part did faith play in Cain's and Abel's sacrifices?

4. Give at least one present-day example of the two types of sacrifices offered by Cain and Abel.

Noah

1. Why was God sorry that He had made man on the earth (Genesis 6:5–7)?

2. Why was Noah chosen by God to build an ark (6:8,9)?

3. What do you think God accomplished through Noah? (Genesis 6:17–22; see also Hebrews 11:7.)

Abraham

1. Abraham holds a unique place in the history of the world. Three religions point to Abraham as the founder of their faith: Christianity, Islam, and Judaism. On the basis of Genesis 12:2,3; 16:4,15; and 17:19, how does each faith trace its origins to Abraham?

2. Why do you suppose God made the request of Abraham recorded in Genesis 22:1,2?

3. Study Genesis 22:8 and give your explanation of it.

4. How does Abraham's willingness picture God's love for us?

LIFE APPLICATION

 What important lesson have you learned from God's response to Cain?

2 Do you think you would have boarded the ark with Noah? Why or why not?

3 How have you and your family been blessed in Abraham as promised in Genesis 12:3?

4 How can the story of Abraham offering Isaac to God in Genesis 22 help your faith to grow?

❖ ❖ ❖

Moses, the Passover, and the Exodus

Jacob, the grandson of Abraham, had taken his family to Egypt to escape a famine. After four hundred years, his descendants had multiplied greatly. A new king of Egypt arose, and because he was concerned about their numbers, he subjected the Israelites to cruel slavery.

Exodus 1 and 2 give an account of this development, of the birth and life of Moses, and of the people's cry to God

Moses

| Exodus 3–27 | Romans 3 |
| Deuteronomy 29, 30 | Hebrews 11 |

for deliverance. God heard their cry and sent Moses to lead them out of Egypt.

❖

Objective: To learn to walk by faith, resting in the Lord

Read: Exodus 3,4,12,14

Memorize: 1 Corinthians 10:13

❖

Bible Study

Moses the Leader

1. Read Hebrews 11:23–29.

Why do you think God chose Moses to lead His people?

2. Read Exodus 3 and 4.

   When God told Moses what He wanted him to do, how did He say the people would react (Exodus 3:18)?

   Whose work was this going to be (Exodus 3:17,20,21 and 4:12)?

   Where did Moses fit in?

3. In Exodus 4, how did Moses respond, and how did God handle those responses?

   Verses 1–9

   Verses 10–12

   Verses 13–17

4. In Exodus 4:1, Moses said of the people, "What if they do not believe me?" When Moses was obedient, how did the people respond (verse 31)?

The Passover

Read Exodus 12.

1. Why was God sending plagues at this time (verse 12)?

2. What was the most vital instruction given to the children of Israel (verse 13)?

3. What are the correlations between Christ's death and the Passover as indicated in these Scriptures?

   Exodus 12:3—John 1:29

   Exodus 12:5,6—Isaiah 53:7; 1 Peter 2:22

   Exodus 12:6—1 Corinthians 5:7

   Blood applied to the two doorposts (sides) and to the lintel (top) created what kind of picture?

4. What do you suppose happened to those who disobeyed the instructions given through Moses?

   What spiritual truth do you believe this illustrates?

5. What does Exodus 12:29 teach about God being a respecter of persons?

How does this apply to the condition of any person who has not received Christ?

The Exodus ("Going Out")

1. One of the most important events in the history of Israel occurred immediately following the Passover. What was it (Exodus 12:40,41)?

2. Compare Exodus 3:7,8 and John 3:16. How do you see them being related?

3. One of the most remarkable and well-known miracles in the world is recorded in Exodus 14. Summarize it in your notebook.

What spiritual truth does this experience suggest to you?

4. While the Israelites were in the wilderness, they had many trials and hardships. Several times in the many years of wandering before coming into the land that had been promised to them, they failed God. (See Exodus 17:1–7; 32:1–6, 15–20; and Numbers 21:4–9.)

What practical value do these events recorded in the Old Testament have for you today (1 Corinthians 10:5–11)?

What wrong attitudes and sins were shown in these examples?

5. In summary of the wilderness wanderings mentioned in 1 Corinthians 10:1–13, what is God's promise to you?

Write out the verse that contains the promise, and claim it.

LIFE APPLICATION

1 God asked Moses a question in Exodus 4:2. What was it?

2 God expects us to use what we have. Moses used a rod; David used a sling; Gideon used lanterns, pitchers, and trumpets. What is in your hands?

3 How do you think God wants you to use what he has entrusted to you?

4 How can you use 1 Corinthians 10:13 in your daily life?

❖ ❖ ❖

Law and Grace

In God's holy Word, the Law of Moses and God's grace are constantly set in contrast.

Under the Law, God demanded righteousness *from* man. The Law was connected with works.

Under grace, God in Christ gives righteousness *to* man, and that righteousness becomes ours by faith (John 1:17; Ephesians 2:8,9).

By the Law we have knowledge of sin (Romans 7:7,8; Galatians 3:19). Paul said, "I felt fine so long as I did not understand what the law really demanded. But when I learned the truth, I realized that I had broken the law and was a sinner, doomed to die" (Romans 7:9, TLB).

Paul laments that, because of his sinful nature, he constantly struggles with wrongdoing. "I love to do God's will so far as my new nature is concerned; but there is something else deep within me, in my lower nature, that is at war with my mind and wins the fight and makes me a slave to the sin that is still within me…Oh what a terrible predicament I'm in! Who will free me from my slavery to this deadly lower nature?" (Romans 7:22–25).

❖

Objective: To understand our inability to keep the law and our need for God's grace

Read: Galatians 3

Memorize: Romans 6:23

This is the struggle of every child of God apart from His grace, which through Jesus Christ delivered us from the guilt imposed by the Law and the bondage created by our sins. Paul said, "Thank God! It has been done by Jesus Christ our Lord. He has set me free" (verse 25).

While Jesus presents the ultimate portrait of God's grace, one cannot fail to see a full gallery of His mercy in the stories of the Old Testament. It is evident from the struggles of man under the Law that deliverance could come only by His mercy and grace. Thus we have a balance between God's judgment of sin and His means of restoration for those who truly trust and obey Him.

❖

Bible Study

The Law

When the "Law" is mentioned, the thing that most commonly comes to mind is the Ten Commandments.

"You Shall Not..." "You Shall..."

The Ten Commandments are listed in Exodus 20 and are repeated in Deuteronomy 5. They are as follows:

I. You shall have no other gods before me.

II. You shall not make for yourself an idol in the form of anything.

III. You shall not misuse the name of the Lord your God.

IV. Remember the sabbath day by keeping it holy.

V. Honor your father and your mother.

VI. You shall not murder.

VII. You shall not commit adultery.

VII. You shall not steal.

IX. You shall not give false testimony against your neighbor.

X. You shall not covet…anything that belongs to your neighbor.

1. Jesus condensed these ten into two in Matthew 22:37–40. What are they?

2. What was James' pronouncement concerning the seriousness of breaking even one of these laws (James 2:10)?

What the Law Does

Read Deuteronomy 29:29 and 30:11–20.

The Law of Moses was a covenant of works. God said, "You shall" and "You shall not." The laws were definite, and the attached penalties were definite if the conditions were not obeyed.

Webster defines law as "a rule of conduct or action prescribed by the supreme governing authority and enforced by a sanction." Law always implies two things: a standard and a penalty.

These laws were presented as God's standard of righteousness for that time. They were literally a yardstick for man. The New Testament reveals that "by the law is the knowledge of sin." Jesus Christ came to "fulfill the law," and now God's standard of righteousness is Christ Himself.

1. How are God's people to respond to the things He has revealed of Himself (Deuteronomy 29:29; 30:11,19)?

2. Briefly, what is the summary of all the Law (Deuteronomy 30:16,20)?

3. How did Jesus Christ summarize the will of God for man in Mark 12:29–31?

4. On the basis of Matthew 5:17, what do you think was Christ's assessment of the Law?

5. Read Romans 3:19–26.

   What does the Law reveal (verses 19,20)?

   To what did the Law bear witness while failing to reveal it fully (verse 21)?

   How has a full revelation been made to us (verses 22–24)?

Grace

1. The Living Bible translation of Romans 3:19–26 will help you understand God's grace. As you read the following passage, underline the words that have special meaning to you.

> The judgment of God lies very heavily upon the Jews, for they are responsible to keep God's laws instead of doing all these evil things; not one of them has any excuse; in fact, all the world stands hushed and guilty before Almighty God. Now do you see it? No one can ever be made right in God's sight by doing what the law commands. For the more we know of God's laws, the clearer it becomes that we aren't obeying them; his laws serve only to make us see that we are sinners.

> But now God has shown us a different way to heaven—not by "being good enough" and trying to keep his laws, but by a new way (though not new, really, for the Scriptures told about it long ago). Now God says he will accept and acquit us—declare us "not guilty"—if we trust Jesus Christ to take away our sins. And we all can be saved in this same way, by coming to Christ, no matter who we are or what we have been like. Yes, all have sinned; all fall short of God's glorious ideal; yet now God declares us "not guilty" of offending him if we trust in Jesus Christ, who in his kindness freely takes away our sins.

> For God sent Christ Jesus to take the punishment for our sins and to end all God's anger against us. He used Christ's blood and our faith as the means of saving us from his wrath. In this way he was being entirely fair, even though he did not punish those who sinned in former times. For he was looking forward to the time when Christ would come and take away those sins. And now in these days also he can receive sinners in this same way, because Jesus took away their sins.

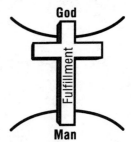

2. Compare Romans 3:20 with Ephesians 2:8,9 and write your conclusions.

   How does keeping the Law make a person feel?

   Should living under grace make you more eager to obey God or less?

   Why?

LIFE APPLICATION

1 How would you explain the difference between Law and grace to someone who was depending upon his own good works to please the Father?

2 What is Christ's relationship to the following:
The Law?
Grace?

3 What is your relationship to the following:
The Law?
Grace?

4 What difference will an understanding of Law and grace make in your desire to please God?

❖ ❖ ❖

Deliverance and Forgiveness

When we think of Joshua and David, each has a distinguishing quality for which he is best known.

Joshua, Moses' brilliant military strategist who eventually led Israel into the Promised Land, is characterized as a *deliverer*. Of the twelve spies sent by Moses into Canaan to survey the territory, Joshua and Caleb alone showed complete confidence that God would help Israel conquer the land. Because of their willingness to obey God, Joshua and Caleb were the only two adults who experienced Egyptian slavery who lived to enter the Promised Land. God appointed Joshua to succeed Moses as Israel's leader and deliverer because he was faithful to ask God's direction in the challenges he faced.

Joshua
Joshua 1–23

David, a shepherd, poet, and soldier who became Israel's second and greatest king, is best known for the principle of *forgiveness*.

An ancestor of Jesus Christ, he is listed in the Hall of Faith in Hebrews 11 and was described by God Himself as "a man who will obey" (1 Samuel 13:14, TLB). Undoubtedly

❖

Objective: To believe the promises of God and maintain fellowship with God, unhindered by sin

Read: Joshua 1,7,8,23

Memorize: Joshua 1:9

he was one of the most famous men of the Old Testament. But he had a dark side as well. He committed adultery with Bathsheba, arranged for the murder of her husband, Uriah, and directly disobeyed God in taking a census of the people.

In spite of his failures, David's unchangeable belief in the faithful and forgiving nature of God is a source of encouragement to us today. David was quick to confess his sins sincerely from his heart, and God never held back His forgiveness (Psalm 32:1–5).

The lesson we can learn from this example is that while God may allow us to suffer the consequences of our sins as He did David, we can count on God's loving forgiveness whenever we fail.

One quality that Joshua and David shared was their confidence in God. This characteristic brought them to the forefront of greatness.

David, more than any other king, was the connecting link between God and His people. It was to this king that God said, "Your family shall rule my kingdom forever" (2 Samuel 7:16, TLB; see also Psalm 89:3,4, 27–29; 132:11). This would

David

| Psalms | 1 Chronicles |
| 1 & 2 Samuel | 1 Kings |

be accomplished through the one Great King who would one day be born of the family of David. This King would Himself live forever and establish a kingdom of endless duration (Isaiah 9:6,7; Luke 1:30–33).

I urge you to study this lesson thoroughly, asking God to help you apply the principles you learn to your life.

Bible Study

Joshua and Deliverance

Joshua's name gives us some insight into the book. His name means "Jehovah is Salvation." It is carried over into the New Testament in the name of our Lord "Jesus."

1. Read Joshua 1:1–9 and list God's promises to Joshua.

   What was the condition on which these promises would be fulfilled?

   Which of these can you apply to your life?

   How?

2. In Joshua 7, why did God tell Joshua to stop praying?

   What does God say to you in Psalm 66:18?

   How can you apply Numbers 32:23 to this passage?

3. What happened after the sin was taken away (Joshua 8:1)?

4. What was Joshua's command to the people before he died (Joshua 23:6)?

5. How do the characteristics of Joshua as deliverer foreshadow Christ's work for us?

David and Forgiveness

1. Read 1 Samuel 24 and 2 Samuel 5 and 12. As you read these chapters, list the verses that indicate the following characteristics of David:

   Submissiveness

   Sincerity

   Boldness

   Trust in God

   Leadership stature

   Sinful passion

   Sorrow for sin

2. The nobility of David's character is seen in many of the recorded instances from his career, including some of those you have just read. He is described as a "man after God's own heart," and as such, he occupies a high position among the heroes of the faith. Jesus' title as the ruler of God's people is "the Son of David."

Many people, however, find the stories of David's terrible sins to be absolutely contradictory to this exalted position of spiritual leadership.

How can you hold up such a man as an outstanding example of "a man after God's own heart"?

If you can answer this question, you will have grasped the essence of biblical faith. Read 2 Samuel 12 again, and then Psalm 32 and 51, which David wrote at that time. (You might find help in Romans 4:1–8 or Luke 7:36–50; 18:9–14.)

3. How did David's experience foreshadow the attitude of Jesus toward sinners? Be specific.

4. How does Christ's roles as King and High Priest relate to deliverance and forgiveness?

LIFE APPLICATION

1 What sin, or problem, do you need deliverance from today?

2 Read Proverbs 28:13. How can you appropriate it for your problem?

3 Read Joshua 24. Circle all the "I's" in verses 3 through 13 and notice all the things God accomplished for the people of Israel.

What do you need Him to accomplish for you?

Pray, asking in faith that God will work on your behalf in these areas.

4 How does your heart attitude compare with that of Joshua and David?

How can you use their example to live a more godly life?

❖ ❖ ❖

Elijah: The Power of a Spirit-Led Man

The most famous and dramatic of Israel's prophets, Elijah was a complex man of the desert who confronted kings. His mission was to drive the worship of Baal out of Israel. Called "the grandest and most romantic character that Israel ever produced,"[1] Elijah exemplifies the power of a Spirit-led man.

He prophesied before King Ahab that there would be no rain or dew apart from his declaration. In Zarephath he raised the widow's dead son to life (1 Kings 17:17–24). On Mount Carmel he called down fire from heaven (1 Kings 18:16–46). And 2 Kings 2:1–12 records how Elijah struck the River Jordan with his cloak and the river divided so he and Elisha could cross on dry land. Then, as Elisha watched, Elijah was caught up into heaven in a chariot of fire.

Through Malachi, God promised to send another prophet like Elijah to Israel who

Elijah
1 Kings 17, 18

❖

Objective: To serve God in power and courage

Read: 1 Kings 17 and 18

Memorize: 1 Kings 18:21

---

[1] Nelson Price, cited in the *Holman Bible Dictionary*, Trent C. Butler, general editor (Nashville: Holman Bible Publishers, 1991), p.411.

would "turn the hearts of the fathers to their children, and the hearts of the children to their fathers" (Malachi 4:5,6). This prophecy was fulfilled in John the Baptist. Luke records the message of an angel to John's father, Zacharias, that his son would be "a man of rugged spirit and power like Elijah, the prophet of old; and he will precede the coming of the Messiah, preparing the people for his arrival. He will soften adult hearts to become like little children's, and will change disobedient minds to the wisdom of faith" (Luke 1:17, TLB).

The Gospels of Matthew, Mark, and Luke record Elijah's appearance with Moses and Jesus on the Mount of Transfiguration. And one of the two witnesses mentioned in Revelation 11:4–6 is thought by many Bible students to be Elijah because of his power "to shut up the sky so that it will not rain during the time they are prophesying."

There is no doubt that Elijah was a Spirit-led man. But the real power of the prophet was not that he could perform miracles. The key to his abilities was his very personal relationship with God.

The same Holy Spirit who empowered the prophet indwells every child of God today. Jesus promised that we will have all the power we need when the Holy Spirit comes upon us (Acts 1:8), and this power will enable us to be fruitful witnesses for Christ as we help fulfill the Great Commission.

Although we may wish to perform amazing miracles for our Lord, our first priority is to focus on our relationship with Him. He can use us only when we are totally and unconditionally surrendered to His plan and purpose for our lives.

❖

Bible Study

Elijah

1. Read 1 Kings 17:1–7. Indicate whether the following statements are true or false.

_____ The cessation of rain is dependent on all these factors: God lives; Elijah lived in His presence; and Elijah's word controlled the rain.

_____ The Bible says that Elijah searched eagerly for the will of God.

_____ The prophet obeyed orders for the immediate future, though he did not know how it would turn out.

_____ Elijah thought the plan was absurd, and hesitated.

_____ The brook dried up, proving he was right.

2. What step of duty have you not taken because you cannot see its outcome?

The Widow

1. Read 1 Kings 17:8–24. Indicate whether the following statements are true or false.

_____ Strict, implicit obedience characterized Elijah.

_____ When her boy died, guilt turned the widow's eyes upon herself.

_____ God desires to remove from our lives now the guilt that can cripple our faith in time of crisis.

2. Do you think it was humiliating to take a step of faith that made him dependent on a very poor widow?

3. Why do you think God deals with us in such a way?

Ahab

1. Read 1 Kings 18:1–18. Indicate whether the following statements are true or false.

_____ Ahab was at least concerned for his animals.

_____ He had refused to acknowledge the real reason for the problem (verses 17,18).

_____ Nevertheless, Elijah recognized the real reason (verses 17,18).

2. Describe a time when you were the cause of a problem for others that you did not acknowledge.

What was the result?

3. How can you avoid this sin (Proverbs 3:5,6)?

Prophets of Baal

1. Read 1 Kings 18:18–40. Write the verse number(s) in which Elijah did the following:

   _____ Rebuked the people for compromise

   _____ Challenged the enemies of God to a contest

   _____ Blasted them with withering sarcasm

   _____ Ordered water poured

   _____ Prayed to God to make Himself known

   _____ Ordered the priests executed

2. How can this incident apply to today?

3. Elijah's prayer in verse 36 provides a superb revelation of the Spirit-led life. Why do you think that is true?

LIFE APPLICATION

1 Describe the relationship Elijah had with God.

2 How does your relationship and power with God compare to Elijah's?

3 How has God's power been exerted through you upon the lives of others?

4 What changes in your mental and spiritual thinking need to take place for you to find the power with God that you desire?

❖ ❖ ❖

Jeremiah: A Witness Who Stood Alone

If you think it is difficult to stand for Christ in your home, on your campus, or in your community, draw some encouragement from Jeremiah.

He was a prophet who endured. He acted as God's faithful messenger in spite of many attempts on his life. His enemies challenged his prophetic honesty. He lived in constant friction with religious and political authorities. And little wonder. He recommended national surrender to the Babylonian Empire and called Nebuchadnezzar, Judah's most hated enemy, the "servant of the Lord" (Jeremiah 25:9; 27:6). Furthermore, he incited his colleagues to desert to the enemy and was accused and convicted of treason.

Objective: To serve God faithfully in the face of discouragement

Read: Jeremiah 1, 20, and 21

Memorize: Jeremiah 23:29

Sometimes he complained to God about the misery of his office. But he was so sorrowful for the fallen condi-

Jeremiah
Jeremiah 1–21

tion of Israel that despite all of his hardships, he persisted in speaking the word of the Lord faithfully and earned the title of "weeping prophet."

Jeremiah is an example to us of sticking to a task despite all odds—especially in a time when many Christians lack long-term commitment to the things of God. Sometimes, like Jeremiah, we must be willing to be a witness who stands alone in the midst of incredible opposition to proclaim the word of God and faithfully obey His commands.

❖

Bible Study

Jeremiah's Call

Read Jeremiah 1.

1. When facing Scripture verses that command you to speak for Christ, have you ever felt, "Why, I could never do that, I have no training for it"?

   What did Jeremiah say (1:6)?

2. To be effective in speaking, one must have something to say. Where do you get the right message (1:7–17)?

   In what way does God touch our mouths today (Ephesians 5:18)?

3. Opposition of the intensity that faced Jeremiah is unknown in America, although it is common in some parts of the world. How can these verses help us overcome situations we face (1:8,18,19)?

Jeremiah's Arrest and Prayer

Read Jeremiah 19:14,15. In verse 14, we see that not only what Jeremiah said but where he spoke (and to whom) were under the Lord's direct guidance. This was also observed in Elijah's life as one of the secrets of effectiveness. The secret is to be filled with God's Holy Spirit. He will lead us to those He wants us to touch. As a result, Spirit-filled Christians share their faith with others at every opportunity. The apostle Paul records in Colossians 1:28, "Everywhere we go we talk about Christ to all who will listen" (TLB).

Verse 15 was Jeremiah's unpopular message in a nutshell: condemnation upon the capital city, Jerusalem; the Babylonian armies would destroy the city. He advised the people to surrender and avoid the horrors of a siege that could not be resisted for long since God was on the enemy's side.

Read Jeremiah 20.

1. How did punishment affect Jeremiah's testimony (20:1–6)?

2. Verses 7–18 are an example of the abrupt interruptions interspersed throughout the book of Jeremiah. What do these prayers reveal about the apparent fearlessness of the prophet?

3. Since his message brought him so much unpopularity, what did Jeremiah consider (20:8,9)?

   Why did he reject that idea?

4. How did his enemies think they could get the best of him (20:10)?

5. What thoughts restored His confidence (20:11)?

6. How can you relate Jeremiah's attitude to your experiences in witnessing for the Lord?

   How can Jeremiah's example help you?

Jeremiah's Prophecy
Read Jeremiah 21.

1. How do you think feelings of despair and frustration influenced the prophet's obedience to God?

2. When asked by the government for a word of comfort and security, what response did Jeremiah give (21:1–7)?

3. What decision did the prophet declare that his hearers must make (21:8–14)?

LIFE APPLICATION

On this chart, list discouragements you may be facing, and what you have learned from Jeremiah's life that will help you cope with them.

DISCOURAGEMENT	LEARNED FROM JEREMIAH

❖ ❖ ❖

The Tabernacle

The Tabernacle and its furnishings have many lessons for us. Examine the diagram on page 377 closely. Notice the three sections: the large area of service, the Holy Place, and the Holy of Holies. Each area was hidden from the others by curtains. When Solomon built his temple after the Israelites had settled in the Promised Land, he followed the same pattern for the inner parts, carefully following God's instructions.

Note the pieces of furniture. The first is the Brazen Altar, which was used for sacrifice and atonement.

Then came the Laver. It was used for cleansing.

Proceeding into the Holy Place, on the right is the Table of Shewbread; on the left is the Candlestick. Straight ahead is the Altar of Incense.

❖

Objective: To understand how the Tabernacle pictures the work of Christ

Read: Exodus 25–27

Memorize: Hebrews 10:10

Beyond this Altar is the Veil of the Tabernacle that hid the Holiest of Holies from the eyes of everyone except the High Priest. In the Holy of Holies we find the Ark, which was the earthly dwelling place of God.

As you study this lesson, you will see how God prepared this Tabernacle, not just for

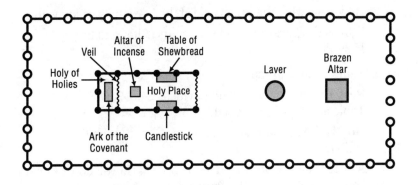

worship and sacrifice, but also as an illustration of the Son He would send to earth.

❖

Bible Study

The Furnishings
Read Exodus 25–27.

1. The Brazen Altar

Read Exodus 29:36,37 and describe how the Altar was used.

Why do you think the Altar was placed just inside the entrance?

Read Hebrews 13:10–16. How does the Brazen Altar reflect Christ's sacrifice?

What sacrifices are we to offer?

2. The Laver

Read Exodus 30:18–21 and describe the Laver and its use.

What is the parallel in Ephesians 5:25–27?

What is our part (1 John 1:9)?

The cleansing is not the forgiveness we receive when we become Christians. It is what we do after we are children of God to be cleansed of our sins.

How does what the priests did at the Laver help us know that?

Why is the Laver placed between the Altar and the Holy Place?

3. Table of Shewbread

Read Exodus 25:23–30 and Leviticus 24:5–9. Describe the Table and how it was used.

How is the Shewbread a picture of Christ (John 6:32–35, 50,51)?

As Christians, God considers us priests (Revelation 1:6). When we partake of the Lord's Supper, what should our attitude be toward the bread (1 Corinthians 11:23,24)?

4. The Candlestick

Read Exodus 25:31–40; 27:20,21. Describe the Candlestick and how it was used.

How is this a picture of Jesus (John 8:12)?

How does this relate to our daily lives (John 12:35,36)?

5. Altar of Incense

Read Exodus 30:1–8. Describe the Altar of Incense and its use.

The Altar of Incense is the reminder of our prayers, which are an incense to God. According to Revelation 8:3,4, what happens to our prayers?

What kind of attitude should we have toward prayer (Psalm 141:2)?

Why do you think the Table of Shewbread, Candlestick, and Altar of Incense were placed inside the Holy Place?

6. Ark of the Covenant

The Holy of Holies was hidden by a veil. Inside we find the Ark, which was the dwelling place of God Himself. What was placed inside the Ark (Hebrews 9:4)?

What was on it (verse 5)?

Who was the only person allowed to enter the Holy of Holies (verses 6,7)?

Why was the Ark separate from the other furnishings?

Why was it placed in the Holy of Holies?

Christ as High Priest

1. How was the Tabernacle set up and sanctified (Exodus 40)?

   What significance did the cloud have?

2. What part did Aaron play?

3. What happened to the veil at Christ's death (Matthew 27:50,51)?

   What did this signify?

4. Describe why Christ is the final High Priest (Hebrews 9:6–14).

5. Compare the old covenant with the new (Hebrews 9:15–23).

6. Christ is both the sacrifice and the High Priest. Read Hebrews 9:24–28. Describe how this is so.

   What is the hope this gives us?

LIFE APPLICATION

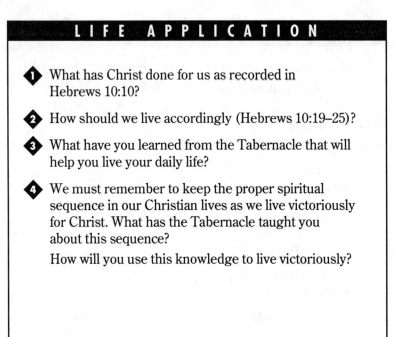

1 What has Christ done for us as recorded in Hebrews 10:10?

2 How should we live accordingly (Hebrews 10:19–25)?

3 What have you learned from the Tabernacle that will help you live your daily life?

4 We must remember to keep the proper spiritual sequence in our Christian lives as we live victoriously for Christ. What has the Tabernacle taught you about this sequence?

How will you use this knowledge to live victoriously?

❖ ❖ ❖

Recap

The following questions will help you review this Step. If necessary, reread the appropriate lesson(s).

Now that we have gone through the Old Testament at a rapid pace, you have some idea of what it contains and what it teaches. Imagine yourself a Jew, possessing only the Old Testament.

Reread: Genesis 4,6,7, 12,22; Exodus 25–27

Review: Verses memorized

1. Can you find God's plan for man in it? Write your conclusions here in your own words.

2. Why did Jesus of Nazareth have to come?

3. How is Jesus pictured in the Old Testament through the following?

   Abraham

   Joshua

   David

   The Tabernacle

4. List some examples of how the High Priest worked in the Old Testament (Exodus 25–27).

5. How is Jesus our High Priest (Hebrews 10)?

LIFE APPLICATION

 How did your study of the Old Testament help you understand the New Testament better?

 Using Hebrews 10:10–18, describe the differences between Law and grace.

How does this affect the way you relate to God?

3 Using the diagram of the Tabernacle, list the ways you can draw nearer to God.

Which is the most significant for you to do today?

4 Right now, thank God for His great sacrifice through Jesus Christ.

❖ ❖ ❖

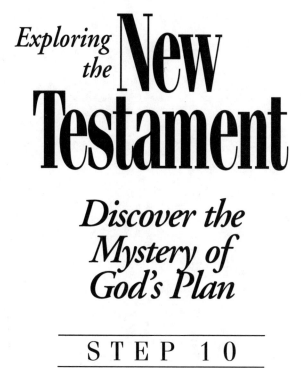

Exploring **New**
the **New**

Testament

Discover the
Mystery of
God's Plan

STEP 10

Matthew

The Gospel of Matthew is the link between the Old and New Testaments. Matthew wrote to the Jews to prove that Christ is their promised Messiah and the eternal King of king and Lord of lords. Therefore, Matthew is careful not to alienate his Jewish readers. Matthew also shows how Jesus fulfilled prophecy and how He is the Person who will bring in God's kingdom.

Because the "Kingdom of heaven" is found thirty-three times in this Gospel, it has been called the Gospel of the Kingdom. The book also shows that followers of Christ are the true people of God and the heirs of the coming kingdom.

❖

Objective: To see the relationship of Christ to the Old Testament, and to understand His role as King of kings

Read: Matthew 21:1–16

Memorize: Matthew 28:18–20

Matthew records Jesus' Sermon on the Mount, the Beatitudes, the Parables of the Kingdom, and Peter's confession of the deity of Christ.

Matthew
Christ as King

START.

It is Matthew's version of the Beatitudes that are memorized in childhood, and it is his form of the Lord's Prayer that we use the most in church today.

❖

Bible Study

Genealogy

Of the four Gospels, only Matthew and Luke give Christ's genealogy. Compare Matthew 1:1–17 and Luke 3:23–38.

1. What differences do you find?

2. Keeping in mind that Matthew presented Christ as King,
   why do you think Matthew wrote the genealogy the way
   he did?

Sermons

In presenting his record of the life of Jesus, Matthew is careful to
record the major sermons that Jesus preached. The longest sermon
on record is the "Sermon on the Mount," which is found in chapters
5 through 7.

1. As you read this sermon, answer the following questions:

   Give one reason Jesus considers it important for His
   disciples to live according to the moral standards of the
   Old Testament Law and prophets (Matthew 5:16).

   What promise does Jesus give that helps the Christian
   overcome his desire for man's praise as he does good
   deeds (Matthew 6:1–18)?

   What assurance does Jesus give to help the Christian overcome his anxiety over physical needs such as food and
   clothing (Matthew 6:25–34)?

2. Read Jesus' sermons recorded by Matthew in the chapters
   listed below and write in your own words the verse that
   means the most to you.

   Chapter 10

   Chapter 13

   Chapter 18

   Chapters 24 and 25

A Vital Question

In Matthew 16:13, Jesus asks a question.

1. Why is answering this question so vital?

2. Read verses 14–16. Why does Jesus say Peter's answer was revealed by the Father?

3. How have you answered this question?

The Great Commandment

Read Matthew 22:34–40.

1. What does Jesus mean when He says that the whole Law and prophets depend on these two commandments?

2. How have you seen Jesus demonstrating the Great Commandment in Matthew's Gospel? Use specific examples.

The Great Commission

Read Matthew 28:18–20. Jesus gave His friends one last commandment before He ascended into heaven. Many call this commandment the Great Commission.

1. How is Jesus' goal different from that of human rulers?

2. In your own words, paraphrase Christ's Great Commission.

3. What does the Great Commission mean to you? Stop

18 And Jesus spoke unto them saying All power is given unto me in Heaven and in Earth

19 Go ye therefore, and teach All Nations Baptizing them in the name of the Father and of the Son, and of the Holy Spirit

20 teaching them to observe All things what solever I have commanded you, and Lo, I am with you Alway, even unto the end of the World.

LIFE APPLICATION

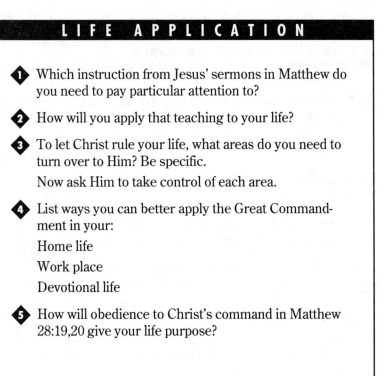

1 Which instruction from Jesus' sermons in Matthew do you need to pay particular attention to?

2 How will you apply that teaching to your life?

3 To let Christ rule your life, what areas do you need to turn over to Him? Be specific.

Now ask Him to take control of each area.

4 List ways you can better apply the Great Commandment in your:

Home life

Work place

Devotional life

5 How will obedience to Christ's command in Matthew 28:19,20 give your life purpose?

❖ ❖ ❖

Mark

Although Matthew precedes the Gospel of Mark in the New Testament, Mark is considered the first of the four Gospels to be written. Possibly written and published in Rome between A.D. 60 and 70, Mark addressed his book to the Roman Christians. Romans were a practical people and did not care about Jewish history and beliefs. The Romans loved action. So Mark writes a brief Gospel full of Jesus' miracles and deeds, not His sermons.

While Matthew described Jesus as a King, Mark tells of His servanthood. Therefore, Mark approaches his Gospel differently. Mark shows how Jesus first directed His public ministry to the Jews, but when their leaders opposed Him, He also went to the Gentile world. However, both Matthew and Mark record the Great Commission of our Lord to go into all the world and preach the gospel.

Mark
Christ as Servant

Although Mark's Gospel is the shortest, it is brimming with the love Jesus showed for others and the mission He came to complete.

❖

Objective: To show the servanthood of Christ and how He cared deeply for people

Read: Mark 14–16

Memorize: Mark 10:44,45

391

❖

Bible Study

Jesus' Ministry

1. Read Mark 10:45. State Mark's objective for writing his Gospel.

2. Read Mark 1:20 and 3:13–35. How did Jesus choose His followers?

   What do these passages say about the qualifications Jesus expects in His disciples?

3. In Mark 1:21–28, how was Jesus described as a teacher?

4. One of the most striking ways in which the Gospel of Mark differs from Matthew is that it places greater emphasis on what Jesus did than what He said.

   What were some of the things Jesus did that caused the religious leaders of His day to be so angry with Him (Mark 2:1–3:6)?

Miracles of Jesus

1. Note the four miracles of Jesus, performed in Mark 4–5:43. List one characteristic of Jesus in each incident.

   Mark 4:35–41

   Mark 5:1–20

   Mark 5:21–23,35–43

   Mark 5:25–34

2. What one thing hinders Jesus from exercising His power and control in the lives of men (Mark 6:1–6)?

Jesus' Death and Resurrection

1. Compare Matthew's and Mark's accounts of Jesus' death and resurrection (Matthew 26–28; Mark 14–16). What differences do you find?

   How does having two accounts help you better understand Christ's sacrifice for you?

2. Describe how Christ the servant is exalted (Mark 16:1–20).

3. How does Jesus combine the qualities of both a king and a servant?

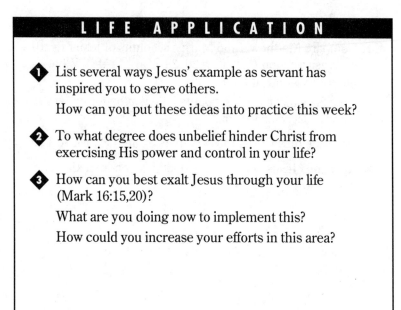

LIFE APPLICATION

1 List several ways Jesus' example as servant has inspired you to serve others.

How can you put these ideas into practice this week?

2 To what degree does unbelief hinder Christ from exercising His power and control in your life?

3 How can you best exalt Jesus through your life (Mark 16:15,20)?

What are you doing now to implement this?

How could you increase your efforts in this area?

❖ ❖ ❖

LUKE 19.10 The SON OF MAN COME TO SEEK AND SAVE THOSE WHO ARE LOST

Luke

The most comprehensive of the Gospels, Luke presents an accurate account of the life of Christ as the perfect Man and Savior. The writer portrays our Lord's concern for His followers and friends and shows His tenderheartedness toward the poor, despised, and sinful. Luke also shows how Christ lived in total dependence on the Holy Spirit.

Luke wrote his Gospel to the Greeks, a cultured people. Luke, an educated Greek himself, knew his readers would be captivated by Jesus as the perfect Man, an idea prevalent in Greek mythology.

Luke
Christ as Man

Luke shows Jesus' human side—with feelings and a love for people, and subject to circumstances. Yet Christ also stands out in this Gospel as being fully God.

MAN +

As a physician, Luke gives the most detailed description of Christ's birth and His childhood. The writer also relates the stories of outcasts such as the good Samaritan, the prodigal, and the thief on the cross. And this Gospel also records more prayers of Jesus than any of the others. *9 PRAYERS*

❖ **Objective:** To understand more deeply Christ's human nature

Read: Luke 2

Memorize: Luke 19:10

395

❖

Bible Study

Introduction

Read Luke 1:1–4.

1. To whom was this Gospel originally written?

2. What evidence is there that the recipient of this Gospel had been given some prior instruction in Christianity?

3. Why did Luke write this Gospel to Theophilus?

Jesus' Suffering

1. One of Luke's great emphases is that Jesus, though He is the Christ, must nevertheless suffer and die at the hands of sinful men (2:33–35; 9:22–31, 13:31–35; 18:31–35; 24:7,25–27,44–47).

   Why do you think Jesus mentioned His death so many times?

2. Read Luke 20–24, the account of the last week leading up to Jesus' death and resurrection.

   What are some qualities of Jesus' character that stand out prominently in these chapters?

   What qualities of character in Jesus' enemies stand out in these chapters?

   Why, then, did men seek to have Jesus crucified?

3. How were the disciples—and thus Theophilus and all the readers of Luke—assured that Jesus' suffering and death occurred according to God's plan, instead of accidentally, simply because of men's evil hearts?

   What difference does that make to you?

Jesus' Prayers

1. Read the three parables on prayer in Luke 11:5–13; 18:1–8; and 18:9–14. What qualities of prayer are described?

2. Now read about some of Christ's prayers (5:16; 6:12; 9:28,29; 11:1; 22:32,44; 23:46). How did Jesus follow through with these qualities?

3. What elements of Jesus' prayers can you apply to make your prayers more effective?

Jesus' Humanity

1. Since Luke writes about the humanity of Jesus, list people whom Jesus touched and the results of His ministry on them.

   6:17–19

   7:36–50

   8:1–3

   15:1–7

   17:11–19

   23:39–43

2. Where do you think Jesus would likely minister today if He were in your area?

Jesus' Resurrection

1. Why do you think the women were the first to discover that Jesus was alive (Luke 23:26,27,48,49,55,56; 24:1–9)?

2. What does that mean to your faithfulness in service to the Lord?

3. What was the reaction of Jesus' friends after His ascension (Luke 24:50–53)?

LIFE APPLICATION

1 Luke presented Christ as the Son of Man. What does that title mean to you?

2 Seeing the types of people Jesus ministered to, how will this affect your mnistry?

List several practical ways you can show the kind of compassion Jesus did.

3 How can Jesus' example of righteousness during suffering help you face crises in your life?

4 Read 1 Corinthians 15:58. Considering the actions of the women during the crucifixion, name one way you can stand firm in your work for the Lord.

❖ ❖ ❖

John

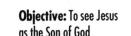

Called "The Gospel of Love," John has won the affection of Christians who turn to it first for inspiration. Because of its universal appeal, this Gospel is the first to be translated into a foreign language or dialect, and it is the most widely distributed of the Gospels.

John seeks to prove conclusively that Jesus is the Son of God and that all who believe in Him will have eternal life. John focused on the uniqueness of Jesus, portraying Him as the Creator who became flesh and dwelt among

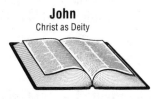

John
Christ as Deity

men as the Lamb of God "who takes away the sin of the world" (John 1:29).

As we view the Gospels together, we see a progression of teaching in each book. Matthew, for example, ends with the Resurrection, Mark closes with the Ascension, Luke gives the promise of the Holy Spirit, and in John our Lord breathes the Holy Spirit upon His disciples and speaks of His return.

❖

Objective: To see Jesus as the Son of God

Read: John 1

Memorize: John 7:37,38

❖

Bible Study

Titles for Jesus
Read John 1:1–18.

1. Why is Jesus called the Word?
   Why is He called the light?
   Why is He called the Son?

2. John also gave other names for Jesus. Write each and a short explanation of what it means.
   6:35
   8:12
   11:25
   14:6

Miracles of Christ

1. Why did John take the trouble to relate the various signs, or miracles, found in his Gospel (John 20:30,31)?

2. Skim through this Gospel and see if you can list the seven miracles of Jesus that John recorded.

Representatives for Christ
Read John 13 and 14.

1. What attitude of the heart must you demonstrate if other people are to realize that you are Christ's representative in the world (13:34,35)?

2. What is God's provision for enabling Christians to be true representatives of Christ in the world (14:16–18)?

Christ's Deity

1. John quotes seven witnesses to the deity of Christ. Who are they?

   1:19,34

   1:49

   6:68,69

   11:24–27

   20:28

   20:31

   10:34–36

2. Why was each person qualified to testify?

The Holy Spirit

1. John also teaches us about the Holy Spirit. How does the work of the Holy Spirit affect your life and ministry?

   3:5

   4:14

   7:38,39

   14–16

2. What is the promise given in John 14:15–31?

The Vine and the Branches

Read John 15:1–8.

1. Describe the relationship between the vine and branches.

2. How can you use this picture to have a more fruitful ministry?

LIFE APPLICATION

❶ According to John 15:16,27, what was to be the
disciples' function after Jesus left the earth?

How are you obeying that command?

What promises can you claim from these verses that
will help you bear fruit?

❷ Read John 21. Summarize what these verses mean to
your ministry for Jesus.

❖ ❖ ❖

The Acts of the Apostles

A sequel to the Gospel of Luke, the Book of Acts portrays the birth and growth of the Christian Church. Acts also is a theological work that builds a strong case for the validity of Christ's claims and promises.

Luke's record of the coming of the Holy Spirit shows that the Church did not start or grow by its own initiative, but as the power of the Holy Spirit empowered the early Christians.

The Book of Acts also describes the opposition and persecution that the Christians suffered at the hands of both Jews and Gentiles. This opposition, however, became a catalyst for the spread of Christianity.

Acts
Works of the Holy Spirit

❖

Objective: To view the dynamic establishment of the first-century church

Read: Acts 2

Memorize: Acts 1:8

Acts is considered the connecting link between the life of Christ and the life of the Church, and is a glimpse into the Christian world that gave birth to the Epistles.

❖

Bible Study

Empowerment of the Holy Spirit

The Book of Acts begins by referring to the material presented in the Gospels as "all that Jesus began to do and to teach" (Acts 1:1). It tells of the works that the resurrected and ascended Christ continued to do through the Holy Spirit poured out on His disciples at Pentecost. Acts 1:8 has often been considered the key verse of this book. Survey the book and answer these questions.

1. What chapters tell of the witness of the disciples at Jerusalem?

   In Samaria?

   To the ends of the earth?

Peter

1. The following are some of the major messages that Peter gave as he witnessed for Christ: Acts 2:14–36; 3:11–26; 10:34–43.

   What was the most important point about the life of Christ that Peter was trying to get across?

2. Read chapter 10. What significance does Peter's experience with Cornelius have for the church?

Paul

Of all the apostles, Paul stands out most prominently in Acts and other books of the New Testament.

1. What kind of man was Paul before he was converted (8:1–3; 9:2; 22:1–5; 26:4–12)?

   When Jesus appeared to Paul on the road to Damascus, what did He tell Paul he was to do (9:4–6)?

2. To whom did Paul seek to minister first at Cypress (13:4–12), at Antioch of Pisidia (13:13–52), and at Iconium (14:1–7)?

To whom did Paul preach after this first group rejected the gospel?

3. In preaching to the Jews, Paul was able to make a point of contact with them by referring to the Old Testament Scriptures. What was the point of contact Paul used in speaking to the pagan Gentiles at Lystra (14:8–18)?

What did Paul do to establish his converts in the faith (14:21–23)?

Romans 15:20 tells us one more thing about Paul's evangelism strategy. What is it?

The Holy Spirit

1. According to these Scriptures, what are some of the ways in which the Holy Spirit empowered the early church?

1:8

4:31

2:4–8; 10:46; 19:6

7:54–60

10:19,20; 13:2–4

11:28; 21:10–13

2. How did the Holy Spirit work through Paul as he ministered at the following places:

Cypress (13:4–12)?

Iconium (13:52–14:3)?

LIFE APPLICATION

1 What is the most important thing you now try to tell others about Christ?

How does that compare with what Peter and Paul preached?

2 What can you learn from Paul to help in your discipling of others?

3 What are some of the ways in which the Holy Spirit is currently empowering you?

❖ ❖ ❖

Romans, 1 and 2 Corinthians, Galatians

Of the 27 books in the New Testament, 21 are letters, with 13 of these definitely written by Paul.

The man God used to write so much of the New Testament, Paul was a Roman citizen, a Jew of Tarsus, a Hebrew of the Hebrews. He was brought up at the feet of a great teacher, Gamaliel, but became a missionary to Jesus Christ. From the day of his conversion,

Romans
Law

1 & 2 Corinthians
Church

Galatians
Grace

Paul's very life was summed up in his own words, "For to me, to live is Christ and to die is gain" (Philippians 1:21).

Objective: To understand the essence of the gospel

Read: Galatians

Memorize: Romans 1:16

Bible Study

Romans

This epistle was written from the city of Corinth to the believers in Rome shortly after

Paul had finished his work in Ephesus. Rome was the center of the civilized world, the great metropolis of a vast empire. The city had already become the home of many Christians.

Paul is telling the Romans the good news concerning the way in which God, in His infinite love, has provided free and full salvation for sinners. Paul's main insistence is that man's justification before God rests not on the Law of Moses, but on the mercy of Christ.

1. Read Romans 1:1–3,16,17.

   What is the main theme of Romans?

   What is the gospel of Christ?

   What does it reveal?

2. Read Romans 3:9–18. Man is sinful and lives a life separated from God.

   Write the five characteristics of a sinful man listed in these verses:

   Verse 9

   Verse 10

   Verse 11

   Verse 17

   Verse 18

   What righteousness does a man have that he can offer God (Romans 3:10)?

3. Read Romans 3:21–28 and 5:1–5.

   What has God declared to you (3:25,26)?

   Therefore, how are you justified (1:17; 3:28; 5:1)?

4. Being justified by faith, what is your spiritual resource (5:5)?

5. Being justified by faith, what is your spiritual worship (12:1)?

6. List five ways in which this sacrifice will affect your daily walk (12:6–13:10).

   Which area do you need to apply most?

I Corinthians

This epistle was written three years after Paul left Corinth. The Corinthian church sent a delegation of its leaders to Ephesus to consult with Paul about some serious problems that had arisen in the church.

1. Read 1 Corinthians 1:17–31. Paul makes it clear that God is wiser than men and chooses the foolish things of the world to confound the mighty.

   How has God ordained that men should hear and believe?

   Whom has He chosen for this task?

   What happens, then, if you boast about what you are doing for God?

2. Read 1 Corinthians 9:22–24.

   Give in your own words definite proof that Paul had forsaken all that he had to follow Christ (verse 22).

   To what does he liken his task?

   Why is this so appropriate?

   What have you given up to help reach someone for Christ?

3. Read 1 Corinthians 13. In verses 4–8, insert your own name in the place of "love" or "charity."

   Which verse does not fit you and what do you think God would have you do about it?

2 Corinthians

Soon after Paul had written 1 Corinthians, he met Titus on his way to Corinth. Titus brought word that Paul's letter had accomplished much good but some were still disloyal, and there were problems with people who put the law before the needs of people.

Paul was physically weak, weary, and in pain. His spiritual burdens were great: first, the maintenance of the churches; second, his concern about the legalists; and third, his anguish over the distrust of him by some members of the churches.

1. Read 2 Corinthians 4:1–6. Notice how carefully Paul handles the Word of God.

   Describe how Paul spreads the gospel of Christ (verse 2).

   Why did God shine into our hearts (verse 6)?

2. What is it that Paul fears and of which we all must be well aware (2 Corinthians 11:3)?

3. Read 2 Corinthians 12:1–10. Paul prayed to be relieved of his "thorn in the flesh" (a physical disability). What was the Lord's answer to his prayer (verse 9)?

   What was Paul's attitude toward the final outcome?

   What lesson can you learn from his experience (12:10)?

Galatians

Some time after Paul left Galatia, certain Jewish teachers began to insist that Gentiles could not be Christian without keeping the Law of Moses. The objective of this epistle is the defense of the gospel of grace that Paul had received by revelation from Jesus.

1. Paul shows that the gospel was not of man, neither did he receive it of man, nor was he taught it of man. What was its true origin (Galatians 1:12)?

2. What is Paul's relationship with Christ (Galatians 2:20)?

   What effect does this have on his daily life?

3. Read Galatians 5:16–21. In this passage Paul lists the works of the flesh. How can we as Christians avoid doing the works of the flesh?

LIFE APPLICATION

1 According to Galatians 5:22,23, what will be the result in your life of this type of walk? List the definite characteristics.

2 Which work of your flesh do you most need to surrender to the Holy Spirit's control today?

Take time to do that right now.

3 Which fruit of the Spirit is God trying to strengthen in your life?

How?

4 What one attitude of Paul's do you desire for your life and ministry?

How will you make it your own?

❖ ❖ ❖

Prison Epistles, Thessalonians, Pastoral Epistles

Ephesians, Philippians, Colossians, and Philemon are called the "prison" epistles because they were written by Paul during his first imprisonment mentioned in Acts 28.

Paul wrote Ephesians to encourage the faith of the believers in Ephesus. In this Epistle, Paul explains the nature and purpose of the Church, the Body of Christ.

In his letter to the Philippians, Paul emphasizes the true joy that comes from Jesus Christ alone. He wrote on the themes of humility, self-sacrifice, unity, and Christian living.

In Colossians, Paul presents Christ as God in the flesh, Lord of all creation, and the

❖

Objective: To examine the character of the apostle Paul as presented in these epistles

Read: Ephesians

Memorize: Colossians 2:6,7

Ephesians
Philippians
Colossians ⎫ Prison
Philemon ⎬ Letters
1 & 2 Thessalonians ⎭

1 & 2 Timothy ⎫ Co-Workers
Titus ⎭

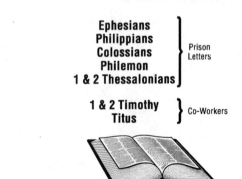

head of the Church. Paul also addresses the problem of false teachers promoting legalism.

In his letter to Philemon, Paul encourages forgiveness for Philemon's slave, Onesimus, who may have stolen from his master and run away. By writing this letter, Paul encourages believers everywhere to treat others with Christian love and fellowship.

In his Thessalonian Epistles, Paul assures believers at Thessalonica of the return of Christ and corrects their misconceptions about the resurrection and the timing of the second coming of Christ. His letters focus on courage in the face of persecution and being prepared for the coming of Christ.

From the time of his first missionary journey, Paul always had co-workers. The Pastoral Epistles—1 and 2 Timothy and Titus— were written to those who were helping him to strengthen the churches he had founded.

Timothy was a young leader, an elder in the church at Ephesus. Paul's first letter to Timothy is a handbook of church administration and discipline. In his second letter, the apostle encourages Timothy to be bold in the face of opposition and persecution and to remain faithful in sound doctrine, loyalty, and endurance.

Titus, a Greek convert, was Paul's representative to the churches on Crete. Paul's letter to Titus tells him how to organize and oversee those churches.

❖

Bible Study

Prison Epistles

Ephesians. The purpose of this letter was to show the Gentiles that they were on an equal footing with the Jews in receiving the blessings of salvation (see Ephesians 2:8–22; 3:6).

1. What had been the prospects of Gentiles receiving the blessings of salvation in previous times (2:11,12)?

2. Through what event were the blessings of salvation made available to all (2:13–18)?

3. From Paul's prayer in Ephesians 3:14–19, list the blessings of salvation that all Christians now enjoy.

4. How can you use this information for encouragement?

Philippians. Paul wrote this letter to the church he had founded (Acts 16) to thank them for the money they sent him for his support while in prison. In writing it, he also sought to overcome the disunity in the church between two women, Euodia and Syntyche (Philippians 4:2). With this disunity overcome, the church could stand firmly together in preaching the gospel without fear to those around them (1:27,28).

1. Read Philippians 1:12–30. What had Paul been doing in Rome that would encourage the Philippians to be bold in proclaiming the gospel (1:13,14)?

2. How did Paul's attitude regarding the future help to encourage the Philippians to stand fearlessly for Christ (1:18–26)?

3. What was Paul's chief reason for being happy about the gift the Philippians had sent him (4:10–19)?

Take time to thank God for the gifts (spiritual and material) that Christians have given you this past week.

Colossians. Paul had never visited the church at Colosse, but reports regarding the increase of false teaching there had reached him in Rome. Since he was an apostle to all the Gentiles, he felt it necessary to write and warn that church.

The false teaching stated that instead of Christ being the only mediator between God and man, there were certain angelic beings through whom man must also go in order to know God. Consequently, Paul's main emphasis in this Epistle is the deity and all-sufficiency of Jesus Christ.

1. List at least three things Paul says about Jesus Christ that show it is unnecessary to seek any additional way to reach God (Colossians 1:12–22).

2. Since Christ is all-sufficient, what is the Christian to do (2:6,7)?

3. What practical effect will submission to the Lordship and uniqueness of Christ have upon the Christian's life (3:1–11)?

4. What evidence of submissiveness do you find in your life?

5. Where do you need to improve in this area?

Philemon. While in prison at Rome, Paul had led Onesimus, a runaway slave, to the Lord. He discovered that this slave's master was Philemon, a personal friend of Paul's living at Colosse. In those days, the penalty for a slave who had run away was either death or brutal punishment. Paul wrote Philemon asking him to forgive Onesimus for what he had done and to receive him as a Christian brother.

This Epistle stands as a great example of the profound change for good that Christ makes in all human relations.

1. State in your own words at least three arguments Paul used to persuade Philemon to receive Onesimus in love.

2. Who do you know that needs this kind of forgiveness?

The Thessalonian Epistles

The first epistles Paul ever wrote were those to the church he had founded at Thessalonica in Macedonia. These were written from Corinth (Acts 18:1–18) soon after Paul had left Thessalonica.

1 Thessalonians. Paul had had to leave Thessalonica very hastily because of persecution (Acts 17:10). The enemies of the gospel there had tried to disillusion the newly won Christians by charging that Paul was only a fair-weather friend who had left them alone because of difficult circumstances. To answer this charge Paul wrote 1 Thessalonians.

1. What effect had the Thessalonians' conversion had on the Christians of the surrounding area (1:7–10)?

2. The lives of those to whom Paul wrote had been changed. How did this prove that those who had preached the gospel to them were godly men (1:5,6)?

3. Give two ways in which Paul's ministry at Thessalonica made it impossible for him to be an insincere person (2:1–10).

4. Think of someone who exemplifies qualities that Paul had. What can you learn from that person's example?

2 Thessalonians. Some questions regarding the circumstances of Christ's second coming had arisen after the Thessalonians received Paul's first epistle. They were troubled because they had to unjustly endure great sufferings and persecutions for Christ (2 Thessalonians 1:3–12). Some also had become slack in doing their work because they thought Christ's second coming would occur at any moment.

1. What do you think the Christian's attitude should be toward persecution (2 Thessalonians 1:3–12)?

2. What is to be his attitude toward work (3:6–15)?

3. How can you apply this to your life?

The Pastoral Epistles

These letters were written in the period between Paul's first Roman imprisonment in A.D. 60–62 (Acts 28) and his final martyrdom under the emperor Nero in A.D. 66. He wrote 1 and 2 Timothy to help Timothy in his work with the church at Ephesus. Titus was written to Paul's co-worker on the island of Crete.

1 Timothy. Read 1 Timothy 6.

1. What are the two things that are necessary for contentment in life (1 Timothy 6:6–8)?

2. What great danger confronts those who seek after riches (verses 9–12)?

3. What attitude should Christians who are wealthy have toward money (verses 17–19)?

4. How does money tempt you?

5. Which verse will help you overcome this wrong desire?

2 Timothy. Paul wrote 2 Timothy just before he was martyred. He writes as though it may be his last word to Timothy.

1. What are the last commands Paul gave him (4:1–5)?

2. What two means will help Timothy remain true to his calling after Paul has gone (3:10,11,14–17)?

3. List several ways this Bible study has helped you remain true.

Titus. Paul wrote this Epistle after his first imprisonment in Rome to encourage Titus and strengthen his ability to minister under opposition. Paul instructed Titus to admonish the people to be "sound in the faith" and hold to "sound doctrine."

1. What are some of the things a Christian should be careful to do in the unbelieving world in which he lives (Titus 3:1,2)?

2. How can you apply verses 1 and 2 to a situation in your life?

3. What reason does Paul give for a Christian living this way (3:3–7)?

LIFE APPLICATION

1 Name two things you have learned from Paul's character in this study.

2 From Philippians 3:1 and 4:4, what approach to life do you think Paul would advise for you?

Is that always possible?

How?

❖ ❖ ❖

The General Epistles

The term "general" is at best an imperfect way to characterize the last eight epistles of the New Testament. It has been selected because, unlike the majority of Paul's epistles that are written to specific churches, most of the recipients of these eight epistles are either churches of some large area or are all Christians (the exceptions are Hebrews and 2 and 3 John).

Hebrews
James
1 & 2 Peter
1, 2, 3 John
Jude

Also, with the exception of Hebrews, these epistles are named for their authors.

❖

Bible Study

Objective: To see the gospel amplified and defined

Read: James

Memorize: Hebrews 1:1,2

Hebrews

The early church called this book "Hebrews" because it was originally addressed to Jewish Christians. In the early days following their conversion through the preaching of some of Jesus' original disciples (2:3), they had become exemplary Christians and had helped supply the needs of other Christians (6:10). They had taken cheerfully the loss of their own possessions as they were persecuted for Christ's name (10:32–34).

However, at the time this letter was written their original teachers and leaders had died (13:7). Now they were on the verge of slipping back from a confession of Christ into the Judaism out of which they had been converted (13:13,14). The writer of Hebrews exhorts the readers to remain true to Christ even at the price of having to shed their own blood (12:3,4).

That writer had to have been an outstanding leader in the early Christian church, but his identity is unknown. Many believe it was written by the apostle Paul, but this cannot be confirmed.

1. What four things must a Christian do, according to Hebrews 10:22–25?

2. Summarize in your own words the two lines of argument that the writer uses to support these commands.

   10:26–31

   10:32–34

3. What attitude did the original readers of this Epistle need to remain true to Christ in the midst of persecution (10:35–39)?

4. How did the Old Testament believers acquire this necessary quality (11:1–40)?

5. In view of the way these Old Testament believers lived, what should you do (12:1–3)?

James

The writer of this Epistle is thought to have been the half-brother of Jesus. Though not counted as one of the twelve apostles, James became a prominent leader in the early Jerusalem church (Acts 15:13; Galatians 1:19; 2:9). Because the name "James" was so common in those days, it is felt that only this James, who figured so prominently in the early church, would have announced himself to the readers of this Epistle without going into any detail as to who he was (James 1:1).

James wrote this Epistle to remind Christians about the qualities of heart and life that should characterize true Christian devotion in contrast to dead orthodoxy. In so doing, he made it clear how a Christian can find joy in Christ even when suffering for Him.

1. Why should the Christian consider adversity a reason for the greatest happiness (James 1:2–4,12)?

2. In what way does the Christian receive the necessary resources to stand for Christ while suffering greatly (1:5–8)?

3. What two things should the Christian always remember when he feels tempted to do wrong?

1:13–16

1:17,18

4. Instead of simply hearing what God has to say in His Word, what should the Christian do (1:21–25)?

What should we do instead of simply talk about being Christians (1:26,27)?

5. Read chapter 5. List several commands that you will apply this week.

Peter

1 Peter. Peter addresses the various churches scattered throughout Asia Minor (present-day Turkey). But like James, Peter's purpose in writing was to strengthen Christians so they could stand firm against the terrible persecutions by the Roman Empire. He begins by pointing out the wonders of the salvation that his readers possess (1:3–12). Then he gives certain commands that when obeyed will help a person to realize the wonders of this salvation.

1. List the five commands Peter gives in 1:13–2:3:

1:13

1:14–16

1:17–21

1:22–25

2:1–3

2. When one fulfills these commands, how does his attitude toward Christ differ from that of those who do not believe and obey Him (1 Peter 2:4–10)?

3. How, in general, does the Christian witness to those around him by his life (1 Peter 2:11,12)?

How, in relationship to the government, does the Christian demonstrate the praises of Christ (1 Peter 2:13–17)?

How, in his relationship with an employer, can a Christian demonstrate the praises of Christ (1 Peter 2:18–25)?

How can a Christian wife best testify of Christ to an unbelieving husband (1 Peter 3:1–6)?

How about a Christian husband (1 Peter 3:7)?

2 Peter. As 2 Timothy records Paul's last words before martyrdom, so 2 Peter was Peter's last message before his martyrdom (1:14; see also John 21:19). This Epistle is a continuation of the theme of 1 Peter. The sufferings that his readers had just begun to endure when that Epistle was written have continued unabated, and Peter's purpose in writing this second Epistle is to encourage his readers to endure steadfastly to the end.

1. From what two sources have the readers heard of God's grace?

1:12–18

1:19–21

2. However, there have always been those whose teaching would keep God's people from the truth. Name three ways to recognize those who are false prophets (2:1–22).

3. What great event should determine the present conduct of Christians (3:10–14)?

How does Christ's return help you live daily?

John

1 John. During his later years, the apostle John settled at Ephesus among Christians who had found Christ through Paul's ministry.

While he was there, a certain false teaching became popular which declared that God did not become truly incarnate in Jesus Christ and that a life of actual holiness was not essential to the Christian life.

The first Epistle of John was written to counteract this heresy. However, it is more than a mere refutation; it is one of the most beautiful and inspiring documents of the New Testament.

The key verse is 1 John 5:13: "I write these things to you who believe in the name of the Son of God so that you may know that you have eternal life."

1. See if you can find at least five tests of this assurance of eternal in the material leading up to 5:13.

1:7

2:3

2:15

3:6

4:7

2 John. It is not clear whether the recipient of this brief Epistle is an individual, or whether the term "elect lady" figuratively denotes a church whose members are her "children" (verse 1).

1. Summarize in your own words the burden of the message John gives to this church.

2. How can you better demonstrate love for those walking in truth?

3 John. The principal characters of this Epistle are Gaius and Diotrephes. As church leaders went from town to town establishing new congregations, they depended on the hospitality of fellow believers. Gaius was one who welcomed them into his home. John wrote this Epistle to thank Gaius for his hospitality and faithfulness and to encourage him in the faith.

1. What example is Gaius to continue to follow in the future (verses 2–8)?

2. What is there about Diotrephes that Gaius is to avoid imitating (verses 9–11)?

3. What do you think an attitude like Diotrephes' can do to church unity?

Jude

Many biblical scholars believe that Jude was another one of Jesus' brothers who was converted after His earthly ministry. He calls himself "the brother of James" (verse 1), and in verse 17 he indicates that he was not himself an official apostle.

1. What was Jude's reason for writing as he does in this Epistle (verses 3,4)?

2. What are two things that Jude wants his readers to remember?

Verses 5–16

Verses 17–19

3. What is the Christian's responsibility in view of the many false teachers that exist (verses 20–23)?

4. Praise God for His qualities found in verses 24 and 25.

L I F E   A P P L I C A T I O N

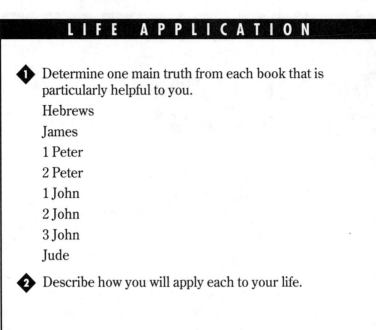

1 Determine one main truth from each book that is particularly helpful to you.

Hebrews

James

1 Peter

2 Peter

1 John

2 John

3 John

Jude

2 Describe how you will apply each to your life.

❖ ❖ ❖

The Revelation of Jesus Christ

❖

Objective: To look at prophecy and prepare for the coming of Christ

Read: Revelation 1–3; 19–22

Memorize: Revelation 21:4

The last book of the New Testament is the record of the revelation that the apostle John received during his imprisonment on the island of Patmos for being a Christian (1:9 and following). Many of the chapters of this book are difficult to interpret. Some of the greatest theologians in the history of the Church have felt unequal to the task of expounding these Scriptures. For example, John Calvin, one of the great reformers, wrote a commentary on every book of the Bible except Revelation.

Despite the fact that the meaning of every part of this book may not be immediately apparent, there is the promise that those who read (not necessarily understand) it will be blessed (1:3).

Though some parts may be obscure, certain ideas do stand out with unquestioned clarity. Chapters 1 through 3 describe Jesus as He appeared to John and record the messages to be sent to the seven churches of Asia Minor. These messages are

Revelation

1–3 Seven Churches
4–18 Prophecy of Future
19–22 Final Redemption

quite clear in their meaning. Chapters 4 through 18 are more difficult, but chapters 19 through 22, which concern those events by which God brings final redemption to the world, are clear for the most part. These four chapters are extremely important to completing the history of redemption outlined since Genesis.

❖

Bible Study

Jesus Christ

1. Write in your own words your impression of Jesus Christ as John describes Him in Revelation 1:9–20.

2. How is this picture of Jesus different from the one of Him as Savior?

The Churches

1. Name the seven churches to whom John was commanded to write, and tell the one main message he was to give to each (chapters 2 and 3).

2. What qualities do you see in your church that are like the ones you read about?

Final Events

1. What great events are described in Revelation 19:1–21?

2. What will be the fate of the devil at the beginning of Christ's thousand-year reign (20:1–3)?

3. What will be the devil's final fate at the end of Christ's thousand-year reign (20:7–10)?

4. What will be the fate of all unbelievers (20:11–15)?

5. List three ways in which the Christian's ultimate destiny will differ from this present existence (21:1–7).

LIFE APPLICATION

1 How can you prepare spiritually for Christ's coming and the events that will be taking place?

2 Below are a few of the commands to the churches. After each, write one way you can obey the command in a specific area of your life.

COMMAND TO THE CHURCH	HOW I WILL OBEY
Ephesus: Keep first love fresh	
Smyrna: Be faithful during trials	
Pergamum: Repent	
Thyatira: Keep My deeds	
Sardis: Keep yourself pure	
Laodicea: Be zealous for God, not lukewarm	
Philadelphia: Keep God's Word	

❖ ❖ ❖

Recap

The following questions will help you review this Step. If necessary, reread the appropriate lesson(s).

1. What is the focus in Matthew regarding the person of Christ?

2. How does Mark differ from Matthew?

3. How did Luke and John each present Christ?

4. What does it mean to bear fruit? (Compare John 15:1–8; Psalm 92:12–15; Galatians 5:22,23; Phillipians 1:11.)

5. What changes took place in Paul's life after he became a Christian?

6. What are the three results of justification by faith (Romans 5:1,2)?

7. How can the Christian be an effective witness for Christ in the midst of sufferings (1 Peter 3:8–17)?

8. Write the names of the books of the Old Testament, listing them by division.

❖

Reread: John 15:1–8

Review: Verses memorized

9. Identify the divisions of the New Testament, and list the New Testament books by division.

LIFE APPLICATION

 Select the book of the New Testament that interests you most. Using the "How to Study the Bible" guide on the following pages, study this book over the next few weeks.

❷ As you study, jot down the points you feel God is leading you to apply to your life.

❖ ❖ ❖

How to Study the Bible

Dwight L. Moody

Someone has said that four things are necessary in studying the Bible: admit, submit, commit and transmit. First, admit its truth; second, submit to its teachings; third, commit it to memory; and fourth, transmit it to others. If the Christian life is a good thing for you, share it with someone else.

Use a notebook as you study the Bible. Write out the answers to the following questions as you study a portion of the Bible:

1. What persons have I read about, and what have I learned about them?

2. What places have I read about, and what have I read about them?

   If the place is not mentioned, can I find out where it is?

   Do I know its position on the map?

3. Can I relate from memory what I have just been reading?

4. Are there any parallel passages or texts that throw light on this passage?

5. Have I read anything about God the Father?

   Or about Jesus Christ?

   Or about the Holy Ghost?

The Christian life is a "good thing" to share with someone else.

6. What have I read about myself?
   About man's sinful nature?
   About the spiritual new nature?

7. Is there any duty for me to observe?
   Any example to follow?
   Any promise to claim?
   Any exhortation to guide me?
   Any prayer that I may echo?

8. What is the key verse of the chapter or passage?
   Can I repeat it from memory?

How to Share Christ With Others

A well-known Christian leader, highly gifted as a theologian, shared with me his frustration over his lack of effectiveness and fruitfulness in witnessing for Christ.

I asked him, "What do you say when you seek to introduce a person to Christ?"

He explained his presentation, which was long and complicated. The large number of Bible verses he used would confuse most people and prevent them from making an intelligent decision.

I challenged him to use the *Four Spiritual Laws* presentation daily for the next thirty days and report his progress to me at the end of that time.

When I saw him two weeks later, he was overflowing with joy and excitement. "By simply reading the booklet to others," he said, "I have seen more people come to Christ during the last two weeks than I had previously seen in many months. It's hard to believe!"

The *Four Spiritual Laws*[1] booklet, reproduced on pages 438 through 444, presents a clear and simple explanation of the gospel of our Lord Jesus Christ.

❖

The *Four Spiritual Laws* presents a clear and simple explanation of the gospel.

---

[1] The *Four Spiritual Laws* booklet can be obtained by writing NewLife Publications, 100 Sunport Lane, Orlando, FL 32809.

This booklet, available in all major languages of the world, has been developed as a result of more than forty years of experience in counseling with thousands of college students on campuses in almost every country on every continent in the world, as well as with a comparable number of laymen, pastors, and high school students. It represents one way to share your faith effectively.

Benefits of *Four Laws*

Using a tool such as the *Four Spiritual Laws* offers many benefits. Let me list some of them:

- ◆ It enables you to open your conversation easily and naturally.
- ◆ It begins with a positive statement: "God loves you and has a wonderful plan for your life."
- ◆ It presents the gospel and the claims of Christ clearly and simply.
- ◆ It gives you confidence because you know what you are going to say and how you are going to say it.
- ◆ It enables you to be prepared at all times and to stick to the subject without getting off on tangents.
- ◆ It makes it possible for you to be brief and to the point.
- ◆ It enables you to lead others to a personal decision through a suggested prayer.
- ◆ It offers suggestions for growth, including the importance of involvement in the church.
- ◆ Of special importance, it is a "transferable tool" to give those whom you introduce to Christ so they can be encouraged and trained to lead others to Christ also. Paul exhorted Timothy, his young son in the faith:

    The things you have heard me say in the presence of many witnesses entrust to reliable men who will also be qualified to teach others (2 Timothy 2:2).

The *Four Spiritual Laws* enables those who receive Christ to go immediately to friends and loved ones and tell them of their new-found faith in Christ. It also enables them to show their friends and loved ones how they, too, can make a commitment to Christ.

Various Approaches

You can introduce the *Four Spiritual Laws* to a non-believer. After a cordial, friendly greeting, you can use one of the following approaches:

- ◆ "I'm reading a little booklet that really makes sense to a lot of people. I'd like to share it with you. Have you heard of the *Four Spiritual Laws?*"

- ◆ "Do you ever think about spiritual things?" (Pause for an answer.) "Have you ever heard of the *Four Spiritual Laws?*"

- ◆ "A friend of mine recently gave me this little booklet that really makes sense to me. I would like to share it with you. Have you ever heard of the *Four Spiritual Laws?*"

- ◆ "The content of this booklet has been used to change the lives of millions of people. It contains truths that I believe will be of great interest to you. Would you read it and give me your impression?"

- ◆ "It is believed that this little booklet is the most widely printed piece of literature in the world apart from the Bible.[2] Would you be interested in reading it?"

Here is a direct approach that you can use when you have only a few moments with an individual:

"If you died today, do you know for sure that you will go to heaven?"

If the answer is yes, ask:

"On what do you base that knowledge? This little booklet, the *Four Spiritual Laws*, will help you know for sure that you will go to heaven when you die."

If the answer is no, say:

"You *can* be sure you are going to heaven. This little booklet, the *Four Spiritual Laws*, tells how to know."

God will show you other ways to introduce this material. The important thing is to keep your introduction brief and to the point.

---

[2] It is estimated that over one-and-a-half billion *Four Spiritual Laws* booklets have been printed and distributed in all major languages of the world.

How to Present the Four Spiritual Laws

1. Be sensitive to an individual's interest and the leading of the Holy Spirit. The simplest way to explain the *Four Spiritual Laws* is to read the booklet aloud to a non-believer. But be careful not to allow the presentation to become mechanical. Remember, you are not just sharing principles, you are introducing the person to Christ. The *Four Spiritual Laws* is simply a tool to help you effectively communicate the gospel. Pray for God's love to be expressed through you.

2. If there is any objection to the term "laws," use the term "Four Spiritual Principles" instead.[3]

3. When questions arise that would change the subject, explain that most questions are answered as you go through the *Four Spiritual Laws*. Or say, "That's a good question. Let's talk about it after we have completed reading the booklet."

4. Be sensitive to the individual. If he doesn't seem to respond, stop and ask, "Is this making sense?"

Millions have received Christ through reading the *Four Spiritual Laws*.

---

[3] You may want to use an adaption of the *Four Spiritual Laws* entitled *Would You Like to Know God Personally?* It is available through your local Christian bookstore, mail-order catalog distributor, or NewLife Publications.

5. Hold the booklet so the individual can see it clearly. Use a pen to point to key areas. This will help hold his attention.

6. In a group, give each person a *Four Spiritual Laws* booklet. Pray with those who are interested in receiving Christ. If only one is interested, be sensitive and in most cases talk with that person privately. Make sure each one understands that Christ comes into his life by faith. If he prays the prayer without believing Christ will answer, nothing will result.

Also be sensitive about whether he wants to pray his own prayer or use the prayer from the booklet. Some will request silent prayer.

7. If someone has already heard of the *Four Spiritual Laws*, ask him what he thought of them, and if he has any questions. If he is interested and the gospel is not clear to him, go over the booklet again.

8. When a person does not receive Christ when you first share the *Four Spiritual Laws* with him, make another appointment if he is interested. Give him the booklet *A Great Adventure* to take with him. (The booklet is available at your Christian bookstore or can be ordered through NewLife Publications.)

9. Pray for the person. Occasionally ask him if he has thought further about your discussion or if he has any questions.

10. Leave the *Four Spiritual Laws* or *A Great Adventure* with the person you have witnessed to whether or not he received Christ. Millions have received Christ through reading these booklets.

Have You Heard
of the
Four Spiritual Laws?

Just as there are physical laws that govern the physical universe, so are there spiritual laws that govern your relationship with God.

LAW ONE

GOD **LOVES** YOU AND HAS A WONDERFUL **PLAN** FOR YOUR LIFE.

God's Love

God so loved the world that He gave His only begotten Son, that whoever believes in Him should not perish, but have eternal life (John 3:16).

God's Plan

[Christ speaking] "I came that they might have life, and might have it abundantly" [that it might be full and meaningful] (John 10:10).

Why is it that most people are not experiencing the abundant life?

Because...

LAW TWO

MAN IS **SINFUL** AND **SEPARATED** FROM GOD. THUS HE CANNOT KNOW AND EXPERIENCE GOD'S LOVE AND PLAN FOR HIS LIFE.

Man Is Sinful

All have sinned and fall short of the glory of God (Romans 3:23).

Man was created to have fellowship with God; but, because of his own stubborn self-will, he chose to go his own independent way and fellowship with God was broken. This self-will, characterized by an attitude of active rebellion or passive indifference, is an evidence of what the Bible calls sin.

Man Is Separated

> The wages of sin is death [spiritual separation from God] (Romans 6:23).

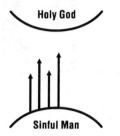

This diagram illustrates that God is holy and man is sinful. A great chasm separates the two. The arrows illustrate that man is continually trying to reach God and the abundant life through his own efforts: good life, ethics, philosophy, and more.

The Third Law gives us the only answer to this dilemma...

LAW THREE

JESUS CHRIST IS GOD'S **ONLY** PROVISION FOR MAN'S SIN. THROUGH HIM YOU CAN KNOW AND EXPERIENCE GOD'S LOVE AND PLAN FOR YOUR LIFE.

He Died In Our Place

> God demonstrates His own love toward us, in that while we were yet sinners, Christ died for us (Romans 5:8).

He Rose from the Dead

> Christ died for our sins... He was buried... He was raised on the third day, according to the Scriptures... He appeared to Peter, then to the twelve. After that He appeared to more than five hundred... (1 Corinthians 15:3–6).

He Is the Only Way to God

> Jesus said to him, "I am the way, and the truth, and the life; no one comes to the Father but through Me" (John 14:6).

This diagram illustrates that God has bridged the chasm that separates us from Him by sending His Son, Jesus Christ, to die on the cross in our place to pay the penalty for our sins.

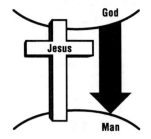

It is not enough to know these three laws...

LAW FOUR

WE MUST INDIVIDUALLY **RECEIVE** JESUS CHRIST AS SAVIOR AND LORD; THEN WE CAN KNOW AND EXPERIENCE GOD'S LOVE AND PLAN FOR OUR LIVES.

We Must Receive Christ

> As many as received Him, to them He gave the right to become children of God, even to those who believe in His name (John 1:12).

We Receive Christ Through Faith

> By grace you have been saved through faith; and that not of yourselves, it is the gift of God; not as a result of works that no one should boast (Ephesians 2:8,9).

When We Receive Christ, We Experience a New Birth
(Read John 3:1–8.)

We Receive Christ Through Personal Invitation

[Christ speaking] "Behold, I stand at the door and knock; if any one hears My voice and opens the door, I will come in to him" (Revelation 3:20).

Receiving Christ involves turning to God from self (repentance) and trusting Christ to come into our lives to forgive our sins and to make us what He wants us to be. Just to agree intellectually that Jesus Christ is the Son of God and that He died on the cross for our sins is not enough. Nor is it enough to have an emotional experience. We receive Jesus Christ by faith, as an act of the will.

These two circles represent two kinds of lives:

Self-Directed Life
S – Self is on the throne
† – Christ is outside the life
● – Interests are directed by self, often resulting in discord and frustration

Christ-Directed Life
† – Christ is in the life and on the throne
S – Self is yielding to Christ
● – Interests are directed by Christ, resulting in harmony with God's plan

Which circle best represents your life?

Which circle would you like to have represent your life?

The following explains how you can receive Christ:

You Can Receive Christ Right Now by Faith Through Prayer
(Prayer is talking with God)

God knows your heart and is not so concerned with your words as He is with the attitude of your heart. The following is a suggested prayer:

Lord Jesus, I need You. Thank You for dying on the cross for my sins. I open the door of my life and receive You as my Savior and Lord. Thank You for forgiving my sins and giving me eternal life. Take control of the throne of my life. Make me the kind of person You want me to be.

Does this prayer express the desire of your heart?

If it does, pray this prayer right now, and Christ will come into your life, as He promised.

How to Know That Christ Is in Your Life

Did you receive Christ into your life? According to His promise in Revelation 3:20, where is Christ right now in relation to you?

Christ said that He would come into your life. Would He mislead you? On what authority do you know that God has answered your prayer? (The trustworthiness of God Himself and His Word.)

The Bible Promises Eternal Life to All Who Receive Christ

> The witness is this, that God has given us eternal life, and this life is in His Son. He who has the Son has the life; he who does not have the Son of God does not have the life. These things I have written to you who believe in the name of the Son of God, in order that you may know that you have eternal life (1 John 5:11–13).

Thank God often that Christ is in your life and that He will never leave you (Hebrews 13:5). You can know on the basis of His promise that the living Christ indwells you and that you have eternal life from the very moment you invite Him in. He will not deceive you.

An important reminder...

Do Not Depend on Feelings

The promise of God's Word, the Bible—not our feelings—is our authority. The Christian lives by faith (trust) in the trustworthiness of God Himself and His Word. This train diagram illustrates the relationship between **fact** (God and His Word), **faith** (our trust in God and His Word), and **feeling** (the result of our faith and obedience). (Read John 14:21.)

The train will run with or without the caboose. However, it would be useless to attempt to pull the train by the caboose. In the same way, as Christians we do not depend on feelings or emotions, but we place our faith (trust) in the trustworthiness of God and the promises of His Word.

Now That You Have Received Christ

The moment you received Christ by faith, as an act of the will, many things happened, including the following:

- ◆ Christ came into your life (Revelation 3:20; Colossians 1:27).
- ◆ Your sins were forgiven (Colossians 1:14).
- ◆ You became a child of God (John 1:12).
- ◆ You received eternal life (John 5:24).
- ◆ You began the great adventure for which God created you (John 10:10; 2 Corinthians 5:17; 1 Thessalonians 5:18).

Can you think of anything more wonderful that could happen to you than receiving Christ? Would you like to thank God in prayer right now for what He has done for you? By thanking God, you demonstrate your faith.

To enjoy your new life to the fullest...

Suggestions for Christian Growth

Spiritual growth results from trusting Jesus Christ. "The righteous man shall live by faith" (Galatians 3:11). A life of faith will enable you to trust God increasingly with every detail of your life, and to practice the following:

G Go to God in prayer daily (John 15:7).

R Read God's Word daily (Acts 17:11); begin with the Gospel of John.

O Obey God moment by moment (John 14:21).

W Witness for Christ by your life and words (Matthew 4:19; John 15:8).

T Trust God for every detail of your life (1 Peter 5:7).

H Holy Spirit—allow Him to control and empower your daily life and witness (Galatians 5:16,17; Acts 1:8).

Fellowship in a Good Church

God's Word admonishes us not to forsake "the assembling of ourselves together" (Hebrews 10:25). Several logs burn brightly together, but put one aside on the cold hearth and the fire goes out. So it is with your relationship with other Christians.

If you do not belong to a church, do not wait to be invited. Take the initiative; call the pastor of a nearby church where Christ is honored and His Word is preached. Start this week, and make plans to attend regularly.

Resources to Help You Witness

A Man Without Equal. A fresh look at the unique birth, teachings, death, and resurrection of Jesus and how He continues to change the way we live and think. Good as an evangelistic tool.

Life Without Equal. A presentation of the length and breadth of the Christian's freedom in Jesus Christ and how believer's can release Christ's resurrection power for life and ministry.

Witnessing Without Fear. A step-by-step guide to sharing your faith with confidence. Ideal for both individual and group study; a Gold Medallion winner.

Four Spiritual Laws. One of the most effective evangelistic tools ever developed. An easy-to-use way of sharing your faith with others.

Would You Like to Know God Personally? An adaptation of the *Four Spiritual Laws* presented as four principles for establishing a personal relationship with God through faith in Jesus Christ.

Spirit-Filled Life booklet. Discover the reality of the Spirit-filled life and how to live in moment-by-moment dependence on Him.

Transferable Concepts. Exciting tools to help you experience and share the abundant Christian life:

How You Can Be a Fruitful Witness
How You Can Introduce Others to Christ
How You Can Help Fulfill the Great Commission

Ten Basic Steps. A comprehensive curriculum for the Christian who wants to master the basics of Christian growth. Used by hundreds of thousands worldwide. (See page 448 for details.)

The Ten Basic Steps Leader's Guide. Contains Bible study outlines for teaching the complete series.

Reaching Your World Through Witnessing Without Fear. This powerful six-session video series can equip your church or small group to successfully share the gospel in a natural way through everyday relationships.

Practical, proven witnessing techniques are illustrated through exciting drama and in-depth training by Bill Bright.

Handy Facilitator's Guide enables lay-people to effectively lead training sessions.

Available through your local Christian bookstore, mail-order catalog distributor, or New*Life* Publications. Call New*Life* Publications at (800) 235-7255, or send E-mail to: newlifepubs@ccci.org

About the Author

BILL BRIGHT is founder and president of Campus Crusade for Christ International. Serving in 152 major countries representing 98 percent of the world's population, he and his dedicated associates of nearly 50,000 full-time staff, associate staff, and trained volunteers have introduced tens of millions of people to Jesus Christ, discipling millions to live Spirit-filled, fruitful lives of purpose and power for the glory of God.

Dr. Bright did graduate study at Princeton and Fuller Theological seminaries from 1946 to 1951. The recipient of many national and international awards, including five honorary doctorates, he is the author of numerous books and publications committed to helping fulfill the Great Commission. His special focus is *NewLife2000*, an international effort to help reach more than six billion people with the gospel of our Lord Jesus Christ and help fulfill the Great Commission by the year 2000.

Ten Basic Steps Toward Christian Maturity

Eleven easy-to-use individual guides to help you understand the basics of the Christian faith

INTRODUCTION: The Uniqueness of Jesus

Explains who Jesus Christ is. Reveals the secret of His power to turn you into a victorious, fruitful Christian.

STEP 1: The Christian Adventure

Shows you how to enjoy a full, abundant, purposeful, and fruitful life in Christ.

STEP 2: The Christian and the Abundant Life

Explores the Christian way of life—what it is and how it works practically.

STEP 3: The Christian and the Holy Spirit

Teaches who the Holy Spirit is, how to be filled with the Spirit, and how to make the Spirit-filled life a moment-by-moment reality in your life.

STEP 4: The Christian and Prayer

Reveals the true purpose of prayer and shows how the Father, Son, and Holy Spirit work together to answer your prayers.

STEP 5: The Christian and the Bible

Talks about the Bible—how we got it, its authority, and its power to help the believer. Offers methods for studying the Bible more effectively.

STEP 6: The Christian and Obedience

Learn why it is so important to obey God and how to live daily in His grace. Discover the secret to personal purity and power as a Christian and why you need not fear what others think of you.

STEP 7: The Christian and Witnessing

Shows you how to witness effectively. Includes a reproduction of the *Four Spiritual Laws* and explains how to share them.

STEP 8: The Christian and Giving

Discover God's plan for your financial life, how to stop worrying about money, and how to trust God for your finances.

STEP 9: Exploring the Old Testament

Features a brief survey of the Old Testament. Shows what God did to prepare the way for Jesus Christ and the redemption of all who receive Him as Savior and Lord.

STEP 10: Exploring the New Testament

Surveys each of the New Testament books. Shows the essence of the gospel and highlights the exciting beginning of the Christian church.

Leader's Guide

The ultimate resource for even the most inexperienced, timid, and fearful person asked to lead a group study in the basics of the Christian life. Contains questions and answers from the *Ten Basic Steps* Study Guides.

A Handbook for Christian Maturity

Combines the eleven-booklet series into one practical, easy-to-follow volume. Excellent for personal or group study.

Available through your local Christian bookstore, mail-order catalog distributor, or NewLife Publications.